# Life on the Home F

## Stories of those who worked, waited and worried during WWII

Julie McDonald Zander

Julie McDonald Zander of
Chapters of Life Memory Books
www.chaptersoflife.com
1-888-864-6937

Based on the written responses of nearly fifty
Rosie the Riveters and the Guys
as well as oral history interviews conducted by
Julie McDonald Zander

Dedication


This book is dedicated to
the Greatest Generation,
those who fought for American freedom
during World War II,
who supported the military
in industrial defense jobs on the home front
or entertained troops,
and who watched the world war unfold
while imprisoned in their own country.

# Rosie the Riveter

By John Martin

Back in the ol' 1940s,
When war had broke out on the earth,
The young men were sent off to battle
To fight for the land of their birth.

These men needed big ships to sail in,
And airplanes to soar o'er the land;
These men needed trucks, tanks and cannon,
And weapons to wield in their hands.

Back home, their moms, wives and sweethearts,
Their aunts and their grandmothers dear,
The ladies next door, and their sisters,
Got themselves into high gear.

They worked at defense plants and factories,
They learned how to rivet and weld,
They built the big warplanes and seaships,
Their workmanship roundly excelled.

Each one had her own disposition,
But they all came to have the same name:
The "Rosie the Riveter" handle,
Raised spirits along with their fame.

You answered the call of your country,
You said, "We can do it," and more,
You armored your young men for battle,
You silenced the dictator's roar.

Your hair bundled up in a hanky,
Your overalls covered with grease,
You were the home-stationed "soldier,"
Who helped win the battle for peace.

Today as we honor our Rosies,
Who came from our own hometown ranks
We think of your great contribution
And offer our most hearty "Thanks."

# Introduction

This heritage book describing life on the home front during World War II blossomed during planning in Lewis County to honor the men and women who held support jobs in defense industries during the war.

We asked eighty-one people to fill out a questionnaire booklet and describe life before the war started, their reaction to news of the attack on Pearl Harbor, rationing, working in war support jobs and other details from more than sixty years ago. Fifty-one people responded to our request, or 63 percent.

The Boeing Company graciously opened its historical archives to members of the Rosie and the Guys Reunion Committee, allowed us to scan photos and newsletters and provided us special permission to reproduce that material in this heritage book.

People who worked at Boeing or in shipyards, armament factories and other defense industry jobs provided photos, identification badges and other memorabilia for us to scan.

Women who served in the United Service Organization, or USO, shared their memories and photos of those war years when they offered friendly faces and welcoming embraces to soldiers and sailors far from home.

Peter Lahmann, one of the Friends of Willie and Joe——a living history group that primarily depicts the regular infantryman of WWII—opened his collection of photos, booklets and other WWII memorabilia for scanning and inclusion in this heritage book.

Proceeds from the sale of this book will benefit the Veterans Memorial Museum in Chehalis, the Lewis County Historical Museum and the Timberland Regional Library Foundation.

# Acknowledgements

Special thanks go to Edna Fund, who chaired the Rosie and the Guys Reunion Committee and provided invaluable help in making this book possible.

She spent countless bleary-eyed hours in front of a microfiche machine at the library reading The Chronicle newspapers from the early 1940s. She recruited teachers and young Rosie Researchers to track down the people who worked in war support positions. And she mailed out questionnaires and solicited donations to pay for printing and binding.

My fellow members on the Rosie and the Guys Committee also deserve praise for contributions to the book and the events honoring the local men and women who worked on the home front.

The Rosie and the Guys Committee consisted of:

■ Maretta Berg of Washington Orthopaedic Center

■ Richard Browning, one of the "guys" at the Boeing branch plant in Chehalis

■ Larry Christomos, a veteran of World War II who represents the American Legion, Grant Hodge Post No. 17

■ Jeannette Dieckman, whose father, uncle, three aunts and a grandmother worked on the home front during WWII

■ Edna Fund, member of the Timberland Regional Library Trustee Board and a volunteer interviewer with the Veterans History Project

■ Dr. Wayne W. Galvin, a board member of the Veterans Memorial Museum and Lewis County Historical Museum, as well as a member of the Chehalis Historical Preservation Committee and a Cold War and Korean veteran

■ Susan Gonzales, a Chehalis Middle School teacher who mentored Rosie Researchers

■ Helen Holloway, a Rosie the Riveter in Chicago who is active in local senior centers

■ Peter Lahmann, a member of the Friends of Willie and Joe and a local and military historian. One uncle, two aunts and a grandmother worked for Boeing during the course of the war.

■ Corene Jones-Litteer, a manager at Timberland Regional Library

■ Tracey Lowrey, Wal*Mart community involvement coordinator

■ John Martin, a United States Postal Service employee in Centralia

■ Sandra Merriman, a reserve police officer with the Centralia Police Department whose mother was a Rosie the Riveter

■ John Miller, a downtown Centralia building and business owner, who is a WWII buff for home front and OPA rationing programs

■ Frances Nugent, a Rosie the Riveter at Boeing's plant in Chehalis and a member of the Centralia Historical Preservation Committee

■ Sandra Sebbas, development director at Timberland Regional Library, represented the Library Foundation's participation in the library's Veterans History Project and the Lewis County project of "Rosies and the Guys"

■ Colleen State, a history teacher at Centralia High School

■ Carole Watson, videographer for the Veterans History Project through Timberland Regional Library

■ Julie Zander, a personal historian and former journalist who helps families, companies and organizations preserve their pasts.

Rosie Researchers from Centralia Christian School, Centralia School District's APEX Program, Chehalis Middle School Knowledge Bowl Team and St. Joseph School found men and women who worked at the Boeing branch plant in Chehalis and elsewhere in war support jobs.

John Martin devoted his evenings to diligently proofreading this book and allowed us to publish his fantastic poem, a tribute he wrote to honor Rosie the Riveters everywhere.

And special thanks go to my husband, Larry Zander, who edited the book for me, and more importantly, kept our house together while I scrambled to finish this book before the 2005 Fourth of July celebration honoring our local Rosies and the Guys.

Funding for publishing this book and activities in Lewis County to honor local war support workers has been provided by:

**Platinum Donors - $500 +**

Altrusa International, Inc.

Boeing Company

Boeing Credit Union

Centralia Monument

City of Centralia

City of Chehalis

Lewis County commissioners

Lewis County Public Utility District

Security State Bank

Sterling Savings

Trans Alta

Twin-Cities Rotary

Wal*Mart

Washington Orthopaedic

**Donors**

American Legion

Book N' Brush

Camp Nine

Centralia Eagles

Chehalis-Centralia Optimists

Chehalis Rotary

Grocery Outlet

Helen Holloway

Lewis County Historical Museum

Palmer Lumber

Peter Lahmann

Pioneer West

Safeway (Centralia, Chehalis and corporate headquarters)

Sandra Merriman

Southwest Washington Fair

Staples

Timberland Regional Library Foundation

Wendy's

**Special Thanks**

APEX Students

Central Aircraft Repair

Centralia Christian School

Chehalis Middle School Knowledge Bowl Team

Chehalis-Centralia Airport

The Chronicle

Dan Mundine of D.M. Construction

DJB Photo

Experimental Aircraft Association Chapter #609

Fire Mountain Civil Air Patrol

Friends of Willie and Joe

Juggling Java

KELA

KITI

Laborers Union

Lewis County Sheriff's Volunteers

Mike Kimbrel family

Rosie Buddies

Sausage House and Deli

St. Joseph School

Summerfest Committee

Timberland Regional Library

Veterans Memorial Museum

Vista Road Jazz Society

Western Ramblers

# Special thanks

Special thanks go to the following Rosie the Riveters and Guys, Japanese Americans and others who shared first-person accounts of their experiences on the home front during World War II.

1. Eugene Donald "Don" Castle

Centralia, Washington

*Booklet*

2. Helen Foote Holloway

Centralia, Washington

*Booklet, photos and donations and oral history phone interview*

3. Dorothy (Hadaller) Hagstrom

Chehalis, Washington

*Booklet, photo, ration cards, union cards*

4. Doris Bier

Centralia, Washington

*Written stories and photos*

5. Dorothy Powell

Salkum, Washington

*Booklet, photos, news clips and write-up about the war's end*

6. Richard Zorn

Chehalis, Washington

*Booklet and ID badge*

7. Eunice Howard

Centralia, Washington

*Booklet*

8. Frances Nugent

Centralia, Washington

*Booklet and photos*

9. Eva Stafford

Chehalis, Washington

*Booklet and baseball team photo*

10. Enid Rogerson

Centralia, Washington

*Booklet and photos*

11. Richard Larson

Chehalis, Washington

*Booklet and photo*

12. Pearl Miller

Chehalis, Washington

*USO photos*

13. Margaret Evelyn (Cowley) Whitford

Milton, Washington

*Booklet and photos*

14. Shirley (Padhan) Erickson

Centralia, Washington

*Booklet*

15. Sarah (Ciranny) Zopolos

Chehalis, Washington

*Booklet*

16. Dale Alexander

Onalaska, Washington

*Booklet and Renton Boeing pin*

17. Mildred Dollarhyde Keen

Chehalis, Washington

*Write-up and photos*

18. Doris Yearian

Salmon, Idaho

*Booklet*

19. Helen C. (Jones) Klindt

Chehalis, Washington

*Booklet*

20. Edward Pemerl

Chehalis, Washington

*Booklet*

21. Mary (Jacobson) Klaus

Onalaska, Washington

*Booklet*

22. Eva (Perona) Hauck

Chehalis, Washington

*Booklet and photos*

23. Ruth Herren

Toledo, Washington

*Booklet*

24. Bob Morgan

Toledo, Washington

*Booklet and photos*

25. Vivian Curry Wood

Ninilchik, Alaska

*Booklet*

26. Margaret Shaver Shields

Centralia, Washington

*Booklet and photo*

# Table of contents

## Chapter 8: Movies, Dances and Athletic Activities

## USO gives servicemen a home away from home

## Chapter 9: War Ends in Allied Victory

## Dropping atomic bombs forces Japanese surrender

## Bibliography and Index

# Life on the Home Front

## Stories of those who worked, waited and worried during WWII

Chapter One

# Recovering from the Great Depression

Attending school, seeking jobs
and helping the Allies

## Dorothy Hadaller Hagstrom

*Dorothy Hadaller Hagstrom lived in a home with a wood stove on a 40-acre farm on Green Mountain, near the community of Riffe, Washington, in eastern Lewis County. The family heated irons on a wood cook stove and "washed clothes with a gas-powered wringer washing machine."*

*She attended first, second and third grades in a one-room schoolhouse on Green Mountain, and then rode a school bus to Mossyrock.*

*"We always planted a garden and had an orchard. Had a flock of chickens and a few rabbits, pigs and veal. Milked around 10 cows. Sold milk to Darigold. We shared with family and neighbors. We canned with zinc lids and rubber. Dried prunes and apples."*

## Dorothy J. Powell

*"I lived with my parents on a farm near Riffe (Lewis County). They got electricity in 1937 when I was 12.*

*"We had lots of farm work, hoeing, haying, animals to feed. People had a lot more time to visit and relax a little. We went to bed at 9:15 when the evening war news was over (the war in Europe began in '39) and got up about 5 a.m. A lot of people didn't have cars, so walked everywhere. If there were events at school, the parents and kids rode the school bus, which would run at night for the event.*

*"Living in Chehalis, we [my aunt and I] had wood heat and a wood cook stove in a little apartment (half an old house on Fifth Street, Chehalis). I had no washer so from February 1943 until April 1947, I washed on a scrub board in a bathtub. I got down on my knees to do it. I washed Harold's*

# Coping with the Depression

As the United States struggled to recover from the Great Depression, the world across both the Pacific and Atlantic oceans rumbled with war.

In 1940 Europe, Nazis under the leadership of Adolf Hitler overran Belgium, Holland and Luxembourg, followed by an invasion of Paris, the French surrender in June 1940 and the Luftwaffe's bombardment of London in the "Battle of Britain."

In China, Japanese troops had already taken over Manchuria and invaded Chinese ports, pressing forward with plans to conquer the country.

But in Lewis County in Washington State, most people went about their business with little thought about the European war overseas or its possible consequences at home.

Instead, they searched for work wherever they could find jobs, planted gardens every spring and canned fruits and vegetables to feed the family and perhaps neighbors during the year, and danced or attended movies on Saturday nights. Some hunted in the woods for recreation and food. Others bought groceries in town at Safeway or another store, where they may have paid 10 cents for a quart of milk, 25 cents for a pound of bread and 35 to 40 cents per pound for steak.

Many of the local grocers purchased fresh fruits and vegetables from Tom Sato, a Japanese American truck farmer who raised crops and a family on 40 acres near Adna.

Nearly one-fourth of the nation's 132 million residents lived on farms and half lived in rural communities or towns under 50,000, with a much higher percentage locally. Agriculture and logging were employment mainstays for Lewis County residents during the Depression and ensuing years, when the national median income hovered around $1,200 a year.

Talk in 1940 might have focused on the high winds in Puget Sound that destroyed the Tacoma Narrows Bridge or the continued difficulty in finding jobs with the nation's civilian unemployment rate at 14.6 percent. Most people heard news first on the radio or read it in the newspapers.

While the president and Congress stated that the United States would

*Cars line Pacific Avenue in Chehalis near Twin City Beauty and the Quick Auto building, which would be converted to a Boeing Aircraft Co. branch plant during World War II.*

remain neutral, the war overseas came closer to home when the government instituted the first peacetime draft.

Elanor Wilber, who now lives in Portland, remembers her mother-in-law complaining about the draft.

"My mother-in-law was so against her four sons going to war that the conversations are neither printable or worthy of repeating. The two older sons were too old to go. My husband's draft number was the first number drawn in Lewis County. He was deferred because he was a logger. The youngest had a medical deferment."

*summer Army uniform that way in Florida. I lived with an aunt in Chehalis who was my age. We both worked at Boeings."*

### EVA M. (PERONA) HAUCK

*"Our family moved to Washington state the last week in December of 1938. Lived in the Adna area one year, then moved to Centralia.*

*"Our family lived almost to the end of Roswell*

*Road. We had wood heat. Mother didn't have a
gas-powered washing machine. Dad later converted and put an electric motor to the machine.
Always had to wash or dry dishes.*

*"Our family always planted a garden and our
mother canned vegetables. We also had a milk cow
for milk and chickens for eggs."*

## JANE DUELL MINEAR

*"I loved my hometown, Chehalis. A safe way of
life. You knew everyone—they knew you. Great,
lifelong friends were created. A much slower pace
there. Simpler tastes. A nice way to grow up.*

*"I lived with my parents in our family home. My
sister Mildred and my sister Alice lived there, too.
Their husbands were in the service. My parents'
family size grew during those years—four small
grandchildren too! Dear Mom!"*

## JUNE G. AYRES O'CONNELL

*"Mossyrock was a wonderful little town. My dad
was a musician and, believe me, music helped
hard times. We had plenty to eat due to Mom,
good neighbors and lots of love."*

## R. J. BOB MORGAN

*"We had a small house and had a wood stove and
wood cook stove."*

## MARGARET SHAVER SHIELDS

*"Late '30s employment was not plentiful, even for
high school grads at that time, although I had
been a sales clerk at Sears—and also had done
farm work.*

*"In Chehalis I lived on a farm. We had wood heat.
We had a huge garden for canning and fresh [pro-*

But other young men didn't receive deferments and entered the armed services. President Franklin D. Roosevelt, who was re-elected to a third term, challenged private organizations to find ways to entertain the servicemen, so the YWCA, YMCA, National Catholic Community Service, the National Jewish Welfare Board, the Traveler's Aid Association and the Salvation Army joined together to create the United Service Organization, or USO, which was incorporated in New York on Feb. 4, 1941.

During the late 1930s and through 1940, the United States continued trading with Japan and other nations. The Carlisle Mill in Onalaska pulled up old logging rail and sold it as scrap metal to Japan, recalls Malcolm "Bud" Berg of Chehalis, who worked on the green chain earning 62½ cents an hour pulling lumber piled six feet high.

"Oh, that mill was tough work for that kind of money. That lumber just kept pouring out, pouring out, pouring out. My brother ran the re-saw."

At the time when Carlisle sent the old rails to Japan, people living in Lewis County worried about it, Berg recalled. They said, "We'll get 'em back in bullets. That's what's going to happen."

The United States and Japan had been squaring off politically for a while, with President Roosevelt condemning Japan's invasion of China in 1937. In 1940, Japan signed a pact with Germany and Italy, aggressors in the war in Europe against U.S. allies Britain and France.

At the time, the average cost for a new home was $6,558, a new car cost $701 and gasoline was 19 cents a gallon.

Most homes in Lewis County had electricity by the late 1930s. Many people burned wood for heat or cooking, while others used coal-fired stoves or coal heat. Many women scrubbed clothes by hand with a washboard, but more and more owned a crank or gas-powered washing machine to make laundering easier. They still hung clothes on a line outside to dry.

If they scraped together two bits, or 25 cents, they could go to the Fox Theater in Centralia or the Pix or St. Helens theaters in Chehalis to watch *The Grapes of Wrath* with Henry Fonda, learning firsthand about the migration of people from the Dust Bowl of Oklahoma seeking work in California. Or perhaps they saw the 1939 classic, *Gone with the Wind*, featuring the charming yet manipulative Katie Scarlett O'Hara and the rakish rogue Rhett Butler, portrayed by Vivien Leigh and Clark Gable, respectively.

*Despite suffering economic hardship along with the rest of the nation during the Depression, the downtowns of Chehalis and Centralia appeared to be thriving in these photos. At right is Market Street in Chehalis with the popular St. Helens Hotel. Below is the corner of Tower and Pine streets in Centralia.*

duce] way up till winter. Had a root house for winter and spring storage."

## RICHARD ZORN

*Richard Zorn remembers his home had a wood cook stove, electricity and a wringer-type clothes washer.*

*"Most of my friends were in school and we sometimes had after-school jobs. Jobs were difficult to get."*

## SHIRLEY PADHAN ERICKSON

*"We lived on a 240-acre farm on Lincoln Creek. We really weren't affected until December 7th. I remember I drove the tractor in haying season, gardening, mowing lawn, etc...*

*"We had dairy cows. We burned wood to heat. We washed clothes in a wringer washer. We had electricity for a number of years."*

## DORIS M. YEARIAN

*"We had just moved from Idaho looking for work because G&P R.R. [Georgia & Pacific Railroad] was closed for good and had to get settled before school started."*

*The family found an old house, although it was "hard to even find one," that burned wood from the mill.*

*"Were just happy and thankful [we] got out of the rain."*

## DOVIE R. (LONG, HALVERSON) WELLCOME

*"I lived in Adna on the farm where I still live. We had electricity and an outhouse. My mother-in-law did my laundry for me until I got a wringer washer. We had cows and my husband had to quit*

*George Burns and Gracie Allen entertained millions of Americans over the radio with the "Burns and Allen" show.*

At the movie theater in 1941, couples might have watched *How Green was my Valley, Citizen Kane, Sergeant York* or *Dumbo.*

Tuning in to the radio, families throughout the country listened to *Burns and Allen, The Red Skelton Show* and *Duffy's Tavern.* On Tuesdays they would have heard *Fibber McGee and Molly.* They listened to music on the radio and probably danced to The Glenn Miller Orchestra's "Chattanooga Choo Choo," which sold more than a million copies, making it the first-ever gold record.

The nation supported Allied troops through the Lend Lease program, providing weapons, ships, planes and other war equipment primarily to the British forces while maintaining the neutral position stated in 1935 to keep the nation out of the European war.

In 1941, Congress banned corporations from doing business with the Nazis. It embargoed shipments of scrap iron and gasoline to Japan. A presidential order in July 1941 froze Japanese assets in the United States.

Isolationists like Robert McCormick, Robert E. Wood and Charles A. Lindbergh, united in the America First Committee, opposed America's entry into World War II.

On Oct. 31, 1941, a German U-boat fired a torpedo and sank a U.S. destroyer, the USS Reuben James, which was escorting a 42-ship convoy, HX-156, with four other destroyers near Iceland. The 115 who died were the first American casualties in a world war the United States had not yet joined.

*When Carlisle Mill at Onalaska, seen above, started pulling up its old railroad track and sending it to Japan as scrap metal, many adults warned that it would come back to the United States as bullets.*

working for Pollom Feed to become a farmer. We had a garden in order to have enough to eat."

She remembers having an icebox before the family bought a refrigerator. They shopped in Chehalis at Safeway run by the Fullers, who then built their own store.

### ETHEL NELSON

Ethel Nelson remembers living in Chehalis and "going to school at St. Joseph in Chehalis, then high school.

"I took tap dancing and baby sat and learned to sew my clothes."

### EUGENE DONALD "DON" CASTLE

"I remember that Chehalis and Centralia were small towns that were the centers of business. We lived in the country and I did chores and milked our cow in the afternoon after school.

"We lived in several country places and burned wood to cook and heat our home. Some of the places had electricity, others didn't. My mother used a washboard and tub."

### EUNICE L. HOWARD

"I lived with my folks on South Tower in Centralia. They had electricity and oil heat."

### JULIA R. FORD MEADOWS

She remembers living in a wood building with "wood heat upgraded to oil heat due to my work." They had a Maytag washing machine and line-dried their clothes.

"As I had no brothers at home, I cut and carried in wood for my mom."

**Hirata, Hatsue Helen**
Drama Club, Senior Play, Orchestra, S. W. W. Music Meet, Entered from Clarkston, Wash.
**Hirvela, Elene Marian**
Secretary of Torch Honor Society, President of O.G.A., Kela Club, Peppers, Congress.
**Hoerling, Robert William**
Hi-Y, Boys' Executive Committee, "C"

# Centralia's only Hawaiian

IN THE SPRING OF 1941, Centralia High School students prepared for the senior prom by decorating the gymnasium with a Japanese motif, including Japanese hanging lanterns.

Hatsue Helen Hirata, a Japanese American from Hawaii and the only Oriental at the school, dressed in a kimono and served punch at the dance, although she normally didn't attend dances because she lived with a Christian missionary family.

"I had the Japanese kimono, which I never wore in Hawaii, but on the mainland I wore it quite often in the church. And so I had that, but I had to have permission first from Mrs. Bacheller, because I'm not going to dance or anything, but they needed someone to serve punch.

"All I did was just go there in my Japanese kimona and serve punch."

Hatsue, who sometimes went by the name of "Helen," lived in Centralia with the Christian missionary family she had met when they lived on her home island of Hawaii. As a teenager, she began ironing, cooking and doing other work for the family after school. When they prepared to leave for the mainland in 1938, they wanted to bring her with them. Hatsue's parents, who both had been born in Japan, spoke no English, so they communicated with the Bachellers through a Christian woman.

Her parents, who had four younger children still at home, let her leave, but only after extracting a promise that the Bachellers would take her with them wherever they went, recalls Hatsue Yoshida, who lives in Kaneohe, Hawaii. She still maintains contact with Betty French Middlebusher, a classmate from Centralia.

Edwin Nelson, Dramatic Coach; Dale Plumb, Peggy Doran, Phyllis Berington, Paul Erzen, and members of the cast.

# WHAT A LIFE

"UNBELIEVABLE" is the only word to describe the troubles that the Aldrich family receive in the three acts of "What a Life" as Henry makes a vain attempt to hold up his father's high scholastic record in order to take Barbara Pearson to a school formal.

All three acts take place in the principal's office where Henry seems to spend the majority of his time, trying to get out of trouble.

The vice-principal, Mr. Jones, is the only one who really understands the boy and who introduces his artistic talent of drawing to his parents who had almost given up, but agreed to send him to art school as a last resort.

Mr. Jones' chief interest in Central High School is not Henry but Miss Shea, the principal's secretary, who finally wins over.

*Page Forty-two*

### Characters

| | |
|---|---|
| Miss Shea | Peggy Doran |
| Mr. Jones | Paul Erzen |
| Mr. Patterson | Clarence Bowlby |
| Miss Pike | Gertrude Aldrich |
| Miss Eggleston | Don Turya |
| Bill | Betty Garvin |
| Miss Johnson | Adrienne Loveridge |
| Mr. Vecchitto | Gerald Flavel |
| Henry Aldrich | Dale Plumb |
| Barbara Pearson | Phyllis Bevington |
| Gertie | Ila Dieringer |
| Mr. Bradley | Earl Conners |
| Mr. Wheeler | Sarah Ciranny |
| George Bigelow | Dick Sharkey |
| Mrs. Aldrich | Donna Tisdale |
| Mr. Williams | Jim Moran |
| Mary | Hatsue Hirata |
| | Jeanne Fusco |
| Students | John Sullivan |
| | Bob Bieker |

*In 1941 Hatsue Helen Hirata attended Centralia High School, where she graduated in May. She then returned home to Hawaii. She is seen with her violin in the orchestra, above, fourth from the right in the front row, and with the drama club, below, second from the right. The 1941 annual also features her photo at the top righthand corner, second from the right, in a full-page feature about a play called 'What a Life.' She remains friends today with Betty French Middlebusher of Centralia, who kindly shared these photos.*

## Margaret Evelyn Cowley Whitford

*"People used to go to town on Saturdays to buy their weekly supplies, so we would always see lots of people we knew. Mom used to take eggs to sell to regular customers. We had electricity, but no phone. A neighbor had an old-fashioned one, a party line that neighbors used for emergencies. No one locked their doors and everyone helped each other, haying and etc...*

*"I lived on Newaukum Hill and went to high school in Adna. My dad worked as a carpenter, building houses in Bremerton, then in Kodiak, Alaska, on the naval base. We had a farm so had cows to milk, chickens to feed and other work. We cooked and heated with wood stoves. We had electricity, but pumped our water from a well. We washed clothes with a wringer washer and hung them on a line to dry. We had an icebox to keep things cold. We would buy a big piece of ice in town on Saturdays.*

*"We always had a big garden even before the war. We canned a lot of food, no freezers."*

## Martha Lahmann Lohrer

*She remembers living on a farm on Joslyn Road, where she "had to work in the fields and do farm chores."*

*"Lived on a farm, had pigs, chickens, goats and forced to plow the fields. In the summer for berry harvest, my dad had some Oakville Indians who lived on our property in tents during harvest. Parents shared produce with them; sometimes after harvest they would bring a salmon for Dad to smoke.*

*"For many years we cooked and canned on a wood stove; eventually had indoor plumbing and hot water tank from woodstove. Always had electrici-*

Hatsue Hirata left Hilo, Hawaii, with the Bachellers, who had two children, Ina and Lewis, aboard the Matson line's steamship Lurline, which carried more than 700 passengers.

They first lived in Modesto, California, where many Japanese Americans attended school with Hatsue during her sophomore year.

"I wanted to stay in California because there were some Japanese people there, you know, in 1938-39. But they said, 'No, I promised your father that I'm going to take you wherever we go.'" Ina remained behind to attend a school in Modesto.

The family left for Anacortes, Washington, where they stayed only a month or so before moving to Lewiston, Idaho, and then across the river to Clarkston, Washington, where she spent her junior year.

"In Centralia, I was the only Oriental in the whole school. Clarkston, Washington, I was the only Oriental. Modesto, California, we had lots of Japanese."

She played violin in the orchestra at each of her high schools.

She recalls her history teacher in Centralia asked in March 1941 if she would be going home early. He seemed to have an inkling that the United States could be attacked, she said. She had made her reservations in January.

She returned home on the Lurline in May 1941, after graduating from Centralia High School. "And you know, I just don't remember about my high school graduation." By then, her family lived in Honolulu.

She said she feels fortunate to have lived in Centralia before the advent of World War II, adding: "I think people were so nice, because knowing that I was from Hawaii, everybody wanted to know—oh, what's Hawaii like, you know.

"Because I was living with this Caucasian family, and they're Christian people so we go to church and all that, we didn't have that discrimination there. Everybody was so nice.

"I mean, every year I went to a different high school. It was hard, you know. But they were all so nice out there. The people, I mean, because it was before the war, I guess. I don't know. But they were so, so nice."

Hatsue Helen Hirata Yoshida, seen in the center, stands next to her high school friend from Centralia, Betty French Middlebusher, who is next to her husband, Gordon. Pictured with Hatsue are her husband, Terio, and their four children. Below, Hatsue (reading the plaque beside Betty) brought her parents, who were born in Japan, with her on a visit to the Pacific Northwest.

ty. We had a washing machine that had to heat water on [the] stove. Outside clotheslines; [in] wintertime [we] had to hang clothes in the house—more difficult for family of eight."

## PAGE G. BENNETT

"I lived on a forty-acre farm with our folks. We had ten to twelve cows, 150 sheep and Mother had 200 chickens. My brother and I had work to do."

## VIVIAN CURRY WOOD

"I lived with my folks on a farm. We had wood heat. Had a wood cook stove and heater in living room. Washed our clothes with a machine in a wash house—huge rinsing tubs and hand-operated wringer. Clothesline in our attic for rainy days. Outside on dry days. No electricity at first."

## FRANCES NUGENT

She said she lived in her "aunt's home in Centralia," which had a washing machine.

## DALE ALEXANDER

"I was raised on a 650-acre farm in eastern South Dakota. Milked cows. Drove tractor for farm work, and went through the Dust Bowl and Depression. But always had a good time even if we had very little money."

## RICHARD LARSON

Life in the 1930s and early 1940s was "pretty quiet," recalls Richard Larson. He lived in boarding houses while working and "took dirty clothes home to Mother."

## BUD BERG

Born the youngest of six children on an Indian reservation in South Dakota, Malcolm "Bud" Berg lived in Indiana for a while before moving to Lewis County when he was almost six. His father, a schoolteacher, settled the family east of Onalaska. He remembers walking across logs on the river and hopping over roots and stumps on the road to Chehalis.

"We had a little old cedar house out there on the old ranch. Dad had taken over the piece of property. Let's see, he had 25 acres. There were 40 acres adjoining him. We had wood heat—and also had oil. Had electricity. Of course, Maytags were very popular in those days. We had one of those. A lot of them didn't have it."

After a year in Nebraska, Berg returned to Onalaska schools and graduated in 1940. He then started working on the green chain, pulling lumber at Carlisle Mill for 62½ cents an hour.

### SARAH CIRANNY ZOPOLOS

"I lived at home in Centralia on my folks' chicken farm. We really never felt the Depression and most all on farms didn't. We had a garden and raised beef and chicken and [had] plenty to eat.

"Picked strawberries at 50 cents a day to buy our school clothes. Didn't know what a hamburger was or a milk shake. We had espresso but didn't know it other than leftover coffee."

### THERESA "TERRY" (WALZ) VANNOY

"In the late '30s I worked for a family south of Minot, North Dakota, for three years. Then went to Minot to be a nurse's aide at the hospital till after both of my parents died. Then my friend and I went to Seattle to get a job in a defense plant."

### EDWARD JOHNSON

"[In] 1932 I graduated from high school. I played a lot of sports, worked at home on the farm and

*This is the cover of a booklet about Boeing provided by Peter Lahmann.*

# Boeing boosts production

AS THE WAR IN EUROPE ESCALATED, defense industries in the United States responded by seeking to boost production of ships, airplanes, armaments and other war material for Allied forces.

The United States government also saw a war coming and, in late 1937 and early 1938, launched a program of rearmament, mobilizing industrial production of ships, tanks, trucks and airplanes. The government spent millions of dollars on wartime production and worked with industrialists to convert automobile and other factories into plants for producing war materials.

In 1941, Henry Kaiser established seven shipbuilding yards on the northern California coast. In Huntsville, Alabama, the War Department located a $6 million ordnance plant next to a new $40 million chemical war plant.

And Boeing Aircraft Co. officials reached into rural communities outside Seattle seeking workers to help build airplanes and construct additional plants.

The company offered a training session at Chehalis Junior High School, which drew loggers, mill workers and farmers seeking higher-paying jobs.

## Richard Larson

Richard Larson worked about four years at Boeing Plant No. 2 in Seattle, starting shortly before the war as a mechanic earning 62½ cents per hour.

"A few years before World War II began, Boeing started an instruction class at the Chehalis Junior High School," Larson recalled. "I love airplanes so I quit my job and enrolled. After finishing the class I went to Seattle Boeing and applied for a job. I was assigned to the graveyard shift.

"A few months later the war started and the radio said the midnight shift would be working but do not use your headlights going to work. My route to work was from Rainier Valley, over Beacon Hill, around the north end of Boeing Field, then to Boeings. When I finally got to work, they said the camouflaging was not completed so go home (without car lights again) and listen to the radio for the next night.

"All reports the next day said we would work so down I went in the dark

Saturday night we went to a local dance hall if we had 50 cents in our pocket."

### RUTH HERREN

"I was still living at home. We had electricity, heated with wood, cooked with wood."

### CLAUDENE MOLLER

"My husband and I were married in September 1941 and moved to Seattle. My husband worked building the Boeing plant in Renton, Washington, for two years and then joined the Navy in 1943. I worked in the shipyards after he joined the Navy.

"I lived in an apartment in Seattle. Electric heat. I washed clothes in the basement of the apartment house in a wringer type washing machine and hung the clothes on lines."

### DORIS (HASTINGS) BIER

Doris Hastings lived in downtown Adna in a home with wood stoves for heating and cooking, a Maytag washer and clotheslines.

### HELEN HOLLOWAY

"I was in school until June 23, 1943. My parents both worked and before I attended school, my grandmother and my mother's siblings looked after me. Chicago was and is a wonderful place—full of parks, museums—the list goes on and on. When I was old enough I began cleaning house, shopping and ironing, helping wherever needed.

"I lived in a walkup third-floor apartment. Six families lived there. One toilet for two families on each floor. Only cold water. Bathed in a galvanized tub. Washed clothes in the above-tub on a washboard. We had electricity and gas for our cook stove. We had a round oak stove for heat and we burned coal after we started a fire with paper and kindling. We *lived a pretty spartan existence. We walked every-where or rode the streetcar. We weren't aware of the 'spartan' stuff. Life was good!"*

### JUNE (WEESE) JOACHIM DESKINS

*Although she lived west of Chehalis in a home with a coal furnace and a washing machine, June Weese Joachim Deskins said, "we all knew what washboards were."*

*"I lived in Pe Ell until eighth grade. My dad worked for Callisons [as] manager of [the] fern plant. In [the] 1930s, we picked ferns and peeled cascara trees and sold [it]. Picked strawberries in summer near Adna for money. [In] 1940, [I] typed for Farmers Home Administration above [the] post office all summer."*

### ENID ROGERSON

*"We lived in Colorado until 1936. We had no electricity for heat, so my brother and I, during the summer we took our wagon out in the pasture and picked up dry cow piles. They were burned for heat."*

### HELEN RIEDESEL-KNOECHEL

*"We lived in an apartment, my sister and I. We both worked. Our heat was probably an oil furnace. We washed our clothes in the washing machine."*

### ELANOR WILBER

*"I grew up in Oakville, Washington. The population was about 400-plus. Everyone knew everybody (and their business). I graduated from high school. Married, moved to Elma, then to Lewis County where my husband logged. I picked ferns. We moved to Chehalis in the Newaukum Valley.*

*"We lived near the Cinebar Store. Eventually we were able to hook up to electricity. Our heat was*

and was told again—no work tonight. Finally on the third night we got back to work. I really enjoyed my four years of work at Boeings.

"The work was routine. I worked on the fuselages. I performed general parts installation and also installed gun sights. Repaired damage done by other workers. There was no dress code."

He joined the Aeronautical Union for mechanics and riveters. He recalled receiving health benefits as well as vacation.

"Everyone was in high spirits."

The job did pose some hazards, Larson said. "My hand was caught in a drill, which tore the skin back. A fellow worker fell off a wing jig and was killed."

## Edward F. Pemerl

Edward F. Pemerl also worked at Plant No. 2 in Seattle, starting in November 1941 and ending in November 1945.

"Rode bus to work at 8 a.m. Later drove and had riders. On swing shift sailed a small boat on Lake Washington."

He completed a ten-month correspondence course and then followed it with two months at an aircraft school in California.

"Needed a job and Boeing was hiring," he said. "Started at 62½ cents an hour. Ended at $1.50 per hour."

He worked for only eleven days on a special assignment in Chehalis, "to make changes on wing parts made in [the] Chehalis plant."

He lived "one year in an apartment, one year in a private home, two years in a University of Washington dorm, one year in wartime housing."

When he wasn't working, he would go to movies or vaudeville shows.

He recalls the Boeing plant as a "very clean place."

"Worked at tables making templates (patterns). No dress code. Very normal."

He also joined the Aeronautical Machinists union Local 751, which

*Escalation of the war in Europe created more demand for airplanes such as the Boeing Aircraft Co.'s B-17, also know as the Flying Fortress. The photo above and the one on Page 12 come from the company's booklet used to recruit new workers. Peter Lahmann provided the booklet.*

charged $1.50 a month in dues. But he said the company didn't offer health care coverage.

"Still have my union book," he said.

After the war, he worked at a Chehalis sheet metal shop for a time before buying a shoe shop and shoe store, which he owned for thirty-two years.

*provided by an oil stove. We did not have a washing machine at first. My husband finally bought an old machine and hooked up a gas motor. I did not get that until after my daughter was born in 1940. I heated the water in a boiler and washed by hand."*

### GEORGIE BRIGHT KUNKEL

*"We had a fireplace, a dining room stove that burned coal and a kitchen stove that burned either coal or wood. We had electricity but my older brothers and sisters had used kerosene lamps and outhouses before our family moved to Chehalis before I was born."*

### HELEN C. (JONES) KLINDT

*Helen C. Jones Klindt remembers washing clothes with a scrub board in the bathtub in her family's coal-heated home.*

### MABEL COOK

*"[We lived in] a two-story house on Gertrude Street in Chehalis. My father paid $4 per month for house rent. I cooked the meals on a wood stove. It had a reservoir on the side for hot water. I washed my clothes on a washboard and hung them on a clothesline. The house we lived in on Gertrude Street was the first house I lived in that had a bathtub and toilet. What a change!*

*"We had no supermarkets in Chehalis at that time that I am aware of. There was a small grocery store on the corner where Kaija's nursery is now located. [For years] we wrote out a list [and] took it to the store where the owner filled and bagged it.*

*"I had my oldest daughter at home as did most women at that time, and two days later I broke out with scarlet fever. One week later most of Chehalis was down with it."*

## WINNIE NICHOLS,
### DAUGHTER OF JERRY AND CRISTLE JOBE

*"In early Chehalis we had an old Maytag washer and used cement sinks on the back porch to rinse our clothes. This was an old wringer washer and was a big improvement for Mom.*

*"When we lived in Coalgate, Oklahoma, the clothes were boiled in a big pot over a fire outside and the bad spots scrubbed on a washboard with home-made soap. The clothes were rinsed in another tub and hung on a clothesline, the chicken wire fence and bushes.*

*"In Chehalis we had a house with an indoor bathroom. In Coalgate we had an outhouse and lived in a one-room log cabin built by my dad and my uncle, L.P. Jennings.*

*"As in Oklahoma, in Chehalis we heated and cooked on wood stoves. We had to build a fire if we wanted to take a bath so the water would heat."*

## JEAN DESPAIN

*"Was born in 1928. Worked on farms of parents, grandparents and uncles. School days. Hometown of Chehalis pretty tame—two theaters, several markets, dances, ice cream parlor across from courthouse.*

*"We had a large garden, orchard, farm animals."*

## EVA STAFFORD

*"Seattle, with an airplane factory in her midst, was a likely place for enemy attacks. For protection large balloons were anchored along the coast and floated in [the] air. Whenever loud sirens sounded everyone had to turn out lights. These times were called blackouts."*

# Bud Berg

Malcolm "Bud" Berg started working at Boeing in Seattle during the summer of 1941.

"I was working at Carlisle Mill pulling lumber on the green chain," said Berg, who was nineteen at the time. "I went to Chehalis and they were having a three-week course over there on riveting, right downtown on Market Street. I thought it would be better than working on the green chain.

"[To take the riveting course] I worked nights at Carlisle. You had to know the length and the size of every rivet by sight. That was a must. You had to pass that test."

He passed the test and started working for Boeing at Plant No. 2 in the wing shop, Shop 303. Plant No. 1 was near the Duwamish River and Plant No. 2, which built body sections, was south and east of Plant No. 1 and a little closer to Seattle, he said.

His wages nearly doubled from 62½ cents an hour at Carlisle to $1.22 an hour, he said. "And later on we got a raise to $1.29."

He worked on wing jigs as the re-work man on swing shift, fixing any errors others made.

They built six wings at one time and each jig had eight wings on it.

"They were going out of there four a day and better."

He said the planes were built with the motors headed down and the tail headed into the air. Overhead cranes picked them up, took the jigs (or frames) off each end and from the part that held the wings.

While working in Seattle, Berg lived in an apartment in Ballard and rode a motorcycle. He also owned a 1940 Pontiac 8, "and if it got too nasty, I drove that car. Motorcycles didn't do well in snow."

Berg met several girls in his apartment building, including an Adna girl named Carol Kay, whom he began dating and married July 19, 1942, at a church in Chehalis.

Chapter Two

# *Japanese Attack Pearl Harbor*

## *Centralia graduate witnesses devastation in Honolulu*

## GEORGIE BRIGHT KUNKEL

*"When the Japanese attacked Pearl Harbor, I was at summer school in Bellingham at what was then called Western Washington College of Education (now WWU). The paper seller was going down our street, yelling, "Pearl Harbor attacked." Some of my friends were considering going into the WAVES or the WACS but for some reason I didn't want to quit my teaching job. I had a profession and could retire from it someday so I didn't want to interrupt my career."*

## JUNE G. AYRES O'CONNELL

*"Heard it over the radio at my parents. I did not realize the horrible side of the whole thing. I was a freshman in high school. Many of our boys in school enlisted immediately."*

## RICHARD ZORN

*"I was at home when we heard it on the radio. We had no idea where Pearl Harbor was."*

## DOVIE R. (LONG, HALVERSON) WELLCOME

*"I was at home and heard [it] on the radio. It was unbelievable. Hard to believe the Japanese could attack the U.S. It all made more sense when I visited Pearl Harbor a few years ago."*

## EUGENE DONALD "DON" CASTLE

*"We lived south of Newaukum Hill Grange above Pleasant Valley. We were getting ready to go to church and our neighbors (Herron family) heard about it on their radio and came across the road and told us of the attack."*

## EVA M. (PERONA) HAUCK

*"I couldn't believe that it happened until we saw it on the news at the Fox Theatre."*

# Japanese warplanes attack

ON SUNDAY, DEC. 7, 1941, AT 7:55 A.M., the first wave of 181 warplanes from Japan, bearing the round red symbol of the Rising Sun, attacked the U.S. Naval Base at Pearl Harbor.

An armor-piercing 1,760-pound bomb set fire to the forward ammunition magazine on the USS Arizona and the explosion and fire killed 1,177 crewmembers. The USS West Virginia and the USS Oklahoma both sank. Other battleships—the USS California, USS Maryland and USS Tennessee—all took heavy damage in the first part of the raid.

Then the Japanese launched a second wave of 170 planes.

Altogether, the Japanese sank or damaged twenty-one U.S. ships, destroyed 188 planes and damaged another 159. Five battleships, three destroyers and seven other ships were sunk or severely damaged.

The attack killed 2,403 people, including sixty-eight civilians—"most of them killed by improperly fused anti-aircraft shells landing in Honolulu," according to the U.S. Department of Navy, Naval Historical Center, *The Pearl Harbor Attack, 7 December 1941.* The wounded totaled 1,178.

The Japanese attack force consisted of six heavy aircraft carriers with more than 350 planes, including torpedo bombers, dive-bombers, horizontal bombers and fighters. Twenty-four supporting vessels accompanied the attack planes. Japan lost twenty-nine planes, five submarines and fewer than a hundred men.

The horrific surprise attack shocked the nation and left its citizens reeling in fear.

Sixteen-year-old Dorothy McMahan was at home preparing for a date with her future husband, Harold Powell.

"It was Sunday at about 10:30 a.m. I was combing my hair listening to music on the radio when it was interrupted to tell about the attack," recalls Dorothy Powell, who lived with her parents on a farm near Riffe in eastern Lewis County.

"I was shocked. First thought—Will [we] be bombed here on the coast? The thoughts of war were frightening.

In photos taken Dec. 7, 1941, at left the USS California is burning. Above, sailors rescue a survivor from the sunken USS West Virginia. Top right is a view of the USS Arizona in flames after an explosion. At right, sailors on the USS Tennessee spray hoses to keep the flames on the USS Arizona from devouring their ship. At bottom right, a photo taken later shows a torpedo hole in the USS California. Below, a drawing shows the location of ships during the attack. At bottom left, the sunken USS Arizona is seen burning.

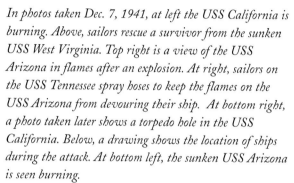

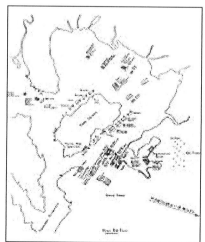

## ETHEL NELSON

*"Worked in Tacoma as a telephone operator. Heard it on the radio. Gave me a big awful scare and hope it didn't happen in the U.S."*

## JULIA R. FORD MEADOWS

*"At home on the radio. It was a shock because Japanese emissaries were in Washington, D.C., talking about peace."*

## RICHARD LARSON

*"I was at a boarding house in Seattle. Heard [it] on the radio. It felt unbelievable."*

## BUD BERG

*"I was going home from work at Boeing, off of swing shift, when it came on the radio—the car. War has been declared against Japan.*

*"Well—here comes them rails! Damn! Everybody knew it then."*

## EDWARD F. PEMERL

*"In my apartment in Seattle. Heard it on the radio."*

## THERESA "TERRY" (WALZ) VANNOY

*"I was working in the hospital in Minot [North Dakota]. It came over the radio. I was very angry. Three of my brothers enlisted shortly after."*

## EDWARD JOHNSON

*"It was on a Sunday morning. [I] was going down to the store at Independence and stopped at my sister's and news came over the radio that Pearl Harbor had been bombed."*

"For many years, we had heard the adults talk about war with Japan. Kids had lots of nightmares about it. Now it seemed it might really happen. We went to Centralia to the movies and newsboys were on the street with The Chronicle's special edition about it.

"When I was growing up, adults often talked about the scrap iron Japan was buying from the U.S. and that someday we'd get it back in bombs."

Well, that day had arrived.

"During the war, at first there was much worry if we'd be attacked by air or by invasion. Our dates were much more serious after Pearl Harbor."

Jane Duell Minear, who lived in Chehalis, remembers hearing the news.

"I was at home on Sunday. My dad came into my room and told me we were being attacked. An unreal feeling. We stayed glued to the radio, and the next day at the office I worked in, we were shaky and unbelieving. Scared."

Immediately, the government issued orders for blackouts to prevent Japan from identifying targets.

Margaret Evelyn Cowley Whitford recalls hearing about the attack and the instructions that followed.

"We were told to put black over the windows at night so no lights were visible outside. We were advised to take first aid classes, so we did."

"The next day at high school, we were called to the auditorium and heard President Roosevelt declare war on Japan," said Shirley Padhan Erickson, who felt "shock and fear of the unknown" when she heard of the attack on the radio at her aunt's home in Tenino.

On December 8th, President Franklin Delano Roosevelt gave a famous speech before a joint session of Congress, which was broadcast over radios to 60 million Americans.

"Yesterday, December 7, 1941—a date which will live in infamy—the United States of America was suddenly and deliberately attacked by naval and air forces of the Empire of Japan ... I asked Congress to declare that since the unprovoked and dastardly attack by Japan ... a state of war has existed between the United States and the Japanese Empire."

A half hour later, the Senate approved the declaration of war 82 to 0, with

At left, torpedo damage sunk the USS Oklahoma, which righted to about 30 degrees on March 29, 1943, while under salvage at Pearl Harbor. Ford Island is to the right of the ship and the Pearl Harbor Navy Yard is left of it. Below left, efforts are taken to right the capsized battleship. Below, the patched USS West Virginia is seen in drydock June 10, 1942, at the Navy Yard.

OFFICIAL U.S. NAVY PHOTOGRAPHS, FROM THE COLLECTIONS OF THE NAVAL HISTORICAL CENTER

the House vote 388 to 1. (The only dissent came from Rep. Jeannette Rankin of Montana, a pacifist.)

"I was ushering at the Fox Theatre on December 7, 1941, when the movie was turned off and the house lights came on," recalls Enid Rogerson.

"The manager of the theatre announced: 'All military personnel report to your bases. President Roosevelt has declared war on Japan.' I felt very sorry for the men. They turned white. We as staff members had to stay until the theater was emptied. When I left, The Chronicle had an extra out and no cars were out."

Margaret Shaver Shields, who worked as a clerk at Fred Meyer in Portland, lived in a rooming house at the time. "Everyone felt panic and terror," she said.

### CLAUDENE MOLLER

"It was on a Sunday and my husband and I were out joyriding and we heard about the war on the car radio."

### DORIS (HASTINGS) BIER

"After Pearl Harbor, [we had] blackout windows, soldier bivouacs on Curtis Hill Road, sentries on [the] Chehalis River Bridge at Adna."

### HELEN HOLLOWAY

"It was a Sunday morning and I was in church. The pastor urged us to go straight home and turn on our radios. We were devastated and I can remember we all cried while President Roosevelt spoke."

### JUNE (WEESE) JOACHIM DESKINS

"I remember my grandfather Tom Weese saying, 'Well, we sold them (Japan) all the scrap metal. Now it is coming back to us in bombs, bullets, airplanes.'"

### HELEN C. (JONES) KLINDT

"Working at S.S. Kreske. [I] heard about it over the radio. Felt terrible because my brother was stationed at Hickam Field and got blown off his bunk."

### HELEN RIEDESEL-KNOECHEL

"It was on Sunday and my brother-in-law was in the service. He had to leave right away. I was in high school and we were all in shock. We heard about it on the radio.

"It was a sad time. I worked at Coffman Dobson Bank. We constantly worried about our boys fighting in the war. Few of the girls had cars. We walked. *Routine: As soon as it started to get dark, we pulled the dark shades over all the windows."*

## ELANOR WILBER

*"We were living in Cinebar in what we refer to as the "first motor home." It was a 36-foot by 8-foot structure. My husband bought it from Ivar Floe. He moved it on his log truck to logging locations. I was taking care of my baby daughter when the news came on the radio. I was shocked that such a horrendous thing could happen to our country. My husband was on his way to Mount Baker to pick up some machinery. He was delayed by the black-out that followed the attack."*

## MABEL COOK

*"At home with my father and my children. We heard it on the radio. Felt angry and helpless!"*

## JEAN DESPAIN

*"At home, sawing wood for winter's cooking and heating. Heard [it] on a portable radio. Worried that [my] brother would be drafted. Worried that it would be over prior to my being old enough to join up."*

## ELLEN IRENE KAIN

*"Being a teenager, my friends and I were roller-skating at the roller rink at Patterson Lake near Olympia."*

## MARTHA LAHMANN LOHRER

*"Radio. Even though only 17, it was very scary."*

## MARY JACOBSEN KLAUS

*"On [the] radio. Disbelief!"*

"In the Monday following, the store was sold out of flour, sugar, coffee by 10 or 11 o'clock in the morning. The store, after an hour or so, rationed to customers."

Three days after the United States declared war on Japan, both Germany and Italy declared war on the United States, which was allied with Britain and France. The United States returned the favor, declaring war on Germany and Italy that same day.

The National Revenue Act raised taxes for the defense effort. The United States froze all German, Italian and Japanese assets. The U.S. Treasury Department issued its Series E War Bonds at 2.9 percent interest.

"When the war started, I tried to enlist," Bud Berg said. "They said, 'You're working at Boeing.' I said, 'Yeah.' And he said, 'Just a minute.' And he pulled the card out and he said, 'No, we can't take you.' I said, 'Why not?' And he said, 'Boeing wants you. You have an efficiency rating of 93 percent and they want to keep you.'

"I tried to get in the Merchant Marine. They wouldn't even take me—because of Boeing. I thought I'd go in—see what it was like over there. But it wasn't to be."

He had blown off part of his thumb and index finger playing with a dynamite cap as a child. "I let go of it but not quick enough." He also had a hernia on his pelvic cavity and the bone was thin on the outside, he said, and the military "didn't want to take me because they thought it might be a detriment."

Dale Alexander, a 1938 Centralia High School graduate, had performed odd jobs and in 1940 worked at a machine shop in Santa Monica, Calif. Six months later, he started working at Lockheed Aircraft in Burbank as a machinist, earning $18 a week. In December 1941, he went home to visit his parents in Centralia.

"I was at Centralia visiting my folks and heard it over the radio when we got home from church. I felt very sad. So I went up and started work at Boeing in December 1941."

A rallying cry for Americans became: "Remember Pearl Harbor!"

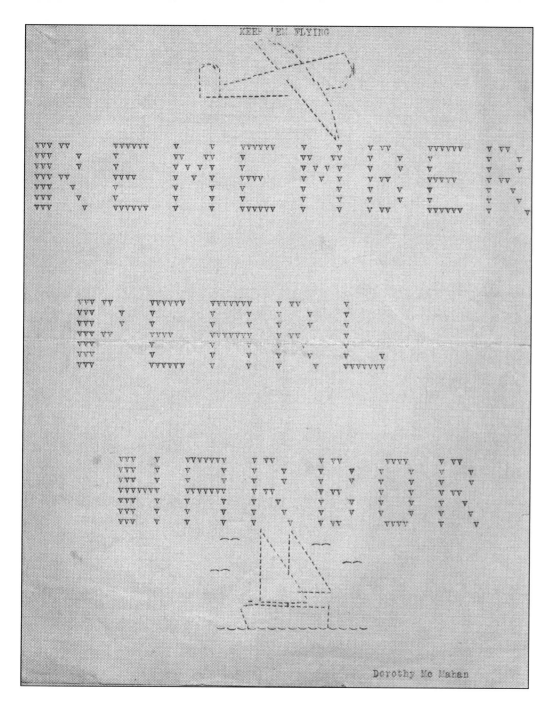

*Dorothy McMahan Powell, a student at Mossyrock High School, used a typewriter to create this depiction of the American rallying cry after Dec. 7, 1941: Remember Pearl Harbor!*

PAGE G. BENNETT

*"I think I was in California."*

R. J. BOB MORGAN

*"I was home. My wife heard it on the radio and came out and told me about it."*

DORIS M. YEARIAN

*In our home at Chehalis, Washington. Words cannot express!*

RUTH HERREN

*"At home. Heard it on [the] radio."*

EUNICE L. HOWARD

*"At my aunt's home in Centralia. Heard it on the radio. Had just graduated from Centralia H.S. and felt scared."*

# *Friendly fire kills civilians*

HATSUE HIRATA SLEPT SOUNDLY in her bed in Honolulu as hundreds of Japanese warplanes soared overhead to drop bombs on U.S. planes and ships at Pearl Harbor on the island of Oahu.

After all, it was Sunday morning. She attended business school Monday through Friday, and helped her parents in their little grocery store on McCully Street.

But she had awakened and heard about the attack by 10 a.m., when she happened to step outside the store for a minute. She watched in horror as, a block away, a U.S. anti-aircraft shell or shrapnel of some sort destroyed a drugstore filled with Christmas decorations.

"It kind of made me scared all day long because, you know, I'm just a block away from where it happened."

Near the department store at King and McCully streets stood a Saimin shop, which sold noodles, and a bakery owned by the Ohtas, friends and relatives of Hatsue's parents.

Kiyoko Ohta, twenty-one, had recently returned from Japan to marry. During a break from work, she had gone to the bakery to see her three-month-old niece, Janet Yumiko Ohta, and enjoy a cup of coffee with her sister-in-law, Hayako Ohta, who was nineteen. Their husbands were brothers.

Then an incendiary bomb or shell exploded on the building.

Hayako's husband rushed to save his family. He carried out Kiyoko, Hirata Yoshida said, and "both of the legs were cut off."

"He put her on the sidewalk and ran in to pick up his wife, but he couldn't find the wife and the baby," she said. Both women and the baby perished. Janet Ohta, who was born August 14, 1941, was the youngest person to die on December 7th.

An older Ohta brother owned a store somewhere else, and his wife was the niece of Hatsue's father.

"Well, knowing that they were my parents' relatives, I was so scared," Yoshida recalls. "I couldn't even drink a glass of water that day."

"We didn't know whether to go up to the mountain, but that's where the

Some of the heaviest civilian damage during the Japanese attack on Pearl Harbor occurred at King and McCully streets. An incendiary bomb set fire to a drug store on the corner and flames spread to level a wide area before the fire department brought it under control. The photo at left, taken by the Honolulu Star-Bulletin, shows the drug store that Hatsue Hirata saw damaged. The photo below shows the charred wreckage of what once was a thriving retail business district at the corner of King and McCully streets, where flames destroyed almost twenty buildings.

planes were shooting, or to the ocean. … We couldn't go to the ocean, because there's all these military people by the ocean, you know. We didn't know where to go."

"So that was the ... scariest morning I had."

Flames destroyed about twenty buildings in the busy retail district of McCully and King streets before firefighters could control the blaze.

Hatsue's father, who worked as a janitor for the Dairymen's Association in addition to owning the store that his wife operated, walked home to check on his family and gather water.

He then walked another mile back to work because all the buses had returned to the bus yard. He wanted to finish the job. Then he walked home again.

*This drug store at the corner of King and McCully streets contained Christmas decorations in preparation for the upcoming holiday when ammunition from American weaponry landed in a Honolulu business district, where Hatsue Hirata's parents operated a store.*

"We were so worried. And that very night we couldn't have any lights on."

Her mother usually prepared meals for about fifteen young men who came from other islands to work in Honolulu. When they first bought the store, the previous owners wanted to make sure these men would still be fed.

"I remember my mom making hamburger for lunch, and nobody came! Sundays they don't serve breakfast but lunch and dinner, and nobody came because of this war thing."

She said a few might have showed up, "but I couldn't even eat because I had a difficult time even drinking water."

"We had to paint our windows black or put [up] all kind of black paper. And we didn't have any school from December 7th till January sometime, I think."

Because many homes had screened tops instead of roofs, they had to put black paper over the top to block out all light. They used to take baths in a furo, a wooden Japanese bathhouse built outdoors, but they had to take them earlier because of the blackouts. Nobody could be out after 10 p.m.

Upon returning to business school, a classmate who lived near Pearl Harbor told her when the bombs started to fall, "she had to run up to the mountains and stayed there till the next morning or something. She was so scared."

"It was very scary for several days, you know. We didn't know where the bombs were going to fall."

Altogether, 32 civilians died in Honolulu from friendly fire, according to the Web site: http://www.gonebutnotforgotten.homestead.com/Civilian Story.html. Only one Japanese bomb landed in the city's industrial area, and it didn't kill anyone. But the American anti-aircraft shells fired in response to the attack claimed lives and destroyed homes, cars and businesses in Honolulu.

"It was one of our own shrapnel; it wasn't Japanese," Yoshida said. "It was American shrapnel that fell."

Chapter Three

# Japanese Americans Imprisoned

## Paranoia prompts military to incarcerate citizens

## Executive Order No. 9066
### February 19, 1942

*Authorizing the Secretary of War to Prescribe Military Areas*

*Whereas, The successful prosecution of the war requires every possible protection against espionage and against sabotage to national defense material, national defense premises and national defense utilities as defined in Section 4, Act of April 20, 1918, 40 Stat. 533 as amended by the Act of November 30, 1940, 54 Stat. 1220. and the Act of August 21, 1941. 55 Stat. 655 (U.S.C., Title 50, Sec. 104):*

*Now, therefore, by virtue of the authority vested in me as President of the United States, and Commander in Chief of the Army and Navy, I hereby authorize and direct the Secretary of War, and the Military Commanders whom he may from time to time designate, whenever he or any designated Commander deem such action necessary or desirable to prescribe military areas in such places and of such extent as he or the appropriate Military Commander may determine, from which any or all persons may be excluded, and with respect to which, the right of any person to enter, remain in, or leave shall be subject to whatever restriction the Secretary of War or the appropriate Military Commander may impose in his discretion. The Secretary of War is hereby authorized to provide for residents of any such area who are excluded therefrom. such transportation, food, shelter, and other accommodations as may be necessary, in the judgment of the Secretary of War or the said Military Commander and until other arrangements are made, to accomplish the purpose of this order. The designation of military areas in any region or locality shall supersede designation of prohibited and restricted areas by the Attorney General under the Proclamation of December 7*

# Families sent to camps

AFTER THE SURPRISE ATTACK AT PEARL HARBOR, many people on the West Coast of the United States started looking askance at their Japanese American neighbors, wondering if they might have some connection to the overseas enemy the nation was fighting.

"Well, nobody really trusted them," said Malcolm "Bud" Berg, who recalls perhaps several hundred Japanese Americans lived in Carlisle Mill's company housing at Onalaska, which he referred to as "Japtown."

"They figured they were sending their money back there. ... How could you tell?"

Some paranoia might have been understandable, but the actions that followed represent what President Ronald Reagan forty years later called "a grave wrong" and "a mistake."

Worrying about possible sabotage at West Coast war production plants, President Roosevelt issued Executive Order 9066 Feb. 19, 1942, authorizing the internment of more than a hundred thousand American citizens of Japanese ancestry and resident aliens from Japan in what he called "concentration camps." Canada issued similar orders to round up 23,000 Canadians of Japanese descent.

The presidential order allowed the military to ban "any or all persons" from up to sixty miles inland from the coastal areas of Washington state south to California and inland to southern Arizona. The government transported many Japanese American citizens, for what it described as their own safety, to sixteen assembly centers throughout the West, including horse stalls at the Puyallup fairgrounds and California racetracks.

Although the order also applied to other residents from hostile countries, only 300 Italian Americans and 5,000 German Americans were interned.

The Japanese Americans suffered the greatest, with 120,000 men, women and children uprooted from their homes and forced to live in barracks and remain confined behind barbed wire for more than three years. Two-thirds of those interned had been born in the United States. Many lost everything they owned.

Japanese Americans already had suffered discrimination in the United

States, with laws passed prohibiting Japanese-born people who immigrated to the country, the issei, from owning land or becoming citizens. Many of these people had moved to the United States between 1884 and 1924—when the country banned further immigration from Japan.

Berg said he attended school with several Japanese American girls, including Teruko Ohata, whose father worked as boss on the green chain during the day, when the Japanese Americans worked.

He remembers the girls were adamant that when the Japanese went into Manchuria in 1937, they "were just trying to help those Chinese."

Berg, who graduated in 1940, worked on the green chain at nights.

"I can tell you this—a known fact—seven of those [men] kept that green chain clean during the day and twenty-seven white men at night couldn't keep it clean. … That's the way they worked. Work ethic. That's why W.A. Carlisle wanted them. And he furnished houses for them."

After the government relocated people to the camps, the families from Onalaska never returned to Lewis County, Berg said.

"None of them came back. They just lived in company housing. They just picked up their belongings and went with 'em."

Vivian Curry Wood, who later worked in Chehalis at Boeing, remembers two Japanese students at her school.

"When the war broke out they had to leave to go to concentration camps. Sad day!"

The story differed a bit in Hawaii, where Japanese Americans made up more than a third of the community's population and much of its work force.

Just after the attack at Pearl Harbor, local officials in Hawaii declared martial law. They started rounding up first generation immigrants from Japan in leadership roles in Hawaii and on the U.S. mainland. Within two days, they arrested nearly 1,300 people.

"All the Japanese schools were closed and the teachers or the principals, they were all interned," Hatsue Hirata Yoshida said. They also took major Japanese store owners, Buddhist monks and priests, and "high society kind of people."

*and 8, 1941, and shall supersede the responsibility and authority of the Attorney General under the said Proclamation in respect of such prohibited and restricted areas.*

*I hereby further authorize and direct the Secretary of War and the said Military Commanders to take such other steps as he or the appropriate Military Commander may deem advisable to enforce compliance with the restrictions applicable to each Military area herein above authorized to be designated. including the use of Federal troops and other Federal Agencies, with authority to accept assistance of state and local agencies.*

*I hereby further authorize and direct all Executive Department, independent establishments and other Federal Agencies, to assist the Secretary of War or the said Military Commanders in carrying out this Executive Order, including the furnishing of medical aid, hospitalization, food, clothing, transportation, use of land, shelter, and other supplies, equipment, utilities, facilities and service.*

*This order shall not be construed as modifying or limiting in any way the authority granted under Executive Order 8972. dated December 12.1941, nor shall it be construed as limiting or modifying the duty and responsibility of the Federal Bureau of Investigation, with response to the investigation of alleged acts of sabotage or duty and responsibility of the Attorney General and the Department of Justice under the Proclamation of December 7 and 8, 1941, prescribing regulations for the conduct and control of alien enemies, except as such duty and responsibility is superseded by the designation of military areas thereunder.*

*Franklin D. Roosevelt*
*The White House, February 19,1942.*

## Nisei Soldiers Fight Valiantly

*A segregated regiment of Japanese American soldiers in World War II fought so courageously it earned distinction for valor and courage in the European theater.*

*The Nisei 442nd Regimental Combat Team, which included the 100th Battalion, became the most decorated group of soldiers in American history, with 3,600 Purple Hearts, 810 Bronze Stars and many other awards. The 100th Battalion won three Presidential Unit Citations.*

*"At full strength the 442nd only numbered 4,500 men, but this unit earned over 3,900 individual decorations," according to The Americans: The Story of the 442nd Combat Team by Orville Shirley, Sons & Daughters of Los Angeles Chapter.*

*The combat team, made up almost entirely of nisei, the American-born children of parents who immigrated from Japan, saw heavy action in Italy, France and Germany, rescued the "lost battalion" from Texas and liberated Dachau concentration camp.*

*In June 2000, the government belatedly bestowed upon 21 Asian Americans—nineteen of Japanese ancestry—the nation's highest military award, the Medal of Honor. The recipients, who each served with the 442nd or 100th Infantry Battalion, joined five other Asians in the regiment previously given the honor, according to the Asian Pacific American Historical Timeline at: http://us_asians.ripod.com/timeline-2000.html*

*Only 441 Medals of Honor have been awarded for World War II service.*

*Shortly after the attack at Pearl Harbor, Hawaiian officials discharged Japanese Americans serving in the Territorial Guard and the National Guard.*

Government officials also discharged Japanese Americans from the Territorial Guard and the National Guard.

And all Japanese Americans, both in Hawaii and on the mainland, had to comply with an 8 p.m. to 6 a.m. curfew and give up their radios, cameras, heirloom swords, flashlights and other items.

After reading the novel *Snow Falling On Cedars* by David Guterson, Hatsue Hirata said she's grateful she was living in Hawaii when the war started. She didn't face discrimination, other than having to turn in her first camera—a box camera—as well as radios. "And those things never came back to us," she said.

They had to paint their windows black, cover their homes with black paper and worry about officials who went door-to-door checking for light leaks.

Hatsue Hirata didn't have classes at her two-year business college for more than a month after the attack at Pearl Harbor. When she returned, carrying a gas mask with her as everyone did, she discovered the Chinese and Korean students missing.

"They all got jobs in Pearl Harbor," she said. "Only the Japanese were left."

One other change affected her family directly.

"One interesting thing I can say is that my parents didn't speak English, you know, so we used to call them by Japanese 'mother' and 'father,'" she said.

But during the war, when people would stop by the store for soda pop or other items, she said, "for us to call them by Japanese wasn't good. …From then on we started to call them Mom and Dad."

But on the mainland, life for Japanese Americans changed dramatically.

In March 1942, General John L. DeWitt, commander of the Western Defense Command, told Japanese Americans living in the Western parts of Washington, Oregon, California and part of Arizona to leave voluntarily, but only about 5,000 people relocated.

So the Army issued its first Civilian Exclusion Order, giving forty-five families on Bainbridge Island near Seattle one week to leave for an incarceration camp. Altogether the Army issued 108 such orders, rounding up Japanese

*This photo shows the barracks at the Tule Lake internment camp, one of ten such camps throughout the United States. Japanese American families, incarcerated in early 1942, lived in these camps for the duration of World War II.*

*These men, along with those in the Army at the time, wanted to prove their loyalty.*

*That's when the 100th Battalion formed, primarily made up of second-generation Japanese Americans, or nisei, from Hawaii. The battalion fought so fiercely it earned the nickname "Purple Heart Battalion," according to Michael Furukawa, whose Web site at http://www.katonk.com/442nd/442nd.htm chronicles the activities of the 442nd Regiment and the 100th Infantry Battalion.*

*Hatsue Hirata Yoshida said her sister's husband was drafted in 1940, before the United States entered the war. After Pearl Harbor, he was placed in the 100th Infantry—what they now call Club 100—which later joined with the 442nd regiment.*

*"He was in Club 100 and he went through a lot," she said. "But they don't like to talk about it.*

*"He was lucky he was able to come home, but many of his friends passed away."*

*The 100th Battalion performed so well that the government rescinded its earlier policy of labeling Japanese Americans as "enemy aliens" and exempting them from the draft.*

*Instead, the War Department created a segregated unit of Japanese American soldiers in January 1943.*

*A month later, President Roosevelt announced formation of the 442nd Regimental Combat Team. "Americanism is not, and never was, a matter of race or ancestry," he said at the time.*

*The 442nd arrived at Camp Shelby in Mississippi in June 1943.*

*A month later, the 100th Battalion received its colors bearing the motto "Remember Pearl Harbor."*

Americans through October 1942.

On March 27, the Army ended the "voluntary evacuation" and prohibited Japanese Americans in the western half of the states from moving.

Japanese American residents were taken to a local assembly center or transported directly to one of ten "relocation centers" or internment camps: Gila River and Poston, Arizona; Jerome and Rohwer, Arkansas; Manzanar and Tule Lake in California; Amache, Colorado; Minidoka, Idaho; Topaz, Utah; and Heart Mountain, Wyoming.

Most of these camps featured makeshift barracks covered with tarpaper, without plumbing or kitchens, in dry desert land surrounded by barbed wire with armed guards in towers pointing their guns inside rather than outside.

Putting people of Japanese ancestry into camps inside their own country didn't make sense to many people.

"I'm an American," Hatsue Hirata Yoshida said. "I'm going to root for America, you know."

Naval Intelligence, the FBI and other officials sources had told the president he didn't need to incarcerate the Japanese Americans, according to Densho: The Japanese American Legacy Project. Densho's Web site quotes J. Edgar Hoover, FBI director at the time, saying: "The decision to evacuate was … based primarily on public and political pressures rather than factual data."

In the fall of 1943, people in the camps had to answer two "loyalty questions." Based on their answers to these questions, they were either transferred to Tule Lake camp in California with other "disloyal" internees or allowed to stay in the camps where they were, according to a chronology of Japanese American History edited by Brian Niiya and published in 1993. Those at Tule Lake determined to be loyal were sent to other camps.

In August 1945, when the Japanese surrendered, about 44,000 Japanese Americans remained in the camps. Others had left for resettlement but they couldn't return to the West Coast. Many worried they would face anti-Japanese hostility if they left.

Tule Lake, the last of the camps to close, shut down March 20, 1946.

Berg remembers when the Japanese Americans were taken to the camps.

"Those that were still around, they scarfed them up and they put them in concentration camps. Even on Vashon Island, they went in there and grabbed [them] up there, running the berry farms. They were so well thought of."

He later worked with a man in the Vashon Island area who was interned during the war. His family had lived on the island growing strawberries and, whenever anyone needed help, he had been there with his tractor.

"The whites thought so much of this guy and his family, they went together and bought his property and held it till the war was over. And when he came back, they turned it over to him."

Eva Stafford also recalled the Japanese internment camps, but offered a story of hope.

"We knew one loyal family with a little strawberry farm who had to go. A kindly neighbor took care of their place and paid the property tax. There is still some kindness in this old world."

But those stories were the exception rather than the rule. Many families lost everything they had.

President Roosevelt rescinded his executive order in late 1944, only a few days before the Supreme Court ruled that the War Relocation Authority couldn't detain loyal citizens.

Altogether, 5,766 Nisei—people of Japanese ancestry born in the United States—renounced their American citizenship. However, most of them later asked to have it returned and 4,978 of those requests were granted.

Regarding the Japanese internment in concentration camps, Berg said, "Well, it wasn't right. No. I didn't think it was the right thing to do. They hadn't done anything. They just worked here is all they did. A lot of us didn't think it was right to do that."

After the war, changes to improve the life of Japanese Americans and other immigrants took place. In January 1948, a Supreme Court ruling opened the door to let natural-born Japanese Americans buy land for their Japanese-born parents.

Six months later, President Harry S. Truman signed an act designed to compensate Japanese Americans for economic losses created by their forced evacuation, but the $38 million didn't alleviate the suffering.

In June 1952, Congress overrode the president's veto to pass a bill granting

*The battalion landed in North Africa Sept. 2, 1943, and fought with the 34th "Red Bull" Division in Africa, then left with them later that month for Italy. The 100th Battalion fought so hard and so valiantly, they earned the respect of the soldiers in the 34th Division.*

*The 442nd Regiment left for war in May 1944 and arrived at Naples, Italy, in June. The 442nd Regimental Combat Team included three infantry battalions, an anti-tank company, a medical detachment and service, cannon and combat engineer companies—and an Army band.*

*The 442nd joined the 100th Battalion and the 34th Division in Europe. The 422nd ended up rescuing the lost battalion, a Texas battalion of 211 men surrounded by German troops in eastern France.*

*The combat team also included the 552nd Field Artillery Battalion, an all-nisei U.S. Army regiment that served in Europe and liberated survivors at Dachau concentration camp April 29, 1945.*

*While the Army overall had a front-line desertion rate of 15 percent, the Nisei 442nd had no known desertions.*

*As Furukawa quotes it, The Story of the Famous 34th Division by Lt. Col. John H. Hougen, Battery Press, 1949, states: "... As men of the 34th observed the battle conduct of the Nisei, they grew to resent the treatment accorded the parents and relatives of these little, brown American Fighters. They resented the confiscation of their property and the herding of their families into concentration camps at home, while their sons were dying by the hundreds in the cause of human liberty. They determined then to raise their voices in protest and to demand justice and recompense for the wrongs inflicted upon these people. The Nisei became true buddies of the 34th."*

*Many Japanese Americans also served in the*

*Military Intelligence Service, a branch of the U.S. Army, using their language skills to help translate enemy documents, interrogate prisoners of war and persuade enemies to surrender.*

*According to the Asian Pacific American Historical Timeline Web site at: http://us_asians. tripod.com/timeline-2000.html: "The Nisei soldiers' 'reward' (when the war was over and they returned to their families) was to discover that they had lost their homes and businesses during their forced relocation!"*

*After the war, in July 1946, President Harry S. Truman received the 442nd Regimental Combat Team on the White House lawn with these words: "You not only fought the enemy but you fought prejudice ... and you won."*

*Staff Sgt. Kasuo Masuda of the 2nd Battalion earned the Distinguished Service Cross, the nation's second-highest medal, while at the same time his sister Mary Masuda and his parents were forced to live in an American internment camp, according to a December 1945 Pacific Citizen article cited by President Ronald Reagan in an August 1988 speech. Two other brothers also served in the military at the time.*

*"Crawling two hundred yards through enemy fire, he secured a 60mm mortar tube and ammunition, and dragged it back to his post," Furukawa wrote. "Missing a base plate for the mortar tube, he used his helmet. For the next 12 hours, he single-handedly fired the mortar without leaving his post, except to run for more ammunition. During that time, he repulsed two counter-attacks. Masuda was later killed on patrol along the Arno River when he deliberately sacrificed himself so the men with him could deliver vital information to their headquarters."*

Japan a token immigration quota and allowed issei to apply to become naturalized U.S. citizens.

In 1968, the government began reparations to Japanese Americans for property they had lost.

Congressional hearings began in July 1981 to investigate the internment of Japanese Americans during World War II and more than 700 witnesses testified about their experiences and the emotional and physical losses they suffered.

The Commission on Wartime Relocation and Internment of Civilians in 1983 determined there never had been any "military necessity" for the unjust treatment of Japanese Americans during World War II. The commission found that the internment stemmed from "race prejudice, war hysteria and a failure of political leadership."

The commission recommended issuing a presidential apology and paying $20,000 to each of the 60,000 surviving Japanese Americans who had been interned.

In August 1988, President Ronald Reagan signed House Resolution 442, providing for individual payments of $20,000 for each surviving internee (60,000 of the original 120,000 interned) and a $1.25 billion education fund. The first redress payments were made in 1990. Also in 1988, the Canadian government issued formal apologies and paid survivors $21,000 Canadian dollars.

President Reagan said signing HR 442 will "right a grave wrong."

"More than 40 years ago, shortly after the bombing of Pearl Harbor, 120,000 persons of Japanese ancestry living in the United States were forcibly removed from their homes and placed in makeshift internment camps. This action was taken without trial, without jury. It was based solely on race, for these 120,000 were Americans of Japanese descent."

"Yes, the Nation was then at war, struggling for its survival, and it's not for us today to pass judgment upon those who may have made mistakes while engaged in that great struggle.

"Yet we must recognize that the internment of Japanese Americans was just that: a mistake.

*Altogether more than 120,000 Japanese Americans lived in makeshift barracks at the internment camps, such as these at Tule Lake, which was built on a dry lakebed in California.*

"For throughout the war, Japanese Americans in the tens of thousands remained utterly loyal to the United States.

"Indeed, scores of Japanese Americans volunteered for our Armed Forces, many stepping forward in the internment camps themselves. The 442d Regimental Combat Team, made up entirely of Japanese Americans, served with immense distinction to defend this nation, their nation.

"Yet back at home, the soldiers' families were being denied the very freedom for which so many of the soldiers themselves were laying down their lives."

*At the end of the war, "the Masuda family was warned by vigilantes not to return from the Gila River Internment Camp to their farm ... But they did," wrote Furukawa, citing Shirley's book, The Americans.*

*And in December 1945, General Joseph Stillwell arrived on the porch of the family's small frame shack in California, the Pacific Citizen article states, and "pinned the Distinguished Service Cross on Mary Masuda in a simple ceremony...to honor Kazuo Masuda, Mary's brother."*

*"In one action, Kazuo ordered his men back and advanced through heavy fire, hauling a mortar. For 12 hours, he engaged in a single-handed barrage of Nazi positions. Several weeks later at Cassino, Kazuo staged another lone advance. This time it cost him his life."*

*At the time, several show business actors paid tribute to the slain hero, including one young actor—Ronald Reagan—who said: "Blood that has soaked into the sands of a beach is all of one color. America stands unique in the world: the only country not founded on race but on a way, an ideal. Not in spite of but because of our polyglot background, we have had all the strength in the world. That is the American way."*

# Adna family told to leave

JOHN SATO WAS BORN IN CHEHALIS in March 1933 and grew up on a farm in Adna.

But unlike his Lewis County neighbors, John Sato spent more than three years behind barbed wire in a prison camp, where he watched his little sister come into the world and his mother leave it.

He is a Japanese American who had what he described as a rather ordinary childhood.

"I grew up on a truck farm," Sato said. "We raised a variety of vegetables, which we harvested and loaded onto a truck and sold … to markets in the Centralia and Chehalis area."

The youngest of four children, John helped his parents on the farm with chores and attended Adna Grade School.

At that time, in the late 1930s, the family consisted of his parents, Tom and Hanako, or "Hana," Sato, who immigrated to Seattle from Japan, and their children: Toshiko, Eddie, Amy and John. Then in 1940, the couple had a fifth child, Irene.

Sometime after Amy's birth in 1931, the family moved south to Lewis County to help run the family farm after Hana's parents died. Her brother, Ted Ohi, was already living at the farm.

In fact, he owned it. That's because federal law prohibited "alien residents," or anyone born in Japan, from owning land in the United States. So Hana's parents, natives of Japan, put the ownership of the farm in the name of their son, Ted, who had been born in America.

John Sato's maternal grandparents had moved to a small community called Littell east of Adna years earlier to work in a sawmill.

"They were able to purchase this little farm," Sato said. "They put it in my uncle's name because at that time they couldn't put it in their own name. He was an American citizen so he was able to own property."

"I would guess the farm was a typical small farm for that period—raising vegetables for market, fifteen milk cows, a hundred or so chickens, couple of pigs, etc.," Sato said.

*Tom and Hanako, or 'Hana,' Sato settled in the early 1930s in the Adna area, where Hanako's parents and brother lived on a farm. They—along with their children Toshiko, Eddie, Amy, John and Irene—were forced to live in an incarceration camp at Tule Lake in California during World War II. At the camp, Hanako gave birth to her daughter Janie and then died six weeks later. The top photo shows Toshiko, Amy, Irene and Janie back at Adna after the war. The center photo shows Eddie Sato. The two youngest girls, Irene and Janie, are seen in the bottom photo. Doris Hastings Bier of Centralia said 'Johnny would never let anybody take his picture.'*

PHOTOS COURTESY OF DORIS HASTINGS BIER

## MINIDOKA, IDAHO

*Opened August 10, 1942.*
*Closed October 28, 1945.*
*Peak population 9,397.*

## POSTON (COLORADO RIVER), ARIZONA

*Opened May 8, 1942.*
*Closed November 28, 1945.*
*Peak population 17,814.*

## ROHWER, ARKANSAS

*Opened September 18, 1942.*
*Closed November 30, 1945.*
*Peak population 8,475.*

## TOPAZ (CENTRAL UTAH), UTAH

*Opened September 11, 1942.*
*Closed October 31, 1945.*
*Peak population 8,130.*

## TULE LAKE, CALIFORNIA

*Opened May 27, 1942.*
*Closed March 20, 1946.*
*Peak population 18,789.*

The entire family pitched in to help with chores, planting seeds, harvesting crops and tending animals. The children all attended Adna schools.

Then the Japanese attacked Pearl Harbor Dec. 7, 1941.

"Well, I was in the third grade when the war broke out," Sato recalled. "When the war broke out, we were all relocated to those camps."

President Roosevelt issued Executive Order 9066 Feb. 19, 1942, caving to political pressure, war hysteria and racists who called for the incarceration of all Japanese Americans on the West Coast. The order authorized the internment of more than a hundred thousand American citizens of Japanese ancestry and resident aliens from Japan.

Immediately after the attack on Pearl Harbor, the government demanded that all Japanese Americans turn in their radios, guns and flashlights.

"Very shortly after Pearl Harbor, we were put on curfew—daylight to dusk—limited to travel in a five-mile area," Sato said.

Since it wasn't harvesting season, the family didn't need to drive to Centralia or Chehalis—except to turn in their personal property to the Lewis County sheriff.

"We finished the school year and shortly after, we loaded on a train that took us to the camp …We went directly to Tule Lake, California."

Packing to leave—without knowing how long they'd be gone—each could bring only what they could carry in a suitcase, primarily winter clothing. They boarded a three-car passenger train at Chehalis, along with Japanese Americans from Raymond and South Bend. It was John Sato's first train ride—a ride that lasted several days.

"But it seemed to take forever to get to the destination. Spent more time sitting on railroad siding than moving. That was because the freight trains had the priority because of the war effort."

While he didn't see any guards on the train, he found them posted at the perimeter of his new home—Tule Lake, California, an incarceration camp featuring rows of wooden barracks encircled by a barbed wire fence and armed guards in towers overlooking everyone.

"There were guard towers, which stood about three stories tall. Initially

*Young Japanese Americans incarcerated in the camps attended school, but John Sato said most of his family fell behind academically during more than three years in the internment camps. Both photos show the grammar school at Tule Lake camp in California. Francis Stewart, a photographer, took all of the photos of Tule Lake internment camp shown in this book.*

PHOTOGRAPH DENSHOPD-137-00170, DENSHO, NATIONAL ARCHIVES AND RECORDS ADMINISTRATION

PHOTOGRAPH DENSHOPD-137-00174, DENSHO, NATIONAL ARCHIVES AND RECORDS ADMINISTRATION

*Instead of a model city, nursery school children at Tule Lake camp played with model barracks similar to those they lived in during World War II. Below, a teacher leads nursery school children in singing 'Twinkle, Twinkle, Little Star.'*

there were guards but within a very short time the guards disappeared since it was unnecessary. Because, you know, we weren't going anywhere," Sato said.

"I mean that the people who had been incarcerated weren't enemies to this country and were doing exactly what they were asked to do. Boys of draft age were drafted and served in the Army. However, most of them volunteered to serve."

As a child, he didn't know exactly how his parents felt about the entire ordeal. "Well, no one was happy about it," he said. "But what could you do?"

The family didn't even have many relatives in Japan—only Tom Sato's half-sister, "but they weren't that close," Sato said.

"Living conditions in those camps were pretty dismal," Sato said. "The living barracks were as minimal as you can get. Floors were diagonal tongue and groove boards. The walls were open studs with diagonal shiplap overlaid with building paper."

The Satos crowded into one end of a barrack, which they shared with at least three other families. For privacy, they hung blankets. If the wind blew over the barren and desolate land, dust poured through the cracks and into the barracks.

"The space we were given was approximately 20 feet by 30 feet. Just a guess. And that was for a family, including a mother, father and five children."

His uncle lived in another area. Everyone slept on Army cots, covered with Army blankets.

"All bathroom facilities were in another building. In our case we had to walk 30 yards or more," Sato said.

Although his parents didn't speak much about the relocation to a camp, Sato said, "I'm convinced that they weren't happy. They were bewildered."

Just over a year after entering the camp, Hanako Sato gave birth to a little girl, Jane, whom everyone called Janie. Six weeks later, Hana passed away.

John was ten.

"We had no real hospital—a makeshift building with staffed doctors who also were interned in to the camps," Sato said.

"Well, we really aren't certain of her illness. After our layman's description of her condition, my son, who is a doctor, has come to the conclusion it must have been some form of cancer. It probably wasn't a heart condition."

"Those days if it were cancer, I don't know what they could have done… You know, there was no diagnosis or anything."

Toshi, the oldest daughter, cared for little Janie, "but I remember we all pitched in," Sato said. The children attended school at the camps, but he said his older siblings had it tough later.

"I think it was more difficult after the camp experience because of mediocre schools and falling back with their peers at Adna.

"I spent the fourth, fifth and sixth grades in camp so although I was behind academically, at that stage of the educational process I was able to pretty much catch up. I like to think I was at least average when I graduated from Adna High School."

They didn't have much to do at the camp. Sometimes they hauled coal to the barracks where each family had a pot-bellied stove for heat and cooking.

"Older kids had organized softball games [and] touch football, which I used to enjoy watching. The camp was built in a dry lakebed. So it was just very barren, no trees."

During their second year in the camp, the Satos and everyone else incarcerated at Tule Lake answered two "loyalty questions" designed to separate the loyal from the disloyal Japanese Americans. Those considered disloyal came from the nine other camps to Tule Lake, while those at Tule Lake considered loyal were sent to other camps in the fall of 1943.

When the Satos—who were loyal Americans—left Tule Lake for the incarceration camp at Minidoka, Idaho, they took along the ashes of their wife and mother, Hanako Sato, who had been cremated after her death.

"And then when my father passed away in 1957, we buried them both together in Claquato Cemetery."

In late summer of 1945, Tom and his family left the camp at Minidoka by train and returned to their truck farm in Adna, only to find it had gone to

PHOTOGRAPH DENSHOPD-137-00076, DENSHO, NATIONAL ARCHIVES AND RECORDS ADMINISTRATION

*In the top photo at left, boys from the lower fifth grade, taught by Mrs. Rhoda McGarva, are playing 'Cock Fight.' In the lower left photo, girls of the lower fifth grade, also taught by Mrs. McGarva, are shown playing 'Two Deep.' Below, sixth-grade students study in Miss Mae Hert's classroom.*

PHOTOGRAPH DENSHOPD-137-00074, DENSHO, NATIONAL ARCHIVES AND RECORDS ADMINISTRATION

PHOTOGRAPH DENSHOPD-137-00077, DENSHO, NATIONAL ARCHIVES AND RECORDS ADMINISTRATION

## TEENAGER PLEADS AT GRANGE
## FOR ADNA TO WELCOME SATOS

*Doris Hastings Bier and her family enjoyed their Adna neighbors, the Sato family: Tom, Hanako, Toshiko, Eddie, Amiko, John, Irene and later Jane. After the war, she said, "some people didn't want them to come home to Adna."*

*"Many people in Grange tried to ban them from returning home—loud, noisy, hateful talk.*

*"My uncle Anton Erp was a close friend and neighbor of Tom's," she said, remembering the Grange meeting when she was only a teenager. "Tears ran down his face while he was talking—chewing them out.*

*"Somebody tried to shut him up. To my amazement I jumped up and told everybody they should be ashamed of themselves and asked if they remembered the oranges and produce Mr. Sato would put on their doorsteps on Christmas. The Satos were friends ... I picked his kids up for Sunday school.*

*"Some yelled at me to shut up and sit down. I was mortified but stood there—had never challenged adults before. I finally sat down."*

*When the Satos returned home, Janie was about three. Mrs. Sato had died in the camp.*

*"I met Mr. Sato in the middle of Market Street by the old bus station. He looked at me. I looked at him. We hugged and started bawling in the middle of the street."*

*She said the kids returned to school at Adna, where they were "very accepted back at school."*

*"Toshiko was my age and kept the family together.*

pasture over the years.

"And the underground irrigation system, which was installed over a period of years—it was galvanized piping in those days—rusted away so ... when we came back from camp roughly three-and-a-half years later, we couldn't go back into that because we couldn't afford to put the irrigation system back in.

"It would have been quite expensive to get the needed infrastructure to get back into truck farming—irrigation, hot beds, etc."

They still owned the farm because it was paid for and belonged to an American citizen, Sato's Uncle Ted. Another uncle, George, who was working in Phoenix when the war broke out, never was incarcerated, Sato said, "probably because Phoenix was far enough inland."

The sheriff's office returned the family's radio, flashlights and cameras.

Although the children returned to Adna schools and struggled to catch up with their peers, Sato said his seventh-grade classmates and the family's neighbors treated them well.

"At Adna, generally it was very good. Yes, very good."

But the family struggled financially to catch up with their neighbors, who had three years to recover from the Depression of the 1930s.

"For me, I think the period after we returned to Adna was the toughest. After three and a half years in camp, with no income for our family, it was a real struggle to get back on a secure financial footing."

Essentially, the family faced poverty.

"Well, we all pitched in and did the best we could. My father worked on the railroad for a while—until we started raising strawberries. My brother Eddie, after graduating from Adna High School, began working for a tire company in Chehalis to help supplement the family income."

Sato didn't remember facing any overt discrimination when they returned home. "People in Adna were very good," he said.

After graduating from Adna High School in 1951, John Sato attended Centralia Junior College for two years, and then he was drafted into the Army at the end of the Korean War. Because a truce had been signed, he

*When Doris Hastings of Adna married Clayton Bier June 13, 1947, they asked Irene and Janie Sato to serve as flower girls. Some people invited to the wedding refused to attend if the girls took part. As Doris Hastings Bier explained it: 'We were there; the complainers weren't.' Also pictured in the photo are the witnesses, Gene and Donna Adams.*

*"I was married June 13, 1947, and Janie and Irene Sato were my flower girls. People said they wouldn't come to the wedding 'if those Japs were there'—both in Adna and Rochester—so we used the Presbyterian Church in Centralia and the girls were the stars of the show.*

*"Tom was so proud of them—he carried them around, one on each arm."*

served on an Air Force base in Japan after basic training, where he lived in Army barracks that "were far superior to where we lived" in the camps.

When he returned home, he attended the University of Washington on the G.I. Bill and graduated in 1960 with a degree in architecture.

"I've been an architect and real estate developer since 1963."

More than forty years after incarcerating its Japanese American citizens, the United States government apologized and tried to make reparations, as recommended by the Commission on Wartime Relocation and Internment of Civilians in its 1983 report called "Personal Justice Denied."

*When they returned from the camps, the Satos returned to classes at Adna schools. Eddie graduated in 1947 in the same class with Doris Hastings. In the class photo, Eddie Sato is second from the right and Doris Hastings is sixth from the left.*

Each of the 60,000 surviving internees received $20,000.

In 1996, a Seattle community group formed Densho: The Japanese American Legacy Project to videotape the life histories of Japanese Americans who were incarcerated during World War II. John Sato is a longtime supporter of the group, which has now recorded more than two hundred stories and collected a thousand photos and documents in its digital archive.

"I've given a lot of thought about it [the internment] through the years and discussed it with my children (adults now). At times I feel like forgetting about it. Other times I think it's good to share this experience with others. I really have mixed emotions.

"I hope this sort of thing doesn't happen again to another group of innocent people."

Chapter Four

# Rationing for the War Effort

*Survivors of Depression*

*learn to make do with less*

## EVA M. (PERONA) HAUCK

*"I remember my folks had to apply for a [ration] book for each member of our family. There were five of us.*

*"When I got married April 8, 1945, my mother had to give the bakery sugar stamps to make my wedding cake."*

## DOROTHY J. POWELL

*"The most difficult was not much gas—no tires! Sugar was very little and difficult to try to bake or can. I didn't do much myself then. People tried to use honey and saccharin for such. The stores had most rationed food, but you couldn't buy much with your allotted stamps. Also there weren't any nylon stockings ... [which] would have been harder for office workers. I walked to work, usually about a mile (to different places I worked). There were lots of drives. My senior year I helped a lot with a book drive for the servicemen.*

*"Everyone saved extra fat rendered out in a can on the stove for the grease for ammunition. We saved toothpaste tubes and turned them in for some metal in them."*

*"I sent many 'care' packages to Harold over the twenty-one months he was overseas in Europe— even light bulbs and fuses the Army didn't have. And lots of food, socks, etc."*

## DORIS M. YEARIAN

*"Rationing was okay and we accepted it as part of helping friends and relatives who were serving. Children and everyone well remember scrap metal drives.*

*"Oh, yes, a victory garden [was] a real adventure for husbands and they all did well, all those fresh*

# People learn to conserve

As the nation fully immersed itself in World War II, changes occurred on the home front to forever alter the makeup of the country.

Fifteen million Americans joined the military to fight overseas, while millions of others left rural communities for the big cities and high-paying jobs in the defense and transportation industries.

In 1942, the Japanese overran troops in the Philippines, forcing General Douglas MacArthur to leave the island with a vow to return, and the Nazi leaders determined a "final solution" for exterminating European Jews. Thousands of soldiers taken prisoner died on the march to Bataan. Allied victories in the Battle of Midway and successful air raids on Tokyo renewed flagging spirits.

At home in America, newspaper headlines screamed the latest war news. Movie screens featured John Wayne as a Fighting Seebee and a Flying Tiger. Newsreels showed the latest battle scenes in a glaring black-and-white panorama. And Life magazine published wrenching photos of soldiers dying on the front lines, bringing the war into the nation's living rooms.

Patriotism hit an all-time high.

"Patriotism prevailed at the highest point on the scale—and the country, from my impression, was more focused and together than at any time since," said John Alexander Jr., of Chehalis, who was a child attending Cascade Grade School at the time.

"Sure there might have been some mistakes, perhaps a flavor of propaganda; but we were in this thing together, and it was a good feeling. ... Vast equipment resources in the hands of citizen soldiers raised in a freedom-loving democracy and supported one hundred percent by the home folks proved to be a winning team.

"And there was no confusion as to who the bad guys were. There were no Jane Fondas. There was Tokyo Rose, but everybody knew she was on the other side. We had Ernie Pyle and Bill Mauldin, who were pro-American and pro-GI."

That's how Helen Holloway remembers it.

"There was no demonstrating or dissent. We only focused on winning that

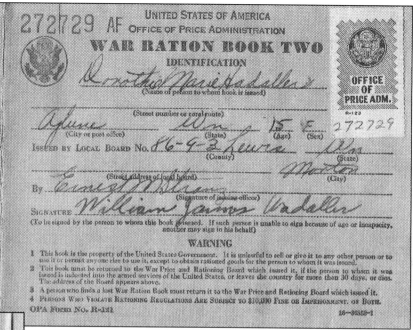

## INSTRUCTIONS

1 This book is valuable. Do not lose it.

2 Each stamp authorizes you to purchase rationed goods in the quantities and at the times designated by the Office of Price Administration. Without the stamps you will be unable to purchase those goods.

3 Detailed instructions concerning the use of the book and the stamps will be issued from time to time. Watch for those instructions so that you will know how to use your book and stamps.

4 Do not tear out stamps except at the time of purchase and in the presence of the storekeeper, his employee, or a person authorized by him to make delivery.

5 Do not throw this book away when all of the stamps have been used, or when the time for their use has expired. You may be required to present this book when you apply for subsequent books.

Rationing is a vital part of your country's war effort. This book is your Government's guarantee of your fair share of goods made scarce by war, to which the stamps contained herein will be assigned as the need arises.

Any attempt to violate the rules is an effort to deny someone his share and will create hardship and discontent.

Such action, like treason, helps the enemy.

Give your whole support to rationing and thereby conserve our vital goods. Be guided by the rule:

"*If you don't need it, DON'T BUY IT.*"

☆ U. S. GOVERNMENT PRINTING OFFICE: 1942    16—30853-1

272729 AF

## UNITED STATES OF AMERICA
### OFFICE OF PRICE ADMINISTRATION

# WAR RATION BOOK TWO
## IDENTIFICATION

Dorothy Marie Hadaller
(Name of person to whom book is issued)

_____
(Street number or rural route)

Adna ____ Wn ____ 15 ____ F
(City or post office)    (State)    (Age)    (Sex)

ISSUED BY LOCAL BOARD No. 86-9-3 Lewis ____ Wn
(County)    (State)

_____
(Street address of local board)    (City)

By Ernest W. Ahrens
(Signature of issuing officer)

SIGNATURE William James Hadaller

(To be signed by the person to whom this book is issued. If such person is unable to sign because of age or incapacity, another may sign in his behalf)

### WARNING

1 This book is the property of the United States Government. It is unlawful to sell or give it to any other person or to use it or permit anyone else to use it, except to obtain rationed goods for the person to whom it was issued.

2 This book must be returned to the War Price and Rationing Board which issued it, if the person to whom it was issued is inducted into the armed services of the United States, or leaves the country for more than 30 days, or dies. The address of the Board appears above.

3 A person who finds a lost War Ration Book must return it to the War Price and Rationing Board which issued it.

4 PERSONS WHO VIOLATE RATIONING REGULATIONS ARE SUBJECT TO $10,000 FINE OR IMPRISONMENT, OR BOTH.

OPA Form No. R-121    16—30853-1

RATION CARDS COURTESY OF DOROTHY HADALLER HAGSTROM

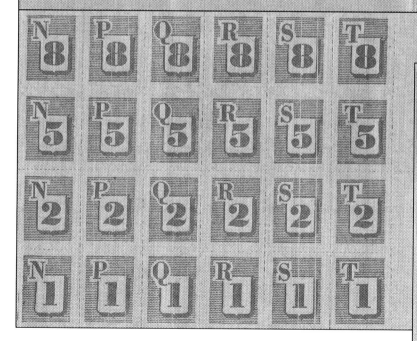

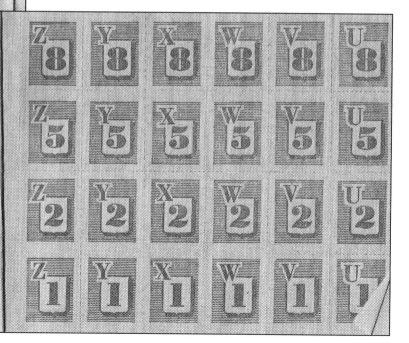

*Ration books limited the amount of sugar, shoes, meat, butter, heating oil and gasoline customers could buy.*

The Stamps contained in this Book are valid only after the lawful holder of this Book has signed the certificate below, and are void if detached contrary to the Regulations. (A father, mother, or guardian may sign the name of a person under 18.) In case of questions, difficulties, or complaints, consult your local Ration Board.

## Certificate of Book Holder

**I, the undersigned,** do hereby certify that I have observed all the conditions and regulations governing the issuance of this War Ration Book; that the "Description of Book Holder" contained herein is correct; that an application for issuance of this book has been duly made by me or on my behalf; and that the statements contained in said application are true to the best of my knowledge and belief.

_Dorothie Marie Hadaller_ [Book Holder's Own Name]
(Signature of, or on behalf of, Book Holder)

Any person signing on behalf of Book Holder must sign his or her own name below

and indicate relationship to Book Holder _William James Hadaller_ _daughter_
(Father, Mother, or Guardian)

☆ U S GOVERNMENT PRINTING OFFICE : 1942  16—26651-1          OPA Form No. R-302

# UNITED STATES OF AMERICA
# War Ration Book One

### WARNING

1 Punishments ranging as high as *Ten Years' Imprisonment or $10,000 Fine, or Both,* may be imposed under United States Statutes for violations thereof arising out of infractions of Rationing Orders and Regulations.

2 This book must not be transferred. It must be held and used only by or on behalf of the person to whom it has been issued, and anyone presenting it thereby represents to the Office of Price Administration, an agency of the United States Government, that it is being so held and so used. For any misuse of this book it may be taken from the holder by the Office of Price Administration.

3 In the event either of the departure from the United States of the person to whom this book is issued, or his or her death, the book must be surrendered in accordance with the Regulations.

4 Any person finding a lost book must deliver it promptly to the nearest Ration Board.

### OFFICE OF PRICE ADMINISTRATION

Nº 106812 -369

People had to apply for the ration books and sign their names. The cardboard tokens below, called red points, were given as change for ration card purchases.

## Certificate of Registrar

**This is to Certify** that pursuant to the Rationing Orders and Regulations administered by the OFFICE OF PRICE ADMINISTRATION, an agency of the United States Government,

(Name, Address, and Description of person to whom the book is issued:)

_Hadaller._   _Dorothie_   _Marie_
(Last name)   (First name)   (Middle name)

(Street No. or P. O. Box No.)   (Street or R. F. D.)

_Winne_   _Lewis_   _Wash._
(City or town)   (County)   (State)

_5_ ft. _4_ in. _120_ lbs. _brown_ _brown_ _15_ yrs. Sex {Male ☐ Female ☒}
(Height)   (Weight)   (Color of eyes)   (Color of hair)   (Age)

has been issued the attached War Ration Stamps this _6th_ day of _May_ 1942, upon the basis of an application signed by himself ☐, herself ☐, or on his or her behalf by his or her husband ☐, wife ☐, father ☒, mother ☐, exception ☐. (Check one.)

_J. W. Overstreet_ (Registrar)   (Signature)

Local Board No. _43_   County _Lewis_   State _Wash._

*Stamps must not be detached except in the presence of the retailer, his employee, or person authorized by him to make delivery.*

WAR RATION STAMP **22**   WAR RATION STAMP **20**
WAR RATION STAMP **19**

_5-166304 g  Canning Sugar 15 lbs._

RATIONING MATERIALS PROVIDED BY DOROTHY HADALLER HAGSTROM

war and bringing our loved ones home again," she said. "Hardships at home were mere inconvenience compared to what our service people had to endure."

At home, to conserve resources for the war effort, the government introduced rationing of gasoline to three gallons a week for non-essential vehicles, and also imposed limits on coffee, sugar, meats, rubber, butter, heating oil and later shoes. Manufacturers quit producing new bicycles and automobiles during the war. Horse-drawn wagons reappeared and the term Government Issue was shortened to GI, referring to anything military.

The Office of Economic Stabilization created controls on farm prices, rents, wages and salaries. Because of rationing and shortages, consumer spending plummeted from $69 billion in 1939 to $38 billion three years later.

"It seems like rationing began shortly after the war began," recalls Holloway, who was living and working in Chicago at the time. "Rationing of shoes was hard but I was always in steel-toed safety shoes and it seemed I spent my life commuting or at work.

"Tried sharing rides but did not appreciate my fellow coarse and vulgar riders. Streetcars were bumpy and crowded but more bearable.

"My mother did all the math and making ration stamps stretch. I could always get a five-cent sandwich or a ten-cent hamburger at work. During the war we collected and recycled everything—rubber, paper, metal—you name it."

She remembers people in Chicago created memorials in empty lots to honor service people fighting overseas. A large blackboard listed the names of servicemen with a blue star beside each name—but a gold star if the person had been killed.

"There was always a flagpole where an American flag always waved."

Americans everywhere did what they could to help win the war.

To obtain metal for war munitions, men, women and children collected scrap iron, foil, gum wrappers, steel, iron and even empty toothpaste tubes. They also collected newspapers and aluminum.

Women gathered leftover grease in cans so the lard could be used to lubricate ammunition.

"There were collection points where people could turn in scrap metal, lard,

vegetables. And wives learned to can vegetables and fruit for winter."

### MARGARET SHAVER SHIELDS

*She remembers sugar and gasoline rationing primarily.*

*"In Seattle I rode the bus, and in Chehalis I shared [rides]."*

*"I don't remember any trading [of ration stamps]—learned to cope and substitute. Lived on [a] farm at Chehalis so had farm food."*

### RICHARD ZORN

*"Stamps were a fair way to handle supplies of food, etc. Tires were hard to get."*

### R. J. BOB MORGAN

*"We remember [rationing] and remember people trying to steal gas from us. I had people riding to work with me."*

### SHIRLEY PADHAN ERICKSON

*"I remember rationing. The only thing that really bothered us was sugar rationing. My mother canned all our fruit and made all our food from scratch. We had everything else. I still have several rationing books.*

*"A big garden was always a must. There were six of us to feed. We only bought things we couldn't produce."*

### DOVIE R. (LONG, HALVERSON) WELLCOME

*"I remember gas and sugar being rationed. We got an allotment for gas for our tractor. So I traded gas coupons for sugar coupons so I could do my canning."*

## ETHEL NELSON

*"During the war I remember scrap metal drives being collected in Centralia City Park."*

## EUGENE DONALD "DON" CASTLE

He remembers *"difficulty getting gas and tires and sugar and shortening. My parents raised food in our garden and we had chickens, pigs and a milk cow. My dad rode to work with another man. I used the car to get home at night after work."*

## EUNICE L. HOWARD

*"Gas, tires, nylon stockings. I think I rode to work with Avard Mandery or sometimes took the city bus."*

## JULIA R. FORD MEADOWS

*[I] shared a ride to work. I remember scrap metal drives. Paper drives."*

## MARGARET EVELYN COWLEY WHITFORD

*"We had ration books for gas, shoes, sugar, meat, and tires and other things. We couldn't buy towels and lots of things. Even chewing gum was scarce.*

*"We shared rides to work because of gas rationing. Once in a while my friends and I would take a weekend off work and take the bus to Seattle or Tacoma.*

*"When nylons came out, I signed up on a list and was able to buy one pair."*

## MARTHA LAHMANN LOHRER

*"We had a farm with [a] large garden and [my] parents shared with me. We also had strawberry fields, blueberries, cherries, apples. We canned*

etc.," Alexander said. "A less sensitive sign seen somewhere that we snickered about was an invitation: 'Ladies, bring your fat cans in.'"

Students collected ten-cent stamps to fill a war savings book and purchase a bond for $18.75 that would be worth $25 in ten years. Classes competed among themselves to collect the most stamps. Often the schools showed just what the students were buying with their stamps.

"There was a diagram of a jeep at the southeast hallway entrance to Cascade School," Alexander recalls. "Even the kids were buying war bonds, and we were doing that by filling stamp books. As I recall it was our classroom's mission to buy the right front wheel for that jeep."

At Adna schools, Doris Hastings Bier remembers school bond drives and collecting war bond stamps for an ambulance.

"We got enough and we traded for a bond," she said. "The bond rally at school was a success. [I] can't remember if we pledged enough for an ambulance or just helped stock one."

People took shifts watching the skies overhead for airplanes in case of a Japanese attack. Bier recalls volunteers serving sentry duty on the Adna Bridge over the Chehalis River.

Elanor Wilber of Portland also remembers watching for planes. "We did plane watching from a tower. We did our schedule of reporting as needed."

"My mom (in the Riffe area) was a volunteer watching for airplanes," recalls Dorothy Powell. "She also got yarn from [the] Red Cross, I believe, and knitted scarves and various items for the Army.

"In Florida I went with the lady where I lived to the Red Cross and helped make bandages, I think from old sheets."

"My first year of teaching I was a warden and had to be ready in case of an emergency," recalls Georgie Bright Kunkel, who worked summers while teaching during the school year. "We studied the shapes of planes so that if we spotted an enemy plane we could report it to headquarters."

With the rationing of butter, many people started using margarine at home—but in white pounds with a coloring packet to make it yellow like butter.

"We went to the milk evaporating plant to get powdered milk and we didn't use butter but used margarine," recalls Kunkel. "The butter industry didn't

## BOOK DRIVE

*april 6, 1943*

The book drive the past two weeks for the Red Cross, sponsored by the V. P. A. proved to be a great success with a total of 1,600 books.

Monday, the deadline being sixth period, found the seniors and sophomores frantically gathering books from every place imaginable. The seniors won in the high school with 340 books while the sophomores were only 30 behind.

The eighth grade won in the junior high with 248 books while the third grade, although the lowest grade in the contest, won the grade school prize with a total of 190 books.

Everyone had a lot of fun and we hope the soldiers will enjoy the books as much as we have enjoyed getting them.

MEMORABILIA COURTESY OF DOROTHY POWELL

*Students at Mossyrock High School collected hundreds of books in the spring of 1943 to send overseas to soldiers on the battlefield. Pictured above is a photo from the high school annual. Dorothy McMahan Powell is standing at the far right end of the truck. The woman at the farthest right in the photo is the teacher. The article at the right, encouraging people to donate books for servicemen, appeared in The Chronicle.*

## Mossyrock Comes Thru In Victory Book Campaign

### 2400 Books Collected In Drive By High School Students

Residents of Mossyrock have contributed 2400 books to the 1943 victory book campaign, ac-

## Donate Books For Soldiers

### With Response Increasing, Lewis County Drive Will Continue Into Next Week

Because results of Lewis county's 1943 Victory Book Week, which opened Monday with an appeal for at least one good book from every household to go to the nation's training camps, have increased daily after a slow start, decision has been made to extend the drive into next week. Collection centers, the public libraries and Daily Chronicle offices in Centralia and Chehalis, reported few books appeared Monday and Tuesday, but Wednesday and Thursday the volume picked up.

OUR MEN NEED BOOKS

SEND ALL YOU CAN SPARE

Scores of excellent books for soldiers, sailors and marines have been given and include fiction and non-fiction not earlier than 1936, and some technical books not earlier than 1935. These contributions were in accordance with regulations of the campaign.

"Trash" Not Desired

However, also received were numbers of books obviously picked from attics and closets. They include volumes much outdated and of little worth to service men who desire, just as do all Americans, to read not only the best, but the newest in books.

Those who have not yet given to the campaign are urged to select one good book from their library. Drive leaders urge: "Give a book you enjoyed reading—for those are the books others will also enjoy."

Reminder is made those who do not wish to give books they value highly, or if they have no books, equally welcome will be the pocket-size books on sale in many stores. All of this type of book is modern or of suitable taste for good reading.

Contribution may be made at either of the public libraries or either of the Daily Chronicle offices in the Twin Cities.

THE CHRONICLE AT CENTRALIA

SEATTLE SHIP YARD WWII
PLANT "B"
CLAUDENE MOLLER
ON LEFT

*Claudene Moller, left, participated in a book drive while working as a sheet metal employee at Todd Shipyard's Plant B in Seattle from 1943 to 1945.*

like the margarine industry cutting into their sales so there was a regulation that margarine could not be produced to look like butter. In each white margarine pound there was a packet of coloring. We would put the white margarine into a bowl and put in the coloring and mix it up and mold it back into the loaf shape."

Of course, in the real world, some people will try to game the system, Alexander said.

"Mother could walk into West's Grocery Store [located where the Chehalis Deli is now], and Elmer Purdue, the proprietor, might offer something like: 'Today I've got a little extra sugar or chocolate, Hester, if you've got the right ration stamps.'"

Sarah Ciranny Zopolos worked at Centralia's Safeway during 1941 and 1942.

"Nylons were scarce and only sold to favorite customers," she recalled. "We had them under the counter at the Safeway store.

"I also worked for Leeds shoe store in Seattle in 1942. [The] store only received a few [nylons] and special customers were able to buy a pair. They had seams."

Others simply traded to obtain the stamps they needed. Jane Duell Minear enjoyed great popularity with the men at work when ration books came out.

"I'd trade the liquor coupons of mine for their shoe coupons," she said, noting that she could walk to work. "I didn't drink but was pretty well shod!"

The government also encouraged people to plant a kitchen garden to relieve food shortages and allow more food for the military men fighting overseas. Some scoffed at the idea as a waste with amateur gardeners doing the hoeing.

And in Lewis County, victory gardens were simply a new name for an old practice.

"We always had a garden before there were victory gardens," said Richard Zorn, who shared a bit about how his family dealt with rationing.

"During rationing time, me and my brother drove to Vancouver near

hundreds of quarts of foods and Mother had a cellar to put them, kept eggs, etc."

## PAGE G. BENNETT

"I had a rationing card and had a rider to take with me to work. Up to 1939 we always had a garden. Then I left home to work out so didn't have [any] garden."

## VIVIAN CURRY WOOD

"Gas rationing. I picked up a close friend daily and took her to work. Dorene Lock was her name. She heard ... that her husband's ship went down in battle. Never found him. (Fred Kiefert.)

"We planted a huge garden. I helped Mom put up vegetables in jars. Dad raised a beef to kill. Mom and I packed it in jars and pressure-cooked it on a wood stove. We also fried pork patties and put them down in a huge crock, covered them with lard and put them ... in the basement to keep cool."

## RICHARD LARSON

"I shared rides. I got special gas coupons because I worked at Boeings. Also shared gas coupons among friends."

## BUD BERG

"I had a motorcycle and I rode it part time. When I worked down here at Chehalis, where [the] PUD is today, I was livin' out at Onalaska, and I picked up a woman over on the other side of Burnt Ridge Hill. Bessie Wright. And then I'd take her back home."

He also gave a ride to Vivian Curry and another girl, who gave him their gas coupons.

"I had new car, per se, little Willys—Americar 1942."

## EDWARD F. PEMERL

*"Had very little trouble with rationing. Did get extra gas to drive to work by having riders and also to drive from Seattle to Chehalis to help on the folks' farm. Also helped in [my] father's shoe repair shop.*

## RUTHIE A. KRAUSE, COURTESY OF HER DAUGHTERS ARLENA ZADINA AND LOIS KRAUSE WELLBROCK

*"We got food rations and Ruth was able to preserve a lot of produce from our vegetable garden and fruit was plentiful in our area. Sugar was not a shortage at our house but coffee was too expensive and Ruth only drank it at Boeing. None of her children learned to drink it. Gas coupons were shared with Mrs. Milam for getting to work and with Esther and Uncle Herman for grocery shopping and church. We did not have a car until after the war ended."*

## RUTH HERREN

*"I recall rationing. Teachers met with the people in their school area to issue rationing stamps (I was teaching). My mother let me use her shoe stamps. We used honey and other sweetening instead of sugar, stretched our meat with casseroles. We lived near enough to walk if gas ran low. We saved scrap metal.*

*"We always had a garden so nothing different there."*

## THERESA "TERRY" (WALZ) VANNOY

*She remembers rationing of sugar, butter and meat.*

*"When I went to work for Boeing, we had a car-pool, six people. We did not do anything to get*

Portland to buy horse burgers," he said. "They tasted a lot like elk meat but with lot of onion weren't bad."

But Jane Duell Minear remembers her father's victory garden.

"We lived on Washington Avenue in Chehalis and had a long area between the curb and the sidewalk where lovely rosebushes bloomed. They were invaded by cabbages, carrots, peppers! Dad loved those vegetables!"

"My mother had a piece of land a few blocks from our home in Chehalis where we grew corn and beans, which we canned every summer," Kunkel said. "We also grew strawberries."

Joseph Anderson, a Boeing branch plant employee in Chehalis, said his son in New Guinea had asked for a shipment of lettuce, radish and onion seeds so he could plant a "victory garden."

"A Victory garden probably seems like a little bit of good old U.S.A. to the boys," Anderson is quoted in the August 1944 Boeing News as saying. "And there are a lot of us here at home who don't bother with a Victory garden."

Even The Chronicle joined the Victory Garden promotion in 1942 with an editorial that stated: "The much maligned victory gardens, and those who have been planting and hoeing them, have at last come into their own and have received recognition for their economic and dietary values."

The editorial went on to say the backyard gardeners' efforts may become an economic asset, with produce prices on the rise, and the fresh food may help build resistance to "one of the most dreaded of diseases," cancer.

"So, keep 'em hoeing, America," it concluded. "There is food, money and health in those backyard vegetable gardens."

At one point, the 20 million victory gardens in America produced a third of all vegetables grown in the country, according to Penny Colman, author of *Rosie the Riveter: Women Working on the Home Front in World War II*, published in 1995 by Crown Publishers Inc. of New York.

In the big cities, Victory Gardens provided a visible sign of patriotism.

Eva Stafford, wife of the late Howard Stafford who worked at Boeing in Seattle and Chehalis, recalls moving to Seattle and having to save gas coupons.

"The gas rationing hit us the hardest as we couldn't very often drive back to

MEMORABILIA COURTESY OF PETER LAHMANN

MEMORABILIA COURTESY OF DORIS HASTINGS BIER

*Conserving gasoline required workers and others to share rides. The riders often gave their gas ration coupons to the driver. Above is a mileage rationing record. At left is Clayton Bier's wallet gas rationing card. Below is a basic mileage ration.*

MEMORABILIA COURTESY OF PETER LAHMANN

food or clothes outside of the rationing allowance.

"We didn't have a garden. We lived in an apartment on the third floor. [We] collected paperback books to send overseas."

### EDWARD JOHNSON

"I don't remember much about rationing. Seems that everything we needed we had. I had riders with me all the time so I had plenty of gas; tires wore out pretty fast."

### CLAUDENE MOLLER

"I remember rationing. I rode the city bus to and from work. Had no problems with food rationing. I remember the scrap metal drives."

### JUNE (WEESE) JOACHIM DESKINS

"Rationing wasn't hard at all. We grew up in [the] 1930s. Everyone had nothing. All mothers knew how to conserve and can anything to eat. We fished and hunted.

"We always had a garden and my mother had a green thumb. Lots to eat."

### HELEN C. (JONES) KLINDT

She remembers gasoline rationing. "Guess we carpooled. Traded stamps with my parents."

### JEAN DeSPAIN

"Keeping track of coupons, books, decals. Shared [a] ride. Had no problem with rationing. Collected scrap iron, copper and aluminum and took [it] to [a] collection station in Chehalis. Collected fat and donated [it]."

### ELLEN IRENE KAIN

"Being a teenager, I was very upset with the shoe

rationing. I needed prom shoes. Especially those green sandals I fell in love with! Our elderly neighbor gave me her shoe coupon—so I could buy those silly green shoes. My dad had a big garden in the back yard. I remember gas coupons and sugar coupons."

## ENID ROGERSON

"My first baby was born in 1943. It was hard to get shoe ration stamps for him. But many of mother's friends gave me their shoe ration stamps."

## HELEN RIEDESEL-KNOECHEL

"They rationed silk stockings. We couldn't get any more silk from Japan. This was before nylons. We didn't suffer here at home. We thought mostly of the boys overseas. I remember the scrap metal drives. I think that was when Chehalis donated the cannon that sat down from the library. I don't remember that rationing was a real hardship.

"Everyone who could planted a victory garden. We also rolled bandages for the wounded, donated blood, blacked out all the windows."

## ELANOR WILBER

"Food was not the only thing that was rationed. Tires and gasoline also. Of course, going to margarine, coloring it in a bag and a pellet of coloring. I shared rides. Meat was one of the hardest items to do without. We took part in the drives. We also saved toothpaste containers."

## JOHN ALEXANDER JR.

"Rationing applied to all materials related to the war effort. Gas was not too much of an issue for our family. Dad lived close enough to the office that he could walk to work. Therefore we seemed

Chehalis to visit with our kinfolks," she said.

"The yard of the place we moved to had been poorly kept, so we dug up the yard and planted our own 'victory garden.' Our next-door neighbor had a beautiful well-kept yard. After watching us dig up our yard, he got his shovel and dug up his nice yard and he, too, planted a garden. There were many community victory gardens in the Seattle area."

Bier and other young people from Curtis, Adna and Boistfort worked in Erett Deck's field at Klaber, where he grew acres of kale and beets, and later in cornfields on the right side of Highway 6 past the turnoff to Boistfort.

"We worked hoeing and harvesting when I was 14. ... We hoed row after row, harvested the crops that were driven to Chehalis to the cannery. School started and we were excused in the afternoon to go to work."

She also helped with corn harvesting at Schollard's Field (later Hamilton Meadows).

"I drove the truck in the field while others picked and loaded the truck. Kids would pick corn and pitch it into truck—got full and used a second truck. Wages were 45 cents to 75 cents an hour. I got 75 cents, as did my friend Dorothy. We were excused from school to work when needed."

Some of the funniest ration stories stemmed from attempts to reproduce nylons or silk stockings—without nylon or silk, which were used to make parachutes and tow ropes.

"Nylon was a war need and soon there were no nylon goods on the market, including women's stockings," Eva Stafford recalled. "At that time women wore dresses (not pants) and nylon stockings. Some women, when they went to social affairs, would paint their legs so they looked like they were wearing nylons."

Mabel Cook, who remembers walking to work and her brother's scrap metal drives, told about making do without nylons.

"Nylon hose were not available during the war but we did have silk hose. The only color we had was gunmetal (gray). When hose were totally unavailable, my friend Opal and I would take 'pancake makeup' and rub [it] on [our] bare legs, then take a pencil and draw a line down the center of [the] leg to look like the seam formed in the hose."

# Tacomans Wait for Butter

More and more Tacomans are beginning to feel the pinch of war and the effects of rationing. With very little meat on hand, many markets have closed business until rationing starts March 29. Others continue in business offering fish and fowl for sale. Butter, too, has been on the short side of the list for some time. When a merchant gets a supply of butter, it doesn't take long for the word to spread. A Tacoma Times photographer happened by a downtown market as long lines formed awaiting an opportunity to get into the market to purchase butter from a merchant who had just received a supply. The photograph above was taken on the Market st. side of the Crystal Palace market Friday afternoon and shows the lineup outside the building. Incidentally, the supply of butter was soon snapped up.

*With meat, butter and other products in scarce supply, Tacoma residents waited in line when they heard this merchant just received a supply of butter. An advertisement in The Chronicle, right, tells readers: 'There is no need to exchange your precious ration points for anything less than Darigold.'*

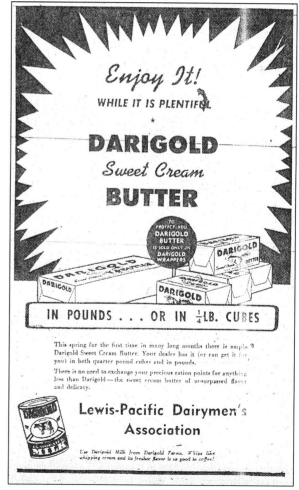

Enjoy It!
WHILE IT IS PLENTIFUL

DARIGOLD
Sweet Cream
BUTTER

TO PROTECT YOU DARIGOLD BUTTER IS SOLD ONLY IN DARIGOLD WRAPPERS

IN POUNDS . . . OR IN ¼ LB. CUBES

This spring for the first time in many long months there is ample Darigold Sweet Cream Butter. Your dealer has it (or can get it for you) in both quarter pound cubes and in pounds.

There is no need to exchange your precious ration points for anything less than Darigold — the sweet cream butter of unsurpassed flavor and delicacy.

Lewis-Pacific Dairymen's Association

Use Darigold Milk from Darigold Farms. Whips like whipping cream and its fresher flavor is so good in coffee!

## Because

**Your money will be safe.** The full faith and credit of the United States Government is pledged for payment of both principal and interest on these United States Savings Bonds.

**Your money will be put to work** at once in the national defense program to protect the freedom and safety of the United States.

| SERIES F | SERIES G |
|---|---|
| Appreciation Bond. Registered. Not transferable. Denominations: $100, $500, $1,000, $5,000, and $10,000. Dated first of month in which payment is received. Matures 12 years from issue date of bond. | Current income Bond. Registered. Not transferable. Denominations: $100, $500, $1,000, $5,000, and $10,000. Dated first of month in which payment is received. Matures 12 years from issue date of bond. |
| 2.53 percent a year, compounded semiannually, when bond is held to maturity. | 2.5 percent a year. Interest is paid semiannually by Treasury check. |
| *Issue price*  *Maturity value*<br>$74.00 will increase in 12 years to $100.00<br>370.00 will increase in 12 years to 500.00<br>740.00 will increase in 12 years to 1,000.00<br>3,700.00 will increase in 12 years to 5,000.00<br>7,400.00 will increase in 12 years to 10,000.00 | This bond is priced at par. It is redeemable at par if it is held by the owner for 12 years from issue date. (See Table of Redemption Values on face of bond, or at any sales agency.) |
| This bond can be registered in—<br>(1) the name of one individual, or<br>(2) of two individuals as co-owners, or<br>(3) of one individual and one individual as beneficiary.<br>This bond can be registered in the name of any association, partnership, trustee, or corporation. | This bond can be registered in—<br>(1) the name of one individual, or<br>(2) of two individuals as co-owners, or<br>(3) of one individual and one individual as beneficiary.<br>This bond can be registered in the name of any association, partnership, trustee, or corporation. |
| Owner is limited to $50,000 of Series F bonds (cost price) or to $50,000 of Series F and Series G, combined, issued in any one calendar year. | Owner is limited to $50,000 of Series G bonds (cost price) or to $50,000 of Series G and Series F, combined, issued in any one calendar year. |
| Owner may redeem bond on 1 month's written notice after 6 months from issue date of bond. Table of Redemption Values appears on face of bond. | Owner may redeem bond on 1 month's written notice after 6 months from issue date of bond. Table of Redemption Values appears on face of bond. |
| At Federal Reserve Banks. Through other designated Sales Agencies. Direct by mail from the Treasurer of the United States, or from any Federal Reserve Bank. | At Fe... Throu... Direc... Sta... |

4

Throughout the war, the government sold savings bonds to raise money for national defense. Students, employees and company branches competed to sell the most savings bonds or raise the most money.

## WHAT ARE *United States Savings Bonds?*

These bonds are direct obligations of the United States Government. They went on sale March 1, 1935. ★ More than 2,500,000 American men and women have placed more than $3,750,000,000 of their savings in these bonds, and their maturity value exceeds $5,000,000,000, as of March 1, 1941. ★ Five billion dollars is the largest amount of money now invested in any single security, and it represents the faith of the American people in the freedom and safety of the United States.

### Why should Savings Bonds be bought?

Today there is further need of safety for the United States and for all its people.

United States Savings Bonds are the quickest way in which you can both serve your country and conserve your earnings. To meet the needs of all our people, the Government now offers three kinds of Savings Bonds:

(1) The SERIES E BOND preserves the character of the Savings Bonds which have proved so popular in the past. This bond is issued to meet the needs of the small investor, who can buy for $18.75 a bond that will appreciate in value in 10 years to $25. Larger bonds up to $1,000 are issued at the same rate of appreciation, which gives an investment yield of 2.9 percent to maturity in 10 years after issue date.

(2) The new SERIES F BOND is issued to meet the needs of people who can invest up to $50,000 a year; and it may also be bought by associations, trustees, or corporations. For $74 they may buy a bond that will appreciate in value in 12 years to $100. Larger bonds are issued at the same rate, which gives an investment yield of 2.53 percent to maturity in 12 years after issue date.

(3) The new SERIES G BOND meets the needs of individuals, associations, and corporations that want current income checks. Offered at par, these bonds bear interest at 2.5 percent per

annum. These bonds, in denominations of $100 up to $10,000, are redeemable at par if they are held for 12 years from issue date.

### What security is behind Savings Bonds?

The full faith and credit of the United States Government is pledged for payment of both principal and interest on these bonds.

Through these three United States Savings Bonds, the Government gives a balanced and complete investment program to the people. Salient facts about each type of bond appear on pages 3, 4, and 5 of this folder. Complete details will be found in Offering Circulars dated April 15, 1941, available at the Treasury Department or Post Offices, Federal Reserve Banks, and other designated agencies.

### How may everyone buy Savings Bonds?

There remains one great army of savers, eager to accumulate funds with which to support the national defense program, to whom the payment of $18.75 at one time is not convenient. For these boys and girls, young workers, clerks, soldiers and sailors, a simple system of saving money with which to buy United States Savings Bonds is provided through Postal Savings Stamps, explained on the next page.

6      7

## POSTAL Savings Stamps

At Post Offices and elsewhere you will now be given a stamp card or album for mounting the kind of Postal Savings Stamp you find easiest to collect.

On the purchase of a 10-cent stamp, you will be given a card on which you may mount 10 of these stamps, and exchange them for $1 worth of the larger sizes.

On the purchase of a 25-cent stamp, you will be given an album on which you may mount 75 of these stamps. When so filled, the album will have a total value of $18.75, the purchase price of a Savings Bond that will appreciate in 10 years to $25.

On the purchase of a 50-cent stamp, you will be given an album to mount 75 of these stamps, total value $37.50, the purchase price of a Savings Bond that will appreciate in 10 years to $50.

On the purchase of a $1 stamp, you will be given an album to mount 75 stamps, total value $75, the purchase price of a Savings Bond that will appreciate in 10 years to $100.

On the purchase of a $5 stamp, you will be given an album to mount 15 stamps, total value $75, the purchase price of a Savings Bond that will appreciate in 10 years to $100.

The completed album is a quick, convenient way to exchange your current savings for United States Savings Bonds.

8

MEMORABILIA COURTESY OF PETER LAHMANN

Drawing a straight "seam" proved to be rather difficult.

"We couldn't buy nylon stockings but you could buy a cream or spray to put on your legs," remembers Dovie R. (Long Halverson) Wellcome.

"But I tried it and it rained and my liquid stockings ran down my legs [leaving them] all streaked and made a mess. It didn't work."

# Grandpa lost ration book

ALTHOUGH JERRY AND CRISTLE JOBE lived on a farm near Coalgate, Oklahoma, when World War II began, a doctor advised them to move west for the welfare of their children.

"Mom and Dad came out to Washington after a doctor told them they needed to bring us kids to a healthy area," said Winnie Nichols, who was about five at the time. But they needed to find jobs before uprooting the family.

"The doctor said they had to leave—to save us kids. They had already lost three children to illness and pneumonia. The doctor recommended Washington state and said they could probably find work picking fruit. So they came out."

The couple left their three children behind on the farm with paternal grandparents. Nichols recalls enjoying life on the farm with a team of mules, two horses and plenty of crops, including peanuts, cotton, corn and watermelons.

"We would go to town in our wagon pulled by our two mules to get groceries and had to give little tabs from ration books to the grocery clerk at Kellog's big grocery," she remembers. "We ate lunch in the wagon yard— bread and bologna and bananas."

Although they had trouble obtaining sugar for making jams and canning, she said the family always had plenty to eat because they lived on a farm with chickens, eggs, hogs, cows and "one pair of shoes for trips to town."

"I was just five years old and though my parents and my grandparents had a stressful time, we kids never suffered."

to have enough gas to make one vacation at the beach each year.

"Mother was a productive gardener anyway and put in a large 'victory garden.' People went to the local farms for eggs and milk, and brought home cream to churn into butter."

FRANCES NUGENT

"Gas—shoes. Foil drives. Selling war bonds."

JUNE G. AYRES O'CONNELL

"Rationing was not difficult for my family.

DOROTHY HADALLER HAGSTROM

"I was still in high school in 1942. Sugar, shoes."

DALE ALEXANDER

"Yes, I remember all the above and just took it as best we could."

Jerry and Cristle found jobs at the cannery in Chehalis, then began working at the Boeing plant.

"When they had saved enough money they sent for us three kids," she said. "We then got on a train (crowded with servicemen) and came out to Chehalis with my grandparents.

"On the trip out, my grandfather got off the train to get food in Cheyenne, Wyoming, and then, thinking the train was leaving, he ran to catch the train and forgot the ration books. We were fortunate that the conductor knew the store name and my grandparents wrote the store requesting that they forward the ration books to us in Chehalis. The people were extremely nice and they did forward our ration books to us."

But the family found housing scarce. The parents, grandparents and three children all crammed into one room in the Crest Apartments, across the corner from Boeing Aircraft Co.'s branch plant in Chehalis. They moved into a three-room apartment as soon as it became available.

"We had a tough time in cramped quarters and Mom and Dad moved us to Doty, Washington, with our grandparents. They came out on weekends on the Greyline bus that went from Chehalis to the ocean beaches."

Finally they found a house in Chehalis and the family reunited under one roof.

"Every year we had a large garden and Mom and my paternal grandmother canned vegetables and fruits from our garden," she recalled. "My parents hunted and we had venison as well as many fish from their weekend fishing trips."

She said her father worked as a farmer and drilled rock in Oklahoma before moving to Chehalis, where he worked as a handyman earning 77 cents an hour at the Chehalis Packing Co. for three months before hiring on at Boeing when the branch plant opened in Chehalis in 1943. He earned $1.35 an hour as a machinist at Boeing, where he worked from Jan. 14, 1944, until Aug. 27, 1945.

Later he worked as a laborer for Rowe and Thompson Co., earning a dollar an hour, and then at Borden's creamery for 87 cents an hour. He held many other laborer jobs later.

Cristle Jobe started working at Boeing as a bucker, holding a rod for a riveter, then later became a riveter.

## "Biggest crop we've ever had"

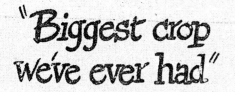

There are thousands and thousands of Long Distance calls every day. Three, five and ten times as many between some cities as before the war.

When your Long Distance call is on war-crowded circuits, the operator may ask you to—"Please limit your call to 5 minutes."

That's especially important these days when wires are needed for the war.

**BACK THE ATTACK— BUY MORE THAN BEFORE**

VICTORY GARDEN

THE PACIFIC TELEPHONE AND TELEGRAPH COMPANY
120 W. Magnolia—Telephone 900    1120 Boistfort—Telephone 950
CENTRALIA                          CHEHALIS

*Patriotism definitely was 'in' during World War II as these advertisements from The Chronicle newspaper show. Many businesses placed a line at the bottom of their ads encouraging readers to 'back the attack' and buy war bonds.*

# Oldtimer Backs Invasion!
## *Why Not You?*

Joe Bilodeau, sled builder of the Weyerhaeuser Timber Company Vail-McDonald Operations, is still hard at it working in the critical-lumber industry. Joe is now 83 years old and a logger for 70 years, a consistent buyer of war bonds and one of the first employees to purchase the extra bond in the Fifth War Loan drive.

V — 5TH WAR LOAN

**Back the Attack! — BUY MORE THAN BEFORE**

Sponsored in the interests of Victory by the

## Weyerhaeuser Timber Company
Vail-McDonald Operations

BOTH ADS FROM THE CHRONICLE AT CENTRALIA

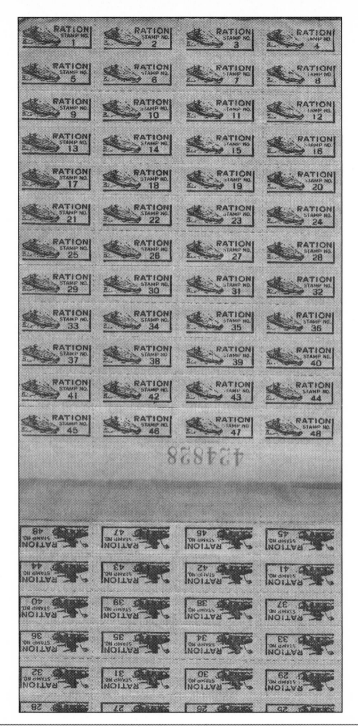

At the same time, Cristle's mother, Grace Burrows Jennings, worked in a munitions plant in Savannah, Oklahoma. Grace Jennings later moved to Chehalis, along with her sisters and brothers. One relative who had two children lived in the Jobes' garage for several years.

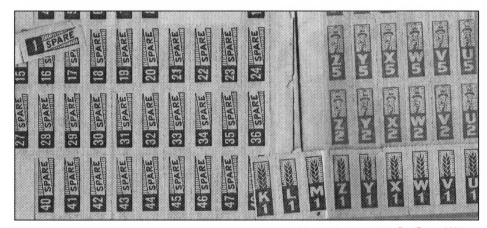

*On a trip from Oklahoma to Washington, Winnie Nichols' grandfather accidentally left his ration coupon book at a store in Wyoming. He wrote to the store owner upon arriving in Washington and the kindly proprietor sent the family the coupon book.*

Chapter Five

# Women Join the Work Force

Defense industries recruit
women, minorities for jobs

## MILDRED DOLLARHYDE KEEN

*Mildred Dollarhyde Keen started working at Triumph Explosives Inc. in Elkton, Maryland, in 1943. She earned $1,793.45 for the year.*

"This was my first move away from home in Virginia to Elkton, Maryland, at the age of 19. I worked in the tracer area, where we pressed powder pellets in tracers for 40mm shells. It was not hard work, just tedious shift work. The plant worked around the clock and we changed shifts on a two-week rotation."

*The town, which had 3,500 residents, swelled to more than 12,000 during the war, according to the Web site at: http://475thmpeg.memorieshop.com/ Elkton/index.html, which refers to these explosives workers as the "boom-boom" girls of World War II. It also quotes newspaper articles from the time, stating that in September 1942 one person died and three people suffered serious injuries in an explosion, and on Feb. 20, 1943, it said more workers were badly injured.*

"The job was stressful because of the imminent danger we knew was around us. In May 1943 there was an explosion in another area of the plant. Everything was shut down for two shifts before resuming production. We heard there were deaths, but never knew how many."

*According to a May 8, 1943, front page headline, "Fifteen Killed; Many Injured by Explosion—Fire."*

"I lived in a company housing apartment with five other girls," Keen said. "We received ration stamps, which we would pool together to buy groceries. There were some fun things to do when we weren't working and plenty of Army and Navy men to date."

### Find The Lucky Girl In Picture -- Is It Your Face?

For the second mystery picture, we give you this random shot taken in the area canteen during the showing of the "Life and Death of the Hornet."

There is a circle around a face in the picture. Look in the circle, and see if the face belongs to you, or anyone that you know.

If the face is familiar, the lucky person will get a 25 dollar bond, free, as a gift from the company.

Here's all you have to do. Report to the TNT Office in the Personnel Building with the picture, and suitable means of identification. There you get the form for getting the bond.

This offer is restricted to those employees who are already buying bonds by the payroll deduction plan, or, those employees who will agree to subscribe for a 25 dollar bond, which, with the free one in the picture, will make a 50 dollar

bond at half price.

If you recognize yourself, c'mon up and tell us about it.

Last month's winner is Rose Holmuller of 534. She is a native of Chesapeake City. Rose was already buying bonds under the payroll deduction plan, so when her next bond comes through, she will have one free, as a gift from the company.

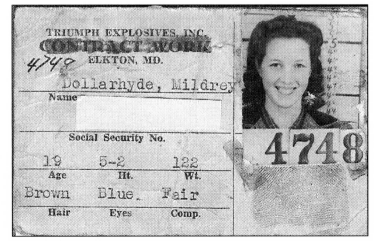

*Mildred Dollarhyde Keen is seated at a table at the bottom right of the above photo, which appeared in The Trident, a publication for Triumph Explosives employees. At left is her worker ID badge.*

PHOTOS COURTESY OF MILDRED DOLLARHYDE KEEN

# Manpower shortage hits

AS MORE MEN LEFT THEIR JOBS on the home front to serve overseas, employers found themselves in early 1943 facing a severe shortage of workers to do business, whether in the defense industry, office supplies or groceries.

But many employers still resisted hiring African-American men, or women of any race, to do the work.

In mid-1941, the leader of the Brotherhood of Sleeping Car Porters, A. Phillip Randolph, met with other black leaders and proposed a massive demonstration in Washington, D.C., to protest the discrimination among employers who refused to hire blacks for war industry jobs.

To avoid such a march by thousands of African-Americans, President Roosevelt signed Executive Order 8802, which established the Fair Employment Practices Commission and prohibited racial or religious discrimination in the defense industries.

On Columbus Day 1942, President Roosevelt urged employers to abandon their prejudices in hiring.

"In some communities employers dislike to hire women. In others they are reluctant to hire Negroes. We can no longer afford to indulge such prejudice."

Malcolm "Bud" Berg remembers when the Boeing Aircraft Co. in Seattle started hiring black men. He said it didn't seem to cause the other workers any problems. "They pretty much got along."

But in other cities, racial tensions created clashes, which peaked in 1943 with thirty hours of rioting in Detroit that left thirty-four people dead.

The government launched propaganda campaigns to persuade women to join the work force, calling it their patriotic duty with slogans such as a 1943 billboard ad that stated: "If you used an electric mixer in your kitchen, you can learn to run a drill press. If you followed recipes exactly, you can learn to load a shell."

Songs also encouraged women to work, such as "Minnie's in the Money," performed by Benny Goodman's jazz band, or the popular tune glamorizing the work of "Rosie the Riveter," commending her for working on the

## HELEN C. (JONES) KLINDT

*"I worked at John Deere in Moline, Illinois, during 1944 and 1945. My job title was riveter. My starting salary was 91 cents an hour ... bucking rivets on the tails of B-17. I wore slacks, long sleeved shirt, snood."*

*She remembers her job at the Rock Island Arsenal Ammunition Plant, where she "bucked rivets," as "very busy" and the morale as "tense and cautious." She didn't recall anyone being injured or killed while she worked there.*

*"All my friends worked at war plants to help the war effort."*

## JUNE (WEESE) JOACHIM DESKINS

*"I and a lot of fellow grads went to Tacoma and worked in [the] shipyards. Both brothers worked there nights and I stayed with them and their wives in an apartment. I worked swing shift and came home at 11:30 p.m. and crossed through Wright's Park. Wow. Can't do that now. Got tired of Tacoma in 1942 and applied at the telephone company on Boistfort Avenue in Chehalis. Business office paid $21 a week."*

*"I worked in Todd Shipyards in Tacoma in 1942 until July 1943. I was paid $52 a week. Came home every weekend with a man who loaded up his car. Ernest Creech (later built bowling alley in Centralia). No dress code at shipyards, except no pants in time office (where I worked 3 to 11:30 p.m.)*

*"Hated living in Tacoma."*

## DALE ALEXANDER

*"I was a machinist at Boeing and made parts for the B-17 and B-29s."*

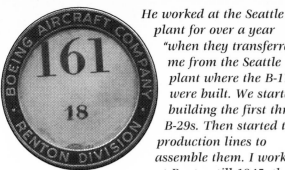

*He worked at the Seattle plant for over a year "when they transferred me from the Seattle plant where the B-17s were built. We started building the first three B-29s. Then started the production lines to assemble them. I worked at Renton till 1945, then went into the service till the end of the war with Japan.*

*Dale Alexander still has his Boeing ID badge, above.*

*"Came home and got into the sawmill business."* He started Alexander Lumbermill in 1949, where, he said, *"my starting salary was not very much."*

## MABEL COOK

*"I worked in the Bremerton Naval Shipyards in the communications department. Repaired equipment. Wore coveralls. We were locked in because all communication to and from the shipyard went through here."*

## EVA STAFFORD

*Eva Stafford, whose husband Howard worked at Boeing both in Seattle and later in Chehalis as assistant foreman, lived in a two-story house near the Seattle plant with wood heat and an electric washing machine but no dryer. They had lived at Chehalis before the war started.*

*"When the war broke out he got a job at the Seattle plant, then we moved to Seattle. Very soon he was promoted to a job as an assistant foreman over a crew (mainly women) who worked on one of the night shifts.*

*"Howard died in 1984."*

assembly line for victory and putting to shame the other girls sipping martinis in cocktail bars.

In 1943, graphic artist J. Howard Miller created a poster for the Westinghouse Corp. depicting a woman with a perfectly made up face and her hair tied in a bandanna, wearing a work shirt with an ID pin on her collar. With her right arm raised, she says: "We Can Do It!"

The same year, Norman Rockwell's Rosie the Riveter appeared on the cover of the Saturday Evening Post.

In 1944, The Chronicle ran a regular column called "Hit the Rivet, Sister," by Ann Pendleton, described as "the real-life adventures of a society girl who goes to work in a war plant."

While Caucasian men accepted the entry of African-American men into the work force, Berg said, they didn't accept it as readily when Boeing hired women in March 1942. But within a year, women made up more than half of the company's work force.

Many men loathed working women—especially married women—during the Depression because they felt the women took jobs that could be helping a man to feed his family.

In 1940 more than 15 percent of all married women worked outside the home and most of the 11.5 million women who held jobs worked because they needed the money, according to oral historian Sherna B. Gluck, in her book, *Rosie the Riveter Revisited: Women, the War and Social Change*, published in 1987 by Twayne Publishers of Boston.

But during the war, Gluck said, an additional 6 million women joined the labor market: 3 million worked in the defense industry, 2 million held clerical jobs, and 1 million worked for the federal government. Women held jobs in shipyards, lumber mills, aircraft plants and foundries or worked as bus drivers, streetcar conductors or office workers.

Many women left low-paying jobs as garment-makers, waitresses, maids and farming for work in defense industries. Sometimes fierce competition for workers forced lower-paying employers who traditionally hired women—such as laundries and restaurants—out of business, according to Penny Colman, author of *Rosie the Riveter: Women Working on the Home Front in World War II* published in 1995 by Crown Publishers Inc. of New York.

*A Simple Guide to*

# BLUEPRINT READING

A TEXT FOR THOSE ENGAGED IN A PRELIMINARY STUDY
OF BLUEPRINT READING

*By*

**WILLIAM N. WRIGHT**
ENGINEERING DEPARTMENT
**BOEING AIRCRAFT COMPANY**
SEATTLE, U.S.A.

AFFILIATE

INSTITUTE OF THE AERONAUTICAL SCIENCES

*After dealing with double-digit unemployment figures during the Depression, the nation found itself without enough workers to build the machinery of war—and do other jobs that servicemen had held before joining the military. Companies sought workers among the ranks of housewives, encouraging them with slogans such as 'We Can Do It!' They also produced guides to teach novices quickly how to help build airplanes with very little training.*

## RUTH HERREN

*"My teacher's salary was small so I needed to earn extra money in the summer. We had a couple of weeks training and then learned the rest on the job. I can't remember the wage but it seemed a lot then.*

*"I worked at Boeings in Seattle during the summers of 1943 and 1944. My job title was inspector.*

*"The first summer I lived with a friend in Rainier Valley, bused to the main plant. I think we started at 7:30, break around 10, noon to 12:30, afternoon fifteen-minute break, off at 4 o'clock. Worked in wing assembly, spot welding.*

*"The second summer I lived in the U District, bused to downtown since I worked at a receiving warehouse—I think on First Avenue or thereabouts. We inspected parts, compared with blueprints.*

*"Noisy in spot welding and we were not told to wear ear protection. My hearing was affected for about two hours after leaving the plant. I was an inspector for wing assembly so had to climb up on the machine to check welds. Pants were required and hair protection.*

*"Morale was good on the job,"* she said, adding that nobody was hurt while she worked there.

*"No health-care coverage. Only benefits were snacks (candy bars, nuts) available at the plant, things hard to find at grocery stores."*

Workers were *"required to join a union even when we were going to work only in the summer."*

*"I was a teacher, just worked the two summers."*

In Vancouver, Washington, she wrote, a schoolteacher earned 75 cents an hour while the same woman could make $1.25 an hour at the Kaiser shipyards. The number of women in unions jumped from 800,000 before the war to 3 million by 1945.

By 1944, ex-homemakers accounted for a third of the people working in defense jobs, and the number of employed women had increased to 18.2 million, according to statistics in *The Life and Times of Rosie the Riveter: The Story of Three Million Working Women During World War II* by Miriam Frank, Marilyn Ziebarth and Connie Field, published in 1982 by Clarity Educational Products of Emeryville, California.

Before the war, the authors wrote, young, single women accounted for most of the working women, while after the war women in the work force were primarily married and over 35.

Berg said to start with in Seattle, the company hired "a bunch of prostitutes" from Alaska and "put them in there." The guys working at the plant didn't like it, he said.

"'Can't get any cheaper than this,' they said. I said, 'I don't care what they are as long as they do their job and don't bend too many rivets and they try to learn. Their private affairs are none of mine.'"

Later his wife, Carol Kay Berg, worked at Plant No. 1 in Seattle, sorting rivets.

"That's a nasty job because those rivets are cold," Berg said. "Can you imagine eight hours of that? And she had to know them by sizes, too."

After they had a daughter, Sharon Irene, April 26, 1943, Berg said his mother took care of the baby while they worked. Altogether they had two sons and two daughters.

As more and more Caucasian women joined the plant, men grew used to working side by side with the opposite sex.

Georgie Bright Kunkel of Seattle, a teacher who worked in the office at Boeing in Seattle and later as a mechanic at the Chehalis branch, held summer jobs at the Port of Embarkation assisting in shipping supplies to Alaska and at the Federal Housing Administration.

"I was a schoolteacher when the war broke out and there wasn't much to do

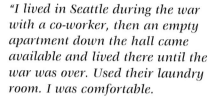

*Rosie the Riveters and men who held jobs in the defense industry earned good money at the time, anywhere from 57 cents to $1.30 an hour. Based on the menu prices below, they didn't have to spend too much of their earnings to buy a decent meal. Above, Triumph Explosives workers belonged to the United Mine Workers of America. At left, Mildred Dollarhyde Keen holds a 40mm shell. Her 1943 W-2 form shows she earned $1,793.45 and had $187.39 withheld for income tax.*

## MENU

### OYSTERS AND CLAMS

| | | | |
|---|---|---|---|
| Half Doz. Raw Oysters | .25 | Large in Milk | .30 |
| Little Neck Clams, Raw | .25 | Clam Stew, Small | .30 |
| Stew, Small In Milk | .30 | Fried Oysters, Doz. | .75 |
| Stew, Small In Cream | .45 | Fried Oysters, Half Doz. | .40 |

### SOUPS

| | | | |
|---|---|---|---|
| Chicken | .15 | Puree of Tomato | .15 |
| Vegetable | .15 | Cream of Tomato | .20 |

### FISH IN SEASON

| | | | |
|---|---|---|---|
| Broiled Spanish Mackerel | .50 | Fried Fillet of Sole | .50 |
| Fried or Broiled Halibut | .50 | Fried Trout | .40 |
| Fried Scallops | .50 | | |

### STEAKS, CHOPS, ETC.

| | | | |
|---|---|---|---|
| Small Steak | .80 | Frizzled Beef, Cream | .50 |
| Sirloin Steak | 1.10 | Veal Cutlet, Tomato Sauce | .50 |
| Tenderloin Steak | 1.10 | Fried Ham | .50 |
| 2 Lamb Chops | .75 | Fried Bacon | .50 |
| 2 Pork Chops | .60 | Baked Beans | .25 |
| Hamburg Steak, Plain | .50 | Ham and Baked Beans | .40 |

### POTATOES

| | | | |
|---|---|---|---|
| Potatoes, Mashed | .10 | Potatoes, Julienne | .15 |
| Potatoes, Lyonnaise | .15 | Potatoes, Plain Fried | .15 |
| Potatoes, O'Brien | .20 | Potatoes, Stewed in Cream | .20 |
| Potatoes, Hash Brown | .15 | | |

### SANDWICHES

| | | | |
|---|---|---|---|
| Tongue Sandwich | .25 | Oyster Sandwich | .20 |
| Tomato Sandwich | .15 | Hamburg Sandwich | .20 |
| Lettuce | .15 | Ham and Egg | .25 |
| Ham Sandwich | .15 | Western Egg | .25 |
| American Cheese | .15 | Combination | .30 |
| Egg | .15 | Chicken | .35 |
| Fried Ham | .15 | Club | .50 |
| Sardine | .25 | Ham and Cheese Combination | .25 |

### SALADS AND RELISHES

| | | | |
|---|---|---|---|
| Hot Chicken | .45 | Potato Salad | .15 |
| Chicken Salad, Mayonnaise | | Cole Slaw | .10 |
| Dressing | .50 | Table Celery | .15 |
| Lettuce and Tomato Salad | .35 | Queen Olives | .20 |

## MENU

### COFFEE, TEA, ETC.

| | | | |
|---|---|---|---|
| Cup of Coffee | .10 | Cup of Postum | .10 |
| Iced Coffee | .10 | Glass of Milk | .10 |
| Pot of Tea | .10 | Cocoa, with Milk | .15 |
| Iced Tea | .10 | Half Cream, Half Milk | .20 |

### DESSERTS

| | | | |
|---|---|---|---|
| Home Made Pies | .10 | Rice Pudding | .10 |
| We bake them ourselves | | Ice Cream | .15 |
| fresh every day | | Pound Cake | .10 |

### EGGS AND OMELETS

| | | | |
|---|---|---|---|
| Eggs, Fried | 2 for .30 | Minced Ham and Scrambled | |
| Eggs, Boiled | 2 for .30 | Eggs | .40 |
| Eggs, Scrambled | 2 for .30 | Ham Omelet | .45 |
| Omelet, Plain | 2 for .30 | Bacon Omelet | .50 |
| Poached Eggs on Toast | .35 | Cheese Omelet | .50 |
| Ham and Eggs | .35 | Jelly Omelet | .50 |
| Bacon and Eggs | .50 | Tomato Omelet | .60 |
| | | Spanish Omelet | .50 |

### VEGETABLES

The finest obtainable - carefully prepared

| | | | |
|---|---|---|---|
| American Green Peas | .15 | Stewed Spinach | .15 |
| Stewed Corn | .15 | Sliced Tomatoes | .20 |
| String Beans | .15 | Fried Onions | .15 |
| Lima Beans | .15 | Stewed Tomatoes | .20 |

### FRUITS IN SEASON

The choicest the market affords

| | | | |
|---|---|---|---|
| Sliced Orange | .15 | Baked Apple | .15 |
| Grape Fruit, Half | .15 | Baked Apple in Cream | .20 |
| Apple Sauce | .10 | Stewed Prunes | .10 |
| Half Cantaloupe | .15 | Strawberries in Cream | .20 |
| Watermelon | .15 | | |

### CEREAL AND TOAST

With Choice Dairy Milk or Cream

| | | | |
|---|---|---|---|
| Grape Nuts, Milk | .15 | French Toast | .20 |
| Force, Milk | .15 | Milk Toast | .20 |
| Corn Flakes, Milk | .15 | Cream Toast | .20 |
| Post Toasties, Milk | .15 | Bowl of Milk with Uneeda | |
| Shredded Wheat, Milk | .15 | Biscuit | .20 |
| Dry Toast | .10 | With Graham Crackers | .20 |
| Buttered Toast | .10 | | |

PHOTO AND MEMORABILIA COURTESY OF MILDRED DOLLARHYDE KEEN

## SARAH CIRANNY ZOPOLOS

*Sarah Ciranny, who was single at the time, worked in the cafeteria at Boeing in Seattle.*

"I didn't have any training," she said.

"I lived in Seattle during the war with a co-worker, then an empty apartment down the hall came available and lived there until the war was over. Used their laundry room. I was comfortable.

*Sarah Ciranny, a 1941 Centralia graduate, worked in the cafeteria at Boeing in Seattle.*

"I worked in the cafeteria. We made green salad in a large stainless steel bowl about six feet on three legs. Also sandwiches and stapled wax paper to half size. Soup was made at a different location. Then on a four-wheel cart we served the workers from the cart. I should say they came and chose the kind of soup and sandwich. Don't remember if they paid or a deduction on their paycheck.

"Everyone was serious and wanted the war to get over and tried to help each other."

She said she didn't face dangers on the job or see any discrimination.

"Met my first 'black' co-worker. Very pleasant and helpful in the Boeing cafeteria. She was tall and very neat."

## THERESA "TERRY" (WALZ) VANNOY

*After living in North Dakota, where the Depression had hit hard as it did in much of the nation, Theresa "Terry" (Walz) Vannoy said, "we needed work."*

"I worked at Boeing in South Seattle from 1943 to

SEATTLE SHIP YARD WWII
SHEET METAL SHOP
BABY SHOWER FOR CO-WORKER
Front row 3rd from left
CLAUDENE MOLLER

*Recruiting women into the workplace also brought a new social activity: baby showers. In the photo above, co-workers at the Todd Shipyards in Seattle hold a baby shower for one of their fellow employees. Claudene Moller is in the front row, third from the left.*

in the summer months but work in the war industry since we couldn't travel anywhere much," she said.

"I think if I had worked as a mechanic in a time that we were not at war I would have felt discrimination," Kunkel said. "However, during wartime women were considered working until—the war was over. Just as women who worked before the war were considered working until—they got pregnant or got married. They were never considered to be a regular part of the work force."

But men working at Boeing didn't see any discrimination.

"I don't recall any racial or sexual going on," said Page G. Bennett, who worked at the Seattle plant as a riveter before transferring to the Chehalis branch plant. "I worked with about any race and color there was. I had mostly women that bucked the rivets for me."

Berg agreed, saying eighty-five percent of the employees were women at some plants and they did "a damned good job."

"They picked it up fast. They had a competitive spirit, and they would get to racing, to see who could get the most done fastest," he said. Then one would make a mistake and they had to call him—the re-work man on swing shift.

But when Boeing started hiring black women, many male workers objected strenuously, Berg said.

"I can say up in Seattle when the blacks first came in, a lot of the guys wouldn't work with those black girls. … They wouldn't work with them. Some of the guys said, 'You ain't putting them with me.' I said, 'They haven't done anything to me.' I treated them just like anybody else.

"They come around to me and said, 'Berg—do you have anything against working with these black girls?' I said, 'No. I don't have anything against working with them. They're here. They're going to stay. Better get along with them.'"

So, he said, the supervisors kept bringing him more black women, since he had no objections to working with them. "I had six of them at one time with me."

He said supervisors "were hiding them out, down on the nacelle on the bottom—the front edge where the motors set—they bolted on with big bolts."

1945. My job title was mechanic (set up). My starting salary was $1.35 per hour and ending at $2.25 per hour.

"We started at 7 to noon. At 12:30 p.m. the whistle blew and [back] to work we went. At 4 p.m. we were off. We worked six days a week.

"I liked working on the planes for the boys to use. I was a driller mechanic on the ailerons and wingtips. [I would] drill holes in aileron skin and clamp metal skin to ribs with a special device, or when that was not needed, we did the same to the wingtips. This was on the Boeing B-17 Flying Fortress. This was a production line. Those parts of the wings were then sent to [the] Renton assembly plant or to the [Wichita] plant.

"First two weeks of school started at $1.35 per hour but received a raise every three months as we progressed through the program. In those days Boeing did not pay a separation pay.

"We had to keep our hair tied up and wear flat-heeled shoes. Had to wear slacks or jeans," she said, adding that she didn't recall any serious injuries at work. "No one was killed, only minor injuries, cuts and bruises."

"We had good morale at the job and at home too. We would have liked to have some nylon stockings.

"We belonged to the airplane mechanic's union. We paid about $15 per month dues. No health coverage outside the workplace. No benefits outside wages."

## CLAUDENE MOLLER

"I worked at Todd's Shipyard Plant B in Seattle, Washington, from 1943 to 1945. My job title was sheet metal shop employee.

*Claudene Moller earned this award after completing a sheet metal training course.*

*"My husband and I were married in September 1941 and moved to Seattle. My husband worked building the Boeing plant in Renton, Washington, for two years and then joined the Navy in 1943. I worked in the shipyards after he joined the Navy.*

*"I wanted to work while my husband was in the Navy during World War II. I was trained on the job.*

*"I helped make metal lockers for ships that docked at our plant. No dress code, but our long hair was protected with a scarf.*

*"My parents worked at Plant A and lived in the apartment next to me. I ate my meals with them and we rode the bus to work together."*

## EDWARD JOHNSON

*"I worked at Boeing Seattle Plant No. 1 and [at] Renton from 1942 to 1945.*

*"I had been working in the woods and got injured—broken cable hit me in the face and ruined my left eye. After I recovered, I took some training and moved to Renton. Got a job at Plant 1, Seattle. My starting pay was 62½ cents per hour. My salary at [the] end was $1.625.*

*"In Renton we lived in an old house that had been broken down into four apartments and we lived in government housing later. When we moved back here I had my house.*
*"We had some training at the Chehalis High*

He said supervisors would tell him they had to hide the women so as to prevent problems, but they needed the help.

According to *The Life and Times of Rosie the Riveter*, during the war years, the presence of black women in industry rose from 6.5 percent to 18 percent—and their wages rose by 1,000 percent over their pre-war income. Overall, within five years, the income of black families rose from 40 percent of what their white counterparts made to 60 percent, the authors wrote.

Helen Kooina Dowling, who moved with her two children from South Dakota to Chehalis to take care of her husband's brother, found working side-by-side with black women a new experience, according to her story in *A Mouthful of Rivets: Women at Work in World War II*, by Nancy Baker Wise and Christy Wise. She said she hadn't had any close contact with African-Americans in the Midwest, but living in Seattle helped to broaden her horizons and teach her about "the different kinds of people who lived in the world and what were some of their problems."

The authors said that war work helped break down regional barriers and enhance understanding of different cultures that make up America.

"There were so many different kinds of people working at Boeing from all over the nation and from all walks of life," Helen Kooina Dowling is quoted in the book as saying.

She said, "It was just a change in our complete society—the migration of people to different places, to war industries."

Disabled or physically challenged workers, who often faced discrimination when seeking employment, found jobs in the defense industry as well.

Berg said Boeing hired what he called "little people" to work in the tail of the plane's body because "they could crawl through there like rabbits, and we couldn't get in there."

While some companies, such as Kaiser, built child care centers for female employees, most women hired baby sitters or asked family members to take care of their children while they worked.

Safety posed a problem in these industrial jobs, which is one reason many companies required women to keep their hair covered in a snood and to comply with dress codes that prohibited loose clothing, high heels and dangling jewelry.

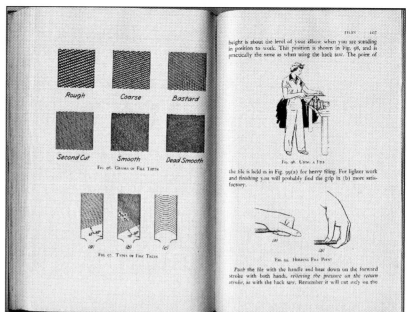

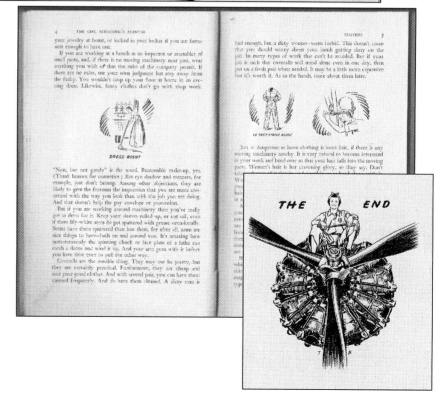

BOOK COURTESY OF EVA (PERONA) HAUCK

*Reading The Girl Mechanics Manual, published in 1944, might very well give a modern-day feminist heart palpitations. In a friendly writing style, the authors talk about clothes being a subject that should interest any woman as well as the importance of safety around equipment to prevent losing an arm 'for after all, arms are nice things to have—both on and around you.'*

*School building. The job was drilling holes.*

*"Boeing workers [worked] steady on the job. Everything [at the plant] was in the open so you didn't have any place to sit down out of sight. I talked to shipyard workers said they went to the bottom of ship and slept.*

*"A typical day, stand at [a] jig and drill holes all day."*

*He didn't experience any problems with morale, dangers or discrimination. He didn't recall the union dues he paid, but noted: "The first morning there was a union man right there to sign you up."*

*He had two children at the time. "My wife stayed at home with kids."*

## MARGARET SHAVER SHIELDS

*Margaret Shaver Shields, who was in her early twenties in the 1940s, enrolled in a four-week class in sheet metal work offered at the Southwest Washington Fairgrounds.*

*"A governmental agency, the National Youth Association (NYA), held 'sheet metal' classes at the Southwest Washington Fairgrounds for interested young people. After a six-week course, Boeing put out a call for workers. Two or three of us went."*

*Then, in May 1942, she moved to Seattle, where she started working at Boeing as an aircraft mechanic earning 57½ cents an hour. She roomed with a Centralia girl, Rhoda Jean Ford Ray (who is now deceased). Both women worked at the Boeing plant—Shields as a mechanic and Ford as a riveter.*

*After Boeing opened a branch plant in Chehalis, she transferred home and worked there into 1945.*

"The women had to wear bandannas to keep long hair out of the machinery, we were told," Kunkel said.

"Every woman came early to stand in front of the mirror and tie her bandanna in the most attractive way she could. I was not concerned over such things and didn't care how mine looked. But other women were primping in front of the mirrors several times a day."

To help new workers learn the job, in 1941 Boeing published *A Simple Guide to Blueprint Reading: A Text for Those Engaged in a Preliminary Study of Blueprint Reading*, written by William N. Wright of the engineering department. The booklet went through many printings during the war.

In 1944, Daniel J. Brimm, Jr., and Ernst Scheifele wrote *The Girl Mechanic's Manual*, published by Pitman Publishing Corporation of New York and Chicago.

Brimm, a former aviation mechanics instructor serving on active duty in the U.S. Naval Reserve, and Scheifele write in a friendly, quaint—albeit condescending—voice to the women. In the preface, they describe it as "slightly unorthodox, but we hope some of the dullness of many instruction books has been eliminated."

Reading the book might give a modern-day feminist a heart attack.

They say the book contains nothing new, just basic facts any mechanic needs, but the need for such information "has become evident to the employers of thousands of girls."

The book starts out: "So you want to be a mechanic. That's swell! Your country needs you, needs the work you can do, needs the planes, tanks, guns, ships, or whatever it is you are going to build. And for every girl that takes a job such as you are about to take or have taken a man is freed for the dirtier jobs we'd still rather our girls didn't do, such as putting Hitler and Hirohito where they belong."

Chapter titles cover your job, clothes, how to act in the shop, figures, more figures, the steel rule, punches, dividers, protractors, squares, calipers, slide and vernier calipers, micrometer calipers, screw drivers, hammers, pliers, clamps, vises, hacksaws, snips, files, twist drills, drills—hand and power, screws, bolts, nuts, studs, wrenches, rivets, materials, understanding drawings and workmanship.

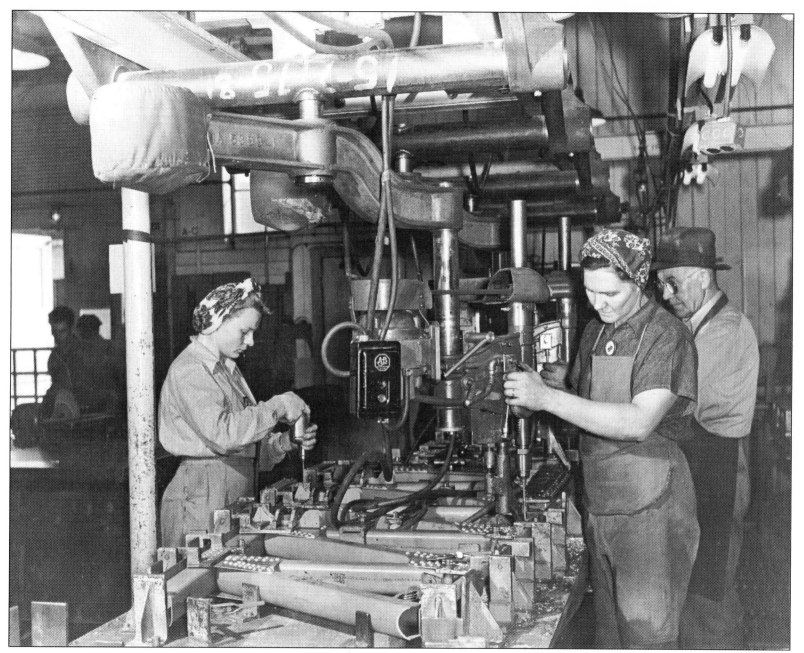

*Margaret Shaver Shields, left, enrolled in a mechanics class at the Southwest Washington Fairgrounds in Chehalis and then applied for a job at Boeing in Seattle. She transferred to Chehalis when Boeing opened its branch plant there. She is working with Autumn Berg Beam of Onalaska.*

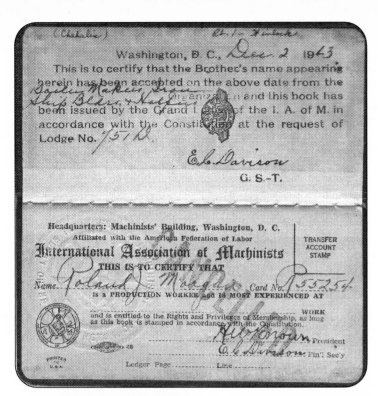

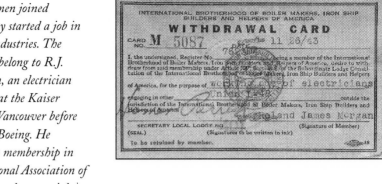

Wartime factory work also proved a boon to unions, which men and women joined whenever they started a job in the defense industries. The booklets here belong to R.J. 'Bob' Morgan, an electrician who worked at the Kaiser shipyards in Vancouver before hiring on at Boeing. He withdrew his membership in the International Association of Machinists (card at top right) so he could join the aeronautical union. He worked at Kaiser, though, during construction of the USS Alazon Bay, which was christened by First Lady Eleanor Roosevelt.

U.S.S. ALAZON BAY

*built by you and your fellow workers,*

*and is your latest contribution to the United States Fleet.*

*You and your immediate family are cordially invited*

*to attend the launching ceremonies*

*Monday noon, April 5, 1943*

*Kaiser Company, Inc.*

*Vancouver Yard*

"You may have never had a hammer in your hand, but you'll find you can do mechanical work just as capably as you run a typewriter, an automobile, a flatiron or a cookstove."

On the chapter about clothes, the authors state: "Now there is a subject which should interest any woman. It has been said that 'clothes make the man.' This may be open to question. It has also been said that clothes make the woman. As a mere man, I confess that they have a lot to do with a girl's attractiveness.

"But, however true or untrue the foregoing may be, there is absolutely no doubt that clothes go a mighty long way toward making the girl mechanic. … If you are not dressed right, you not only won't be able to do your work efficiently, you may lose your hand, your arm or your life. Don't think the last is an exaggeration. More than one mechanic has had a loose sleeve or necktie catch in moving machinery and been dragged right into it. When such a thing happens, you are lucky if you go only to the hospital. You are more than likely to wind up on a very cold slab. Plenty of others have.

"Another thing. Rings and bracelets are pretty, but not in the shop, for if you wear them, some day you might not have a finger or arm on which to wear them.

"But if you are working around machinery then you've really got to dress for it. Keep your sleeves rolled up, or cut off, even if those lily-white arms do get spattered with grease occasionally. Better have them spattered than lose them, for after all, arms are nice things to have—both on and around you. It's amazing how instantaneously the spinning chuck or face plate of a lathe can catch a sleeve and wind it up. And your arm goes with it before you have time even to pull the other way."

"Just as dangerous as loose clothing is loose hair, if there is any moving machinery nearby. It is very natural to become interested in your work and bend over so that your hair falls into the moving parts. Woman's hair is her crowning glory, so they say. Don't take a chance of losing it—and possibly your head along with it. Wear a net, a cap or a kerchief."

But even training workers, emphasizing safety and imposing dress codes couldn't prevent injuries and deaths.

While the United States lost 500,000 servicemen during the war, the Office of War Information reported in early 1944 that 37,600 workers had died in industrial accidents. Another 210,000 had become permanently disabled and

*When she entered the plant, guards would check her ID button at the door and open her lunch sack or pail. She'd go to the workstation, which was already set up for the day's work. She'd leave for lunch when the bell rang, then return to work and finish when the bell rang again at quitting time.*

*"I enjoyed it," she said of her job as a Mechanic 3 in assembly of parts. "No dress code except work clothes and hair covered. You worked steady.*

*"We had fun, just jawing with everybody, but when we were working, we concentrated. It wasn't something you could take lightly."*

*Morale was good. "People felt proud to doing their part in the war effort.*

*"We all had a thought in our minds that we were helping our friends and relatives who were serving. We did our part. We felt patriotic."*

## PAGE G. BENNETT

*"I was in California for schooling and when I was done with it went to work in Douglas aircraft as a riveter. I worked for Douglas aircraft in California in late 1940."*

*He then worked at the Boeing plant in Seattle as a riveter, and later in Chehalis. He worked for Boeing from 1941 until 1945. He started at 62 cents an hour.*

*"You had a badge with the shop number where you worked. Mine was the wing shop, 303. I started riveting when the wing was in the jig.*

*"Then after doing that for about a year, I did pick up riveting after the wing was on the floor after the inspector marked the lead rivets.*

*"I worked the graveyard shift. You worked six and*

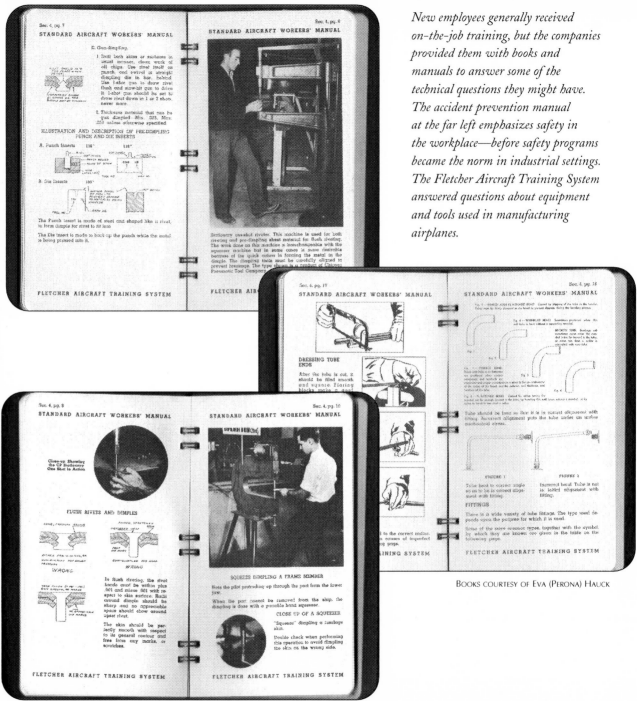

*New employees generally received on-the-job training, but the companies provided them with books and manuals to answer some of the technical questions they might have. The accident prevention manual at the far left emphasizes safety in the workplace—before safety programs became the norm in industrial settings. The Fletcher Aircraft Training System answered questions about equipment and tools used in manufacturing airplanes.*

4.5 million suffered temporary disabilities, the report stated.

The war years also changed the dynamics of the population, with families swarming north and west to seek those higher-paying jobs in defense industries. Many big western cities, including Portland and Seattle, saw their populations swell by more than a third, according to a history paper by Amanda Bevers published in 2004 called *Rosie the Riveter Goes West: The Mobilization and Migration of Women Workers During World War II*, published on the Internet at: http://www2.ups.edu/faculty/dsackman/400papers/fall2004/bevers.htm

For example, Clark County in Southwest Washington saw its population grow from 18,000 in 1941 to more than 100,000 by the end of the war, according to the Clark County Web site at: http://www.co.clark.wa.us/aboutcc/proud_past/WW2.html The population increase put pressure on housing, prompting builders to develop six neighborhoods within eighteen months to house shipyard workers, according to Colman.

Portland's mayor declared a week in June 1943 to be "Working Women Win Wars Week."

Newspaper editorial pages joined the government in praising the efforts of women workers during the war.

On June 18, 1942, The Chronicle editorial page gave these women a literary pat on the back:

"Now it is the 'emergency girl.' She is the product of the war emergency. She is wiser than the flapper, less self-centered than the career girl that Hollywood exploited, and has more charm than glamour.

"The emergency girl of 1942 is not necessarily engaged in vital defense work. She may be a housewife, but, as such, she is helping her country by her little economies and her planning of diets to build healthy, strong children. She may be a stenographer or a saleswoman, but she has her own little niche in the wartime scheme of things.

"The term 'emergency girl' is one that may be well applied to all American women. Old and young, they are shoulder to shoulder with their men, providing spiritual as well as material support. It has been suggested that as a subtitle to 'emergency girl' the term 'grit girl' might be applied. That, too, is fitting."

*a half hours and got paid for eight hours. Then in the daytime I drove bus for Seattle. I drove from downtown to White Center.*

*"Working at Boeing in Seattle the morale was very good. At Chehalis it was good also.*

*"There was always danger but I don't recall any real danger. I was on the safety committee, also the grievance committee.*

*"We had our son born in 1942, but my wife didn't work out [so she] was home to take care of him."*

*Servicemen on leave often walked along the lakefront in Chicago.*

# Three jobs in one day

JOBS WENT BEGGING DURING THE WAR. Just ask Helen Holloway, who worked at three different defense industry plants in one day!

In March 1944, the day the Rock-Ola Manufacturing Co. in Chicago finished its government gun contract, Helen Dilbo Holloway walked down the city street, lunch in hand, and into another factory.

"I was placed at a bench to solder wires to parts for radios in tanks," she recalls. "Two hours later at lunchtime a man holding a mike told everyone to gather outside the factory as we were 'on strike.'

"I took my lunch and started walking and eating as I walked to another factory. I stopped at Bendix Aviation (making parts for fighter aircraft), was hired, finished my lunch and began my new job. I was so surprised that anyone would strike! Jobs went begging and we were all so vital to the war effort. I would not strike."

Along with most Americans, she felt patriotic during the war and wanted to do her part. She had worked summers, nights and weekends while attending school, so graduating in June 1943 meant she could find a full-time permanent job. Everywhere she worked, the company sent her to school anywhere from two to six weeks so she could learn the job.

"I had a very high mechanical aptitude in all my testing. I was an only child and my dad wanted a boy—what can I tell you!"

While her fiancé, Merle Foote, served overseas in New Guinea, she worked first at Rock-Ola Manufacturing from 1943 until March 1944, then at Bendix Aviation until November 1944 and finally at Dodge from December 1944 until May 1945.

"The one thing that stands out in my mind now is the noise and constant din," she recalled. "Everything quit when the whistles blew for lunch or shift changes."

She traveled an hour each way on a streetcar to Rock-Ola, where she earned 50 cents an hour test firing .30-caliber carbines and disassembling, cleaning, inspecting and reassembling rifles.

"My first job firing rifles," she recalled, "someone forgot the plug in a rifle and when the gunsmith picked it up, a bullet in the chamber was fired and

HELEN 7/43 HEADED
FOR WORK AT ROCK-OLA
MFG. TEST FIRING 30-CAL
CARBINES.

*Helen Dilbo Foote Holloway worked at Rock-Ola Manufacturing test firing .30-caliber carbines. She is dressed in her 'Rosie' outfit at the far left. Above is the Chicago neighborhood where she lived during the early 1940s. At left is a parade featuring military men on a Chicago street.*

Photos courtesy of Helen Foote Holloway

*Helen Dilbo Foote Holloway is seen in her Chicago neighborhood wearing a much dressier outfit than the clothes she wore to work in the defense industry.*

another gunsmith across the room was shot in the leg. There were less spectacular injuries."

Every place she worked had its own uniform or dress code. If you worked around machinery, you couldn't wear dangling jewelry or clothing. You also had to cover your hair—and a tragedy at Bendix Aviation confirms why women wore snoods, or kerchiefs, over their hair.

"At Bendix a girl got her hair caught in her drill press and was scalped and died. It only took seconds."

Holloway earned a dollar an hour at Bendix as an inspector of aircraft parts for fighter planes. Again, she traveled an hour each way. After arriving, she'd punch in, then pick up job allocations, blueprints and the necessary drill bits and tools needed.

"I went to each of twenty machine operators—prepared machine, job and test-ran a few parts to see measurements were accurate and let operators take over. Because I was responsible for mistakes, and all metal was in short supply, I inspected each operator's output regularly throughout my ten-hour shift. At the end of each workday, I spent an hour or more doing paperwork."

Each of the factories had a small infirmary to take care of industrial accidents, and Dodge had a small hospital on site. "At the time I worked there it was the largest building under one roof in the USA," she said.

While working at the Dodge Chicago plant, she said, "several people were run over by a forklift and I remember one was killed."

At Dodge, she completed four weeks of training to become a Magna-Flux operator and inspector, earning $1.20 an hour. For this job, she traveled almost two hours each way.

"I worked at a large machine containing a tank that held kerosene and iron filings. The machine had a foot pedal that opened and closed two jaws. Parts were put between jaws—you pushed a large button on the side of the machine with your hip while hosing the kerosene on the part. The iron particles would align themselves around any defect for the inspector to see.

"Magna-Fluxing looked like a modern dance done rapidly—very rapidly—and was almost comical to watch. Needless to say I always had someone hesitate as they walked by when I was shooting parts."

*During the war, with her sweetheart serving in New Guinea, Helen Dilbo bided her time by running heavy equipment, test firing carbines and inspecting the work of machine operators. A closer look at the equipment shows the name 'Helen' scratched near the seat.*

Although she didn't have children, those women who did usually left them with extended family. "Never heard of day care," she said.

Women might have faced inappropriate comments occasionally, but they took care of it themselves.

"Men had more respect for women in those days and even if something was said or done, a withering look or a 'hit the road' was enough to restore propriety!"

With African-Americans working side-by-side with whites, she said, several times racial tension erupted at the Dodge Chicago plant.

"Workers fought it out in the (basement) tunnels between shifts," she said. "Those incidents were rare. People got along because we had a common goal.

"We were all on a mission to help our troops win the war quickly. The camaraderie was amazing. We all discussed our letters and our loved ones who served. We supported each other and laughed and cried together. We looked forward to each new day with hope that the war might end."

# Go play with what?

*Doris Hastings Bier, left, was only a teenager when she applied for a job at the Mount Rainier Ordnance Depot. She applied there because, at sixteen, she was too young to work at Boeing, which was geographically closer to home, She excelled at her work and won a coveted 'E' award for excellence.*

A CO-WORKER AT THE MOUNT RAINIER ORDNANCE DEPOT told sixteen-year-old Doris Hastings Bier to go play with dolls.

"We women were really a test to see if we could do the work and be effective," she said. "Some men disliked us very much. Others were encouraging."

Bill, a man from Chehalis about the age of her dad, knew her family.

"He was angry at women doing men's jobs—told me to go home and play with dolls," she remembers.

In May 1944, she and a fellow student had applied for war support jobs. After physicals at Madigan Army Hospital, they answered pages of questions in an aptitude test. Bier attended mechanics training at Clover Park School in Lakewood, where she graduated second in a class of thirty women.

"We studied books and hands-on," she recalled. "To graduate we were given a wash tub full of engine parts and a key. Only thing assembled was a carburetor. Two chances with the key to start our engine—mine did and I was headed for work at the depot."

A friend at school who shared her toolbox didn't pass the test, so she wound up working in the steam room rather than on the assembly line.

The assembly line job working on truck and Jeep axles paid $1.50 an hour—"men's wages," she said, which "didn't endear me to the older men working there."

"I was the only female on the line. We checked out tools after [punching the] time clock and headed to our stations. All our axles and parts came overhead on a cable—straight from the steam room. We'd swing the basket over to our table and go to work."

On the job, she wore coveralls and steel-toed shoes with her hair either short or in a bandanna. She rode a Greyhound bus to Tacoma and boarded there during the week, sharing a ride with four others to reach the base.

"We rode bicycles all over Tacoma," she recalled.

*Doris Hastings Bier is pictured above Dec. 25, 1941, with her brother-in-law, Roy Robbins, center, and her brother, Donald Hastings, at Fort Lewis. At right, she received this certificate for completing the Basic Mechanic Learner program at Clover Park school in July 1944.*

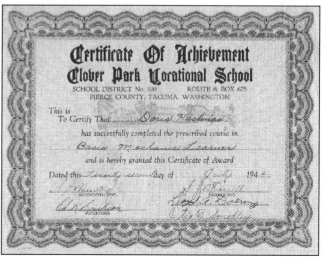

*When Doris Hastings Bier earned recognition for her excellent work, a co-worker thought she had been called away from her job to be fired! The pin at left is awarded for excellence. The one on the right she received upon graduating from Mechanic School at Clover Park in Lakewood.*

Her first job was a Diamond T truck axle—and she'd had no schooling on that. The foreman helped her with the first one and then left her alone to cope.

Her first tool kit proved too heavy for her to lift, so somebody helped her carry it.

"Most everyone was helpful and friendly. They would tease me."

Except for Bill.

Bill kept complaining about her, saying she wasn't doing her job or went so fast she got grease on the brake shoes and paint where it didn't belong. "We painted everything Army green and marked each axle with our initials and number."

"Got so bad one day the head foreman came over, took my completed axle apart and inspected it, put it back together, shook my hand, patted my shoulder and said: 'Good job, keep it up.'"

She would complete two axles before morning break, two after the break and four in the afternoon. "Bill did five maybe all day."

She recalls one very memorable afternoon.

"I was called from work one afternoon by my foreman. Bill thought I was getting fired! I was taken to Gray's Field at Fort Lewis and received an "E" pin for good work!"

They gave her a carnation, took her photo and drove her back to work. She was one of perhaps ten people to receive the award for "outstanding work—especially at my age."

"Walked in and Bill got steamed. He thought I finally had gotten fired! Instead I got an award. He called my dad and told him I was a troublemaker and [told him to] make me go home!

"My dad was proud of me and laughed at him. Even the tool room guys stuck up for me and gave me a huge rolling toolbox."

One time, she said, she wound up with a nasty headache. "A bolt shot across an aisle and hit my head," she said.

Another time while she was working, she felt somebody looking over her shoulder. But it wasn't the boss—or Bill. Instead, it was "an Italian prisoner of war looking for cigarettes."

"Six of them walked away from Fort Lewis and ended up at the depot—polite and curious about we women working like men," she recalled. "They wandered around awhile before somebody turned them in. They waved at us from the back of the truck surrounded by armed guards.

"I enjoyed the job and the respect I got from most of the men. Hated to quit and go back to school."

Chapter Six

# Blue Stars and Gold Stars

Military men on the minds of
girlfriends, parents, friends

## ELLEN IRENE KAIN

*"We lived in the small town of Yelm. I remember when a family lost a family member in the war, they hung a star in their window.*

*"My cousin Johnny Conklin was killed in Hawaii when it was hit. My schoolmate Eddie Vancil also was killed. My boyfriend Francis Heath was killed in the Battle of the Bulge in Europe.*

*"They [her family] talked about how sad it was when someone lost a son or family member."*

## EVA M. (PERONA) HAUCK

*"I had one uncle in the Navy and one uncle in the Army. My first check was $52.89 and 25 cents was taken out once a month toward a war bond."*

## JUNE G. AYRES O'CONNELL

*"My future husband was in the submarine service on the USS Aspro #309. I had many friends in the service."*

## RICHARD ZORN

*"Older brother Bob was in [the] Army during the invasion and fighting in France."*

## R.J. BOB MORGAN

*"[I had a] brother in the Army transport service."*

## JOYCE MARKSTROM VENEMON

*The late Chehalis City Councilor told a reporter in 1989 that all three of her brothers served in the military during World War II.*

*"Almost everybody there had brothers, husbands or dads in the war. You were pretty patriotic."*

# Waiting and worrying

MOST OF THE YOUNG WOMEN who took jobs in the defense industry knew young men fighting overseas.

Some followed their husband from one base to another in the United States, and then bid him farewell as he left for the battlefront, not knowing whether she'd ever see him again.

Many of the older women bid farewell to sons—some who never returned home.

Throughout America, people posted blue stars in their windows to indicate how many family members were serving in the military. A gold star meant their loved one had made the ultimate sacrifice for his country.

Sixty percent of the women who entered the workforce for the first time were over 35, while 22 percent were 20 to 24 and 17 percent between 14 and 19, according to statistics compiled by Miriam Frank, Marilyn Ziebarth and Connie Field and published in *The Life and Times of Rosie the Riveter: The Story of Three Million Working Women During World War II.*

Women with husbands serving overseas were three times as likely to work as wives whose husbands were not away from home, according to the authors' figures. And some of those husbands never returned home.

Virginia Willhite, plant nurse at the Chehalis Boeing branch plant, learned in April 1944 that her husband, Army Air Force Maj. Theodore Willhite, was killed in action over Italy, according to the April 1944 edition of the Boeing News, a newsletter produced for employees working at the plants.

"When the telegram arrived, Mrs. Willhite was fighting off pneumonia," the newsletter stated. "Major Willhite died never having seen his twenty-month old son, who was born shortly after the father was sent overseas."

The same item reported that Chehalis production clerk Ida Joslyn's son had failed to return from a bombing raid over Germany.

Dorothy Hadaller Hagstrom also knew the pain of losing a loved one in the war.

"In June 1944 my oldest brother James was drafted in the Army," she said. "He was killed in the Battle of the Bulge."

*No matter where their loved ones served, family members on the home front worried about their safety and prayed for their safe return. The photo at top left shows a bomber in flight and the photo above is a fighter. At left is a photo of ships from the Puget Sound Shipyards recruiting booklet.*

PHOTOS COURTESY OF PETER LAHMANN

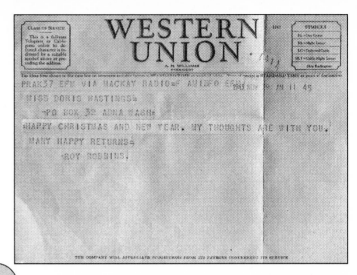

Family members and friends maintained contact with their loved ones serving overseas through V...—mail, official United States mail services for the armed forces, and telegrams, such as the one at right from Roy Robbins wishing his sister-in-law, Doris Hastings, a Merry Christmas and Happy New Year.

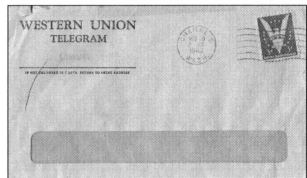

TELEGRAM COURTESY OF DORIS HASTINGS BIER

V-MAIL COURTESY OF PETER LAHMANN

She also lost many classmates.

Dorothy Powell followed her husband Harold to Army bases in Pennsylvania and Cape Cod, remaining with him as long as possible, from July 1, 1943, until March 31, 1944. After he shipped overseas, she left Florida April 11, 1944, to return to Riffe in Lewis County.

"I had to wait there until I knew where he was being sent in case I could go where he was sent," she said. "The Army never told the men where they were going."

But he went into combat and she returned home, where she joined the war effort as a Boeing worker.

In addition to her husband, she had one brother, an uncle five years her senior, seven first cousins and six in-laws from Harold's family serving in the military.

"Many other cousins and almost all the boys in my class that I knew," she said. "I think every class of those several years lost someone. I had two second cousins [taken] prisoners of war; several in the Lewis County area we knew were prisoners. Two boys died from my neighborhood. Two more died after the war; they committed suicide due to war injuries."

Some lost friends when the war began—at least for the United States—in the Japanese attack at Pearl Harbor.

"My high school friend, Jimmy Reynolds, was killed at Pearl Harbor on the Arizona," said Jane Duell Minear. "My brother, Floyd Duell, was in the Navy—a pharmacist mate on a hospital ship. He returned safely after some scary experiences."

At home her family often discussed the latest war news.

"We talked about the war. 'When would it be over?' 'Were our loved ones OK?' 'We are sick of rationing.' All the time knowing how lucky we were compared to other countries and the people there. But it was an exciting time, too, to be alive and part of it all."

Margaret Shaver Shields also lost a personal friend when the Arizona sank. Her brother served in the Navy, as well as many friends and cousins, including one in the 6th Army Rangers.

"I remember we always compared notes about what we heard from different

### SHIRLEY PADHAN ERICKSON

"My husband was in the 13th Army Air Force in the South Pacific for three years. I was fortunate and didn't lose anyone close to me."

### DORIS M. YEARIAN

"Our friends in Salmon, Idaho, [were] in the service. Well do I remember our neighbor's son, first in Lemhi County [Idaho] killed, and the blue star in the window turned to gold."

### DOVIE R. (LONG, HALVERSON) WELLCOME

"Three brothers [served]—Bruce Long in the Army at California, Don Long in the Navy overseas, and Buck Long in the Coast Guard in the States—and a friend, George McClung."

### ETHEL NELSON

"E.R. Bud Nelson (my husband) EM 3/C was on DD destroyer in the South Pacific. [My] twin brother [was a] lieutenant colonel in the Army Air Force—China and Japan and India. Brother Harry Hallman was a second-class boatman's mate in the Aleutian islands by Alaska.

"One thing we [the family] all prayed they would come home safe and they did. Thank the Lord."

### EUGENE DONALD "DON" CASTLE

"My sister was a WAVE and her husband was a sailor. My other brother-in-law was in the Army and served in the South Pacific where he was wounded and sent home."

### EUNICE L. HOWARD

"My husband was in the 11th Airborne Division and served in the Pacific. I lost many friends in both Europe and the Pacific."

## JULIA R. FORD MEADOWS

*"Two brothers [in the] Navy [served] all over. One sister in the WAVES in Washington, D.C. [They were] Egbert Arthur Ford and Donald Ford, deceased, and sister Rhoda Jean Ford Ray."*

## MARGARET EVELYN COWLEY WHITFORD

*"Several of my uncles were in the war in the Army. Some school friends also. Several were killed. My uncles served in Europe and survived.*

*"We looked forward to getting short censored letters from family members in the Army overseas and shared them with others. We sent cookies and popcorn to the men."*

## MARTHA LAHMANN LOHRER

*"Not family. [A] good neighbor's son was a pilot and killed. After graduating from high school, I was accepted in the United Nurses Cadet Corps. Was proud to serve and graduated as R.N. Practiced nursing for fifty years. Still do a little when needed. I specialized in ICU and CCU, cardiology and neurology. Had many years of ongoing education required."*

## JEAN DESPAIN

*"Brother in Army, friends in Army, Navy and Coast Guard. Couple of friends died in combat.*

*"Most talk was about those in [the] service and about the victories of our troops."*

## DALE ALEXANDER

*I had two older brothers; we were all in the service at the end of the war."*

family members and close friends who were in the service," she said.

Sarah Ciranny Zopolos had three brothers serving in the military: Nick, in the infantry in Germany, and Louie and Sam in America.

"We talked about how sad to have a brother, son, Dad and all men away without being with their families," she said. "Our mother really never showed sadness in front of my sister and I. Must have been hard for her to have three sons in the service. The Lord spared them and thankful for that."

"People hung a star in their window for each son serving in the armed services," said Winnie Nichols, daughter of Jerry and Cristle Jobe. "My dad was at first exempted in Oklahoma as he was farming. After he came out here he was reclassified as 1A but never had to go to the armed services as the war then ended."

She said an uncle in the Marines won an award at Iwo Jima for defending his position against Japanese attackers and another uncle served in the Air Force after the war. Her husband, Wallace William Langille, was wounded by shrapnel while serving in the Army in communications and airborne reconnaissance in the Philippines.

War news covered front pages of newspapers, and newsreels shown at theaters brought the fight home to people. Many bought war bonds to support their loved ones overseas and help the nation achieve victory.

The entire community worked to raise money for the effort. Ads sponsored by businesses throughout the Twin Cities—Centralia Knitting Mills, Weyerhaeuser Co., Pacific Telephone and Telegraph—encouraged readers to purchase war bonds.

Centralia Rotary Club members took charge of the Fifth War Loan campaign in June 1944 for the city, opening with a meeting where Rotarians pledged to buy $16,450 worth of bonds.

Retail clerks competed with one another to sell the most bonds, with the Centralia Chamber of Commerce commending Mrs. Donna Knowles, an employee at Poore's apparel shop, for selling $8,150 worth of bonds during the drive while Mrs. Genette Miller from Profitt's placed second by selling $8,000 worth of bonds. Both women received a $25 war bond.

By the end of July 1944, the city of Centralia had surpassed its goal during the bond drive by raising $813,832.58—more than $13,000 above its quota, according to J. C. McNiven, the city's war savings chairman. Nearly half of that money came from individuals, which was much higher than the national average.

Students held book drives to gather reading material for the soldiers overseas. Newspaper editorial pages urged readers to recycle 8 million tons a year of paper, which was essential for the war effort as it was used to wrap food, protect ammunition and produce blueprints, among other things.

Vivian Curry Wood, whose father had served in World War I, waited for news of her brother when he served in Germany, where she lost a close friend.

Then came the news (reported in the Boeing News) in 1944 that her brother, Staff Sgt. Newt D. Curry, a waist gunner of the Flying Fortress bomber dubbed "With Love and Fifties," received a second Oak Leaf cluster medal for his service as a member of the Third Bombardment division, which President Roosevelt cited for its shuttle-bombing of plants in Germany.

Her husband also served in the Navy Air Force.

While heroes emerged in battles, the war created many widows and broke the hearts of countless mothers and fathers.

In August 1944, the Boeing News newsletter again reported two Chehalis workers received sad news via War Department telegrams. James Bradshaw learned that his son was killed in action in Europe, and Katherine Bruen learned that her son, also stationed in Europe, had been wounded.

Georgie Bright Kunkel said her oldest brother, Raymond Bright, suited up for WWII but never served as the war was over right after he joined. Her youngest brother, Norman Bright, served in the Army Mountain Rescue Unit, and her oldest sister, Anne Williams, was in the Army Nurse Corps as a second lieutenant serving in Africa and France.

"She said that in Africa they were to have received summer uniforms but they were sold right off the dock before they ever reached the hospitals," Kunkel recalled. "She would walk into the town near the hospital and see civilians wearing the nurse uniform that she should have received. She used to use her helmet for a wash basin when she was in North Africa living in a tent."

She also wrote to her future husband, who served overseas from 1943 to

### EVA STAFFORD

*"Howard had two brothers in the Army and one sister in the WAVES."*

### RICHARD LARSON

*"Two brothers were in [the] Army. And number of friends [were] in the military. Several were killed."*

### EDWARD F. PEMERL

*"One brother—field artillery. Lost high school classmates."*

### RUTH HERREN

*"No family members in the military, but several schoolmates were lost."*

### THERESA "TERRY" (WALZ) VANNOY

*"I had three brothers in the Army. All came back, but some had lingering malaria. Lost several friends.*

*"We watched the newspapers for news and that was the most we could do."*

### EDWARD JOHNSON

*"I can't remember anyone from here. I had a nephew who was in the Navy.*

### CLAUDENE MOLLER

*"Husband—Navy—South Pacific; cousin—Bill Nicholson—Army Air Force (killed in action); brother—Dean Nicholson - Navy, Tarawa; brother—[also] Bill Nicholson—Navy."*

### DORIS (HASTINGS) BIER

*"Brother-in-law in [the] Army Rangers at Bataan*

*and Guam. Cousins in [Europe] in the Army at the Battle of the Bulge. Lost one schoolmate in battle on the beach in the first wave at Omaha Beach.*

*"Vicious circle in wars. Some came home badly wounded [in] mind or body; others were buried overseas; some disappeared. My dad came home [from WWI] gassed—bad lungs. Died in 1929 when I was two."*

*"My husband's cousin was twenty years old and was a Wing Commander of a B-17 bombing from England. He lost a few friends. He came home and never flew again. If he couldn't drive or take a train, he wouldn't go."*

## HELEN C. (JONES) KLINDT

*"Friends, yes. Army—Hickam Field—brother. Navy—New Zealand—brother. Army—Okinawa—brother. Navy—Farragut, Idaho—brother.*

*At home when the talk turned to the war, she said, we would "hope that my brothers would all get home safe."*

## ENID ROGERSON

*Everette (brother) [in the] Seebees and Dale (brother) [in the] Army.*

## HELEN RIEDESEL-KNOECHEL

*She had brother and two brothers-in-law as well as many friends both in the Army and Navy.*

*"Two of the men from Coffman Dobson Bank were killed that I know of.*

*"Most of all we worried about our relatives and friends who were overseas. There were so many who didn't come back."*

1945 with the British in a private ambulance corps called the American Field Service in the India/Burma campaign. Later he served with the U.S. Army directly after V-E day May 8, 1945, in repatriation efforts in Italy and again under the British in the liberation of the Bergen-Belsen concentration camp in Germany.

"I would send the words to all the popular songs to my guy overseas," she said, noting that she taught school in Centralia and shared an apartment with another teacher.

"We sent care packages to my sister overseas and I sent my future husband things he needed. One time he asked for a bottle of ink and I put it into an Ovaltine can with packing around it. When he got it he was expecting a great Ovaltine drink and when he opened it, here was this ink which he needed but at the time it was a disappointment."

Helen Holloway, who lived in Chicago at the time, remembers many uncles, cousins, friends, neighbors and classmates serving in every branch of the military.

"I was in high school until 1943 and my classmates quit school to enlist and many died in action," she said. "The front wall of our school auditorium was covered with blue and many gold service stars. All of our assemblies began with prayers for our service men and women."

Her future husband served overseas in New Guinea, and she could hardly wait for him to return home. After finishing her war industry jobs, she worked as a long distance telephone operator. He arrived home Dec. 23, 1945, and they married Jan. 1, 1946, and settled the following month at Kosmos in Eastern Lewis County.

During the war years, she said, "morale was high as a rule." Employees competed for the latest production award or to fill a quota.

"As I look back on those days, it seems like all we did was pray, work and write letters. Someone coined the phrase, 'There are no atheists in foxholes.'

"All in all, we kept plugging away and waiting and hoping for the day the war would end," she said.

"Highs came with victories for our troops. Bad times were bad war news. Worse times were when friends, neighbors or loved ones were wounded or that horrible telegram came from Uncle Sam!"

*While servicemen fought the battles overseas, other men, women and children did what they could on the home front—collecting scrap iron, buying war bonds and working in the defense industries.*

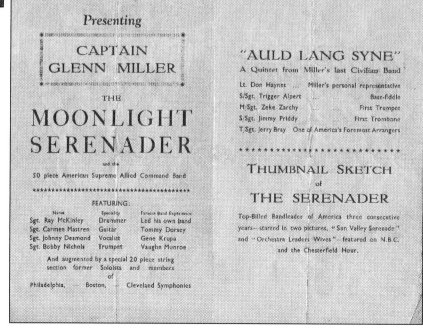

MEMORABILIA COURTESY OF PETER LAHMANN

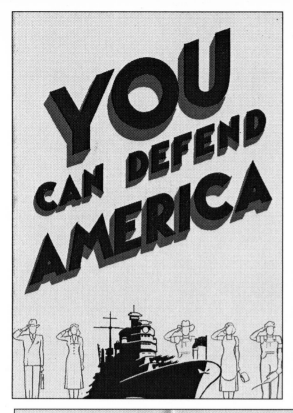

*The government encouraged patriotism on the home front with publications such as this one: 'You Can Defend America.'*

## TODAY

**America fights . . .**

**Fights in a total war.** Builds arms—ships, tanks, planes and guns. Trains millions of men.

But is this enough?

Our enemies fight with force of arms, *and with ideas.*

What is America's Big Idea? Is it big enough to win?

Has America the super-force of a fighting faith? Does she build character? Teamwork? The will to sacrifice?

Has America mobilized all these armaments for

. . . and thirty million Americans ask :

. . . ?"

**PLENTY !**

## AMERICA NEEDS

# *Teamwork in Industry*

WAR IN INDUSTRY can sabotage any armament program. It can cripple a nation while its forces fight heroically

France failed in the factory be front. Her people forgot how to ployers refused to sacrifice. Men her zero hour desperation was no s ... s lost.

... must win the battle f ... ... e to win the war. E ... r, every employer, ev ...

... at more on the prod ... the battle front.

... know how to work ... every man for himse ... —whatever his job.

... work with all we've g ... ... half its cylinders— ... h of her power has be ... ... waste on the land. W ... e of men.

... work together. Fricti ... ... re than friction in m ... r says, "More time ... ... mpers than through i ... ... workers destroy team ...

... ness, they sell out their country. Then the gains each

## AMERICA NEEDS

# *A United* *Nation*

BEHIND AMERICA'S FIGHTING FORCES must stand a united people.

Nations in Europe have gone down because their people couldn't get together. They were at war inside themselves. They refused to face facts. They were caught unprepared. Even as the storm broke men schemed to get more for themselves. Groups fought for their own rights until the enemy swept away the rights of all.

National unity is the heart of national morale. If a nation is united no fifth column can slip through and sabotage its strength.

A crack football team isn't all made up of quarterbacks. Every man has his part. Each depends on all the others. So with the nation. Unless we have national teamwork someone is likely to take the ball away from us.

"Teamwork," said Knute Rockne, "is a combination of self-sacrifice, brains and sweat." It means working together for America. Honest teamwork between government and business, labor and management, union and union, Republican and Democrat, city and farm.

Teamwork cannot be built by high talking and low living, by fine ideals and selfish lives.

Unity is more than agreeing on what we like or whom we hate. It is not a question of who's right, but of what's right.

A united people will have the spirit which no disaster will shake and no danger weaken.

A united people will build the new America. A nation set free from fear, hate and greed. A nation that holds the secret of a new world.

AMERICA'S FIGHTING MEN NEED

SHIPS, TANKS, PLANES AND GUNS

AMERICA'S FIGHTING SPIRIT NEEDS

*Sound Homes*

*Teamwork in Industry*

*A United Nation*

THESE BUILD TOTAL STRENGTH

THESE DEPEND ON <u>YOU</u>

MEMORABILIA COURTESY OF PETER LAHMAN

# Fiancé, brothers saw action

NOLAN JOACHIM SERVED IN THE NAVY aboard the USS California in the Lingayen Gulf on Jan. 6, 1945, when a kamikaze pilot slammed into the 600-foot-long battleship's fire-control tower, killing 203 of its 1,500 crewmembers.

All the while, the 1942 Centralia High School graduate's girlfriend waited for him at home, working for the war effort at the Todd Shipyards in Tacoma during 1942 and later as a service representative in the business office at Pacific Telephone and Telegraph in Chehalis.

After the tragic suicide attack, the USS California returned to Bremerton for twenty-one days, and Nolan Joachim and June Weese married at the Methodist Church in Chehalis March 17, 1945.

They collected gas stamps to honeymoon at Long Beach, but when they returned, she had to say goodbye to him again when he sailed again for the war in the South Pacific, where June had two brothers serving as well—Arnold Weese in the Army Air Force and Harry Weese in the 9th Infantry Division. Harry, now 88, won the bronze star for digging U.S. soldiers out of a cave that had collapsed.

"We got mail once in a while, except my husband never touched land for ten months and then later one year," she recalled. "He ate beans and rice three times a day."

Against the wishes of her brothers, she had applied to join the WAVES, which stood for Women Accepted for Voluntary Emergency Service.

"My brothers didn't want me to join the Navy—said only the crummy did—so I joined anyway," she said.

She rode the bus to Seattle and at Navy headquarters removed her clothes and donned a gown behind a curtain for a physical exam.

"I heard a loud scream next to me, and I was next and no clothes to leave in," she said. "Found out the gal had a very bad appendix and when the doctor poked her, she let out a terrible scream. We had to pass a written exam and tie ropes (good Girl Scout training) and [identify] pictures of tools. My dad had all of them so [I] passed with flying colors."

She was never sworn in, but returned home to wait for her assignment as a

## ELANOR WILBER

"My brother was sent to Alaska for the duration. We didn't know where he was until a friend from our hometown read his APO address and gave us his location. Some of the boys I went to school with lost their lives on the beaches of Normandy."

## MABEL COOK

"Friends. Wayne Selby was in the Air Force. His plane was shot down. We had talked about getting married when the war was over.

"The first car I owned was given to me by a serviceman I was dating. He was getting ready to ship out overseas and didn't need it anymore. He was a pilot and was later shot down and killed over Germany."

## MARY JACOBSEN KLAUS

"[I had] two brothers as soldiers."

## JOHN ALEXANDER JR.

"We were not immune to the tragic consequences of war, as the tentacles of the conflict reached into our community. One example was Jeri Hughes, my tap dancing teacher who married a young man. He was anxious to get into the conflict early and volunteered for the RAF. It is assumed that he was lost over the English Channel.

"I also remember a quiet and somber gathering in the surrounds of what is now Silver Brook with the Keesee family. Lorne Keesee was home on furlough and was relating some of his experiences as a B-24 bubble gunner. The thought that he would soon be going back to war was causing some eyes to mist over."

*June Weese Joachim Deskins' brother Harry, left, won a bronze star for digging soldiers out of a cave that had collapsed. He is seen above in Hawaii.*

gunnery instructor at Hunter's College in New York. As an experienced trap-shooter, she had been around guns all her life.

The Chronicle even wrote about her plans, saying: "Miss June Weese, recently accepted for enlistment in the WAVES, is awaiting orders to report for her indoctrination at Hunter's College in New York. She is the daughter of Mr. and Mrs. Melvin C. Weese. She graduated from Chehalis High School and at present is employed by the Pacific Telephone and Telegraph Company in Chehalis."

Working for the phone company for twenty-seven years, she "answered complaints, typed, filed and in emergencies had to work other duties."

"All telephone operators were required to wear silk dresses, stockings and high heels, and no one saw them except the lady chief and lady assistant chief," she said.

"We had to go to the hospital and go in the operating room and give blood (in work clothes). I have O-positive so I had to go often. My dad would say 'June, someday you will need that blood.'"

She said her brothers met by chance for a few days in Hawaii.

During the war, a newspaper published a poem written by her brother, Corp. Arnold Weese, who served with a bomb squadron, as the poem's title says, "Somewhere in the Central Pacific."

Somewhere in the South Sea Islands where the sun is like a curse,

And each long day is followed by another slightly worse,

Where the flies are thicker than the island coral sands,

And the white man dreams of finer, cooler, cleaner, dryer lands.

Somewhere in the Central Pacific where a white woman is never seen;

Where the sky is never cloudy and grass is always green.

Where air raid sirens wail nightly, robbing man of blessed sleep;

Where there isn't any whiskey, and the beer is very weak.

Somewhere in the Central Pacific, where mail is always late,

Where Christmas cards in April are considered up-to-date.

*Harry Weese drew on this piece of burlap that had contained ammunition and then sent it to his mother from the South Pacific. At top right, Harry Weese of Tacoma, left, is reunited overseas with his brother, Arnold Weese of Little Rock, Arkansas. The poem Arnold wrote was printed in a military publication.*

Where we always sign the payroll, but never get a cent,

Though we never miss the money 'cause there is no place to get it spent.

Somewhere in the Central Pacific, where the soldier longs and sighs,

And the lumbering sea turtles come upon the beach to die.

Take me back to the mainland, to the girl I love so well,

For this God-forsaken island is too damn close to Hell.

Recalling the service of her husband and brothers, Deskins notes that the "only thing I can say that helped the USA—all or most in service were 18, 19, 20 years old [and] used to being told to do something and not ask why."

They may have smoked, but the men didn't do drugs. And as "Depression kids," they were used to hardship, living in rough areas, being hungry and not complaining, she said. They learned to "work as hard as you were required—and work harder even more."

★ Corp. Arnold Weese, serving with a bomb squadron against the Japs, has submitted the following poem, "Somewhere in the Central Pacific," to this column for publication:

Somewhere in the South Sea Islands where the sun is like a curse,
And each long day is followed by another slightly worse,
Where the flies are thicker than the island coral sands,
And the white man dreams of finer, cooler, cleaner, dryer lands.
Somewhere in the Central Pacific where a white woman is never seen;
Where the sky is never cloudy and the grass is always green.
Where air raid sirens wail nightly, robbing men of blessed sleep;
Where there isn't any whisky, and the beer is very weak.
Somewhere in the Central Pacific, where mail is always late,
Where Christmas cards in April are considered up-to-date.
Where we always sign the payroll, but never get a cent,
Though we never miss the money 'cause there is no place to get it spent.
Somewhere in the Central Pacific, where the soldier longs and sighs,
And the lumbering sea turtles come upon the beach to die.
Take me back to the mainland, to the girl I love so well,
For this God-forsaken island is too damn close to Hell.

PHOTO AND MEMORABILIA COURTESY OF JUNE WEESE DESKINS

*Dorothy Powell
kept track of
every article in
The Chronicle
regarding
her cousin,
who became
a prisoner.*

ARTICLES FROM THE
CHRONICLE COURTESY OF
DOROTHY POWELL

# They work for 'Missing Men'

TWICE IN A WEEK Royden Wagner, Sr., received fateful messages from the war department while at work in the Chehalis plant. The first, July 8, brought the grim news that his son, Royden, Jr., was missing in action at the Italian front.

The second message, July 14, said the man had found his way back to his outfit, and was uninjured. No better news ever reached the Wagner family. The Wagners have another son in the service, stationed with the Army Combat Engineers in Mississippi.

Their experience could be repeated—sometimes with sad variations—many times, for thirty-two long months of war the conflict has reached into nearly every home.

Many sons, brothers, husbands and other relatives of Chehalis workers are on faraway fighting fronts; some have been killed, some are missing—although as men in the Air Forces say, "M for missing" can mean anything, or everything, or nothing. To employees here, such ties make all the more important the need to stay on the job each day, building the Fortresses and Superfortresses that will hasten loved ones' safe return.

Under the heading of "why we work and fight" you can list Wanda Blankenship, shop clerk, whose father is in radar work with a Navy scouting squadron. In his year and a half in service, he has gone the length and breadth of the Pacific, including Japan's home waters.

Dorothy Davis, a recent hire, dedicates her work to a brother with the Army Air Forces in the European theater, and to another brother who was lost in Italy May 23 serving as a paratrooper.

Mrs. Pearl Zimmerman, a mechanic, works for the return of her husband, Victor, a private with an armored force in France. Of employees who are alone, Esther Miller, teletype operator, has two Navy brothers, a pharmacist's mate and a navigator, in the South Pacific. The husband of beginner mechanic Maca Hill is a prisoner guard in Italy. Vivian Schoelkoff, riveter's assistant, has two brothers in Europe, one in the A.A.F. and one a Seebee. Delores Smith's Navy brother is in New Caledonia and her sister is a Marine. Audrey Smith's brother is in the Army.

A war going on? They know it, these people, and they want to do everything they can to shorten it.

*This article appeared in The Boeing News' Chehalis edition July 28, 1944.*

**Smile Girl**

Wanda Blankenship is smiling because she's happy over the recent visit of her uncle, Sgt. Hilman Perkins, while he was home on furlough from the icicle islands. The icicle islands? Where are they? Why, they're the Aleutians! Wanda's uncle, who has been on several bombing missions over the Kuriles, reports the Aleutians make the Japs shiver just thinking of them.

*The photo and caption above
appeared in The Boeing News'
Chehalis edition August 25,
1944.*

# Chapter Seven

# Lewis County Helps War Effort

## Employees earn national awards for excellence

## MARGARET SHAVER SHIELDS

*After a year in Seattle, Margaret Shaver Shields transferred to the Chehalis plant, which opened in June 1943 to make airplane parts and tail sections for the Flying Fortresses, or B-17s.*

*"I walked to State Street to wait for Father to get off [work], after which we drove home," she said. "We shared to save gas; also I did not have a car at the time and we made gasoline stretch."*

## DOROTHY HADALLER HAGSTROM

*"I worked at Boeing in Chehalis during June and July and August 1945. My job title was riveter. I worked from 4 p.m. to midnight.*

*"I lived in an apartment on State Street when I first started working. I didn't like walking home by myself so I moved down to the old Tagland apartment building where the new courthouse building is now. Got acquainted with a girl by the name of Polly Blankenship who lived there with her sister and worked at Boeing with Harold Kinnamon and I. She and Harold are deceased. I married her brother Floyd in 1946. He is deceased since 1958."*

*"Hair had to be covered. I bought hats at the plant. I assisted Harold Kinnamon as he riveted wing sections along with Polly Blankenship as the other assistant."*

## EVA M. (PERONA) HAUCK

*"I worked at Boeings in Chehalis during June 1944 to July 1945. I started working sometime around the middle of June in 1944 about two weeks after I graduated from Centralia High School.*

*"Walked about a mile and a half to meet my ride at [the] east end of [the] viaduct in Centralia. Clocked in before 4 p.m., then waited for the day shift to leave. I was a 'C' mechanic and I drilled*

# Three firms win awards

EVEN THE SMALLER COMMUNITIES such as Lewis County, rich in willing workers but located eighty miles from the major population centers, proved fruitful in providing manpower—and womanpower—to aid in the nation's production of war materials.

At least three companies in Lewis County won national honors and acknowledgement for their work during World War II.

In June of 1944, when Boeing won the Army-Navy "E" award, all of the branch plants celebrated as well, since workers at the branch plants helped Boeing break airplane production records.

Two months later, in August 1944, the National Fruit Canning Company of Chehalis was among a dozen western food processing plants awarded the War Food Administration's "A" award for outstanding achievement in the industry—based on quality production, good labor-management relations, healthful working conditions and low absenteeism.

The award—similar to the Army-Navy "E" award for excellence and maritime "W"—came with a coveted "A" flag and honor pins for employees.

And in May 1945, the Rowe and Thompson Company—which built prefabricated barracks at plants in Chehalis and Tacoma—won the Army-Navy "E" award for excellence in manufacturing of war materials.

Three-fourths of the manufacturing of barracks, designed for use in the Southwest Pacific, was done at the Chehalis plant. Owners of the company were Robert Thompson, Earl Rowe and Austin Bee.

Another local company involved in producing materials for the war was the St. Helens Manufacturing Company and its owner, A.R. Badger, who accepted a government contract to produce a new type of fumigation unit for military use, according to a March 1943 article in The Chronicle.

At that time, Badger said he expected the plant on Fords Prairie to operate day and night shifts. The company had manufactured incubators, brooders and boats in the county for forty-five years, initially in Toledo.

He also said his company was one of only three in the nation producing fumigators for the military.

But Boeing's branch plant in Chehalis proved to be the biggest defense

*'Rosies and the guys' work on the assembly floor of the Boeing branch plant in Chehalis in December 1943.*

*holes in the wing parts for B-29 planes.*

*First I had to check out a drill and bit, being sure to get the right size 'bit.' These wing parts were later sent to the riveter who riveted struts to these parts. We had 'jigs' which the pattern was on, then made an aluminum sheet, which was clamped down, then a metal pattern laid on top and it was clamped down also. I drilled holes on two or three different wing parts. The finished product with sent to the Seattle plant to be installed in the B-29 planes.*

*"Shortly after I started working, we attended classes at the R.E. Bennett School, where we learned various parts that we worked on. No previous training.*

*"Since I worked on swing shift, we got a little more. My starting wage was 80½ cents an hour. When I made 'B' mechanic, I got 92½ cents per hour. My highest check was $78.62.*

*"All of us women had to have our hair covered with a bandanna and wear trousers. Morale was very good. We were all trying to help in the war effort.*

*"According to my check stub, $1.50 was taken out monthly for group health insurance or union dues. I don't remember which.*

*"I do remember that when I started working at Boeings we did not have a telephone in our house. Since I was working in a defense plant, I was eligible to have a phone put in our house."*

### Frances Nugent

*"In June 1945, at the age of eighteen, I graduated from high school. My sister, Roberta, and I were limited in ways to participate in the war effort and to earn money for college. We applied for jobs at*

industry manufacturer in Lewis County, at one time employing about 700 workers—many of them women.

Boeing opened the Chehalis branch Nov. 15, 1943, and it closed just after the war ended in mid-August 1945.

Yet Rowe and Thompson's 125 employees might be the county's unsung heroes in manufacturing barracks for military men serving in an area where malaria from mosquitoes posed one of the greatest health risks.

Rowe and Thompson designed the barracks for use in the tropics, adding such features as continuous window screens fitted with a glass substitute and ventilators along the sidewalls and over-hangings to carry off tropical rains, according to articles in The Chronicle.

Each basic unit contained 900 separate parts, and when put together, extended 20 feet by 48 feet. Additional sections could be linked together to form large hospitals or other buildings.

In January 1944, the company obtained $2,230,000 in Army engineering contracts to build 2,804 barracks for use in the Pacific area. Before that, Thompson primarily ran Lincoln Creek Lumber Co. and Rowe's company was in Tacoma.

The company designed special machines to conserve labor in the cutting of barracks parts. The Tacoma plant cut most of the plywood while the Chehalis plant cut other wood parts and assembled the barracks into packages for shipment.

When the company received its Army-Navy "E" award, singer Harold Quick led the community in song and Virgil Lee, Chehalis Chamber of Commerce president, served as master of ceremonies. The 362nd Armed Service Forces band from Fort Lewis provided music.

In his citation, H. Struve Hensel, assistant secretary of the Navy, described the award:

"For meritorious and distinguished service to the United States of America, the Army-Navy production award is hereby presented to the men and women of the Rowe and Thompson Company. By their unflagging spirit of patriotism—by the acceptance of high responsibility—by the skill, industry and devotion they are showing on the production front of the greatest war in history—they are making an enduring contribution, not only to the preservation of their country, but to the immortality of human freedom itself."

At right, Evelyn Stedham and Lorraine Hamilton rivet on the assembly floor of the Boeing branch plant in Chehalis Dec. 9, 1943. Below, Virginia Harlow, right, a reporter for The Chehalis Bee Nugget, interviews Boeing workers Marjorie Fuhrman and Imogene Pease.

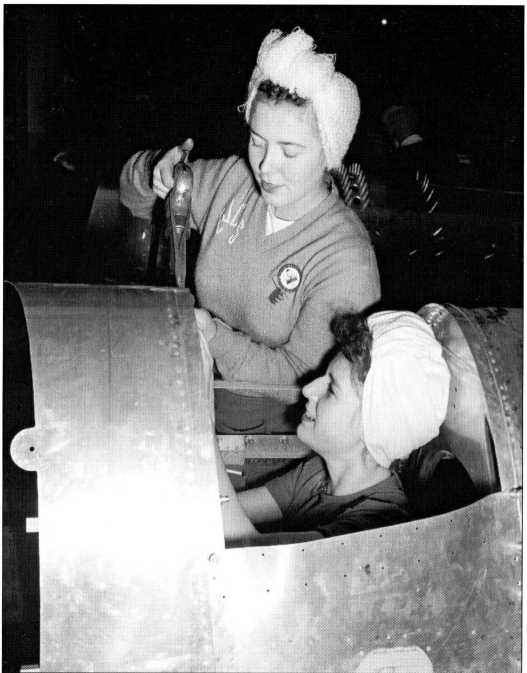

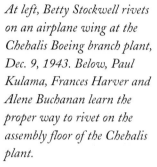

*At left, Betty Stockwell rivets on an airplane wing at the Chehalis Boeing branch plant, Dec. 9, 1943. Below, Paul Kulama, Frances Harver and Alene Buchanan learn the proper way to rivet on the assembly floor of the Chehalis plant.*

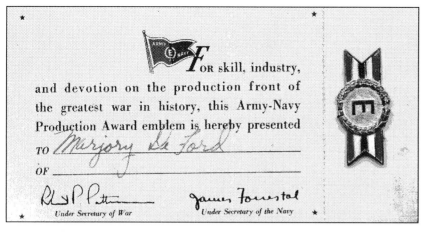

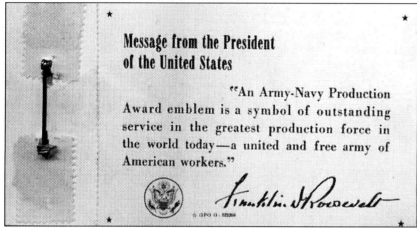

For skill, industry, and devotion on the production front of the greatest war in history, this Army-Navy Production Award emblem is hereby presented

TO *Marjory De Ford*

OF

_Robert P. Patterson_
Under Secretary of War

_James Forrestal_
Under Secretary of the Navy

## Message from the President of the United States

"An Army-Navy Production Award emblem is a symbol of outstanding service in the greatest production force in the world today—a united and free army of American workers."

_Franklin D Roosevelt_

MEMORABILIA COURTESY OF PETER LAHMANN

*When companies won awards for excellence, they received a flag to fly above their buildings, while their employees received pins attached to a card with a message from President Roosevelt.*

"The award consists of a flag to be flown above your plant and a lapel pin which every man and woman at your plant may wear as a symbol of high contribution to American freedom," declared Robert P. Patterson, undersecretary of war, in a June 6, 1945, article in The Chronicle.

"This award is your nation's tribute to your patriotism and to your great work in backing up our soldiers on the fighting fronts," he said.

the Chehalis Boeing Plant and to our surprise were hired. It was a proud experience we never forgot.

"No memory of pay or training. Wore long pants, flat shoes, hair covered by a bandanna. Spent lunch with co-workers on the lawn of Chehalis Library. Very upbeat.

"I lived across the Nisqually River and the property on the other side was Fort Lewis. The Army used this site for maneuvers such as building a pontoon bridge, which they then practiced bombing. Drove in blackout maneuvers."

### JANE DUELL MINEAR

"I worked at Boeing Aircraft in Chehalis during 1943. My job title was secretary to the night supervisor (swing shift).

"I would be at work around 3 or 3:30 p.m. Our shift ended around midnight, as I recall. I didn't have training. I had been a secretary for the Federal Land Bank office just before I left for Boeings."

"My older sister Mildred Duell Fetters ... was the timekeeper, and a good one! Her husband, Joe, was in the Army, and she was raising two little girls, and her job was very important to her.

"My sisters worked at Boeing, and I was dating a fellow who worked there as a foreman so [I] heard a lot about it. I quit my job as a secretary and hired on at Boeing. Don't remember my wage.

"I worked in an office. We wore slacks, always, it seemed. I didn't work on the production line, so was able to dress pretty much as usual. But, we had never worn pants like we did starting then, and continuing till today.

"I would think the morale was good. At home, my

*mother and dad worried about my brother a lot. And my sisters missed their husbands, but they were not overseas, and that helped a lot. They eventually joined them.*

*"I remember there was 'flirting' [at the plant] but I didn't get involved. Many of the supervisors, foremen, were married, but not above a leer or two.*

*"Most of the women I knew best at Boeings were my age. Single, and not too long out of high school.*

*"I didn't belong to a union. I only stayed at Boeings a few months. I went to work as deputy city clerk of Chehalis and was there till I married in 1945.*

*"Like I said, in many ways it was a 'crazy' time. My dear mother suddenly had three daughters who were going off to work at hours that weren't 'the norm.' Definitely not getting off work at normal hours. Wearing clothing that wasn't what they usually had worn to a job. But, working with all their hearts for 'the war effort,' and for the people close to them to get home safe and sound.*

*"Women, as you know, were never 'just housewives' again!"*

WINNIE NICHOLS,
DAUGHTER OF JERRY JOBE AND CRISTLE JOBE

*Jerry Jobe worked for Boeing from January 14, 1944, till August 27, 1945. His wife, Cristle Von Jennings Jobe, worked there from May 8, 1945, until Aug. 22, 1945. She received 92 cents an hour as a riveter.*

*"Jerry started as a riveter and then became a quality assurance person who checked the work of other riveters and corrected bad rivets. Jerry and Cristle worked on B-17 and B-29 wings."*

# Boeing opens branch plants

DESPITE ITS BEST EFFORTS, Boeing didn't have enough employees to meet increasing demands for airplane production in the Seattle area.

So officials devised a plan: If you can't bring the workers to you, go to the workers.

To that end, in May 1943 the company established a branch plants section and sought advice from the U.S. Employment Services about communities with thriving labor forces.

With Albert W. Jacobson appointed branch plant manager, the company began establishing smaller plants throughout Western Washington where parts for the B-17 could be made and then shipped to Seattle for assembly.

Workers obtained two weeks of training while the plants were constructed, then started work when the doors opened. Later, employees could sign up for supplemental training, such as courses in blueprint reading, aircraft inspection and mechanic fundamentals.

The first of these branch plants, Plant 681, opened in Aberdeen on Aug. 15, 1943, followed by Bellingham Plant 683 Oct. 4, Everett Plant 687 Oct. 13, South Tacoma Plant 684 Oct. 15, Chehalis Plant 685 Nov. 15 and North Tacoma Plant 686 in December.

Each of the plants made different parts for the plane. For example, Aberdeen concentrated on building stringer turrets, top gun emplacements and side gun panels while Chehalis constructed pilot and co-pilot seats, wings and lower turret mounting assemblies.

"Boeing in Seattle soon reached the point where it couldn't meet the demands for planes," recalls Eva Stafford, whose husband Howard worked at the plant in Seattle.

"They then established an auxiliary plant in Chehalis. Howard was then transferred from there to the Chehalis plant. We were happy to get back to our home grounds, and we found a spot for another 'Victory Garden.'"

"When they went to Chehalis, I transferred down to be close to [my] hometown," said Page Bennett, who had worked at the Seattle plant. He played on the baseball team in Chehalis.

Army inspectors oversaw work at the branch plants as well as at the main

*Boeing established its branch plant in Chehalis at the corner of Pacific Avenue and Park Street. The building above was constructed in the mid-1920s by Harry B. Quick for his harness company, which he later converted to an auto company. His daughter, Marge Murray, said he lost everything during the Depression. The Lewis County PUD had purchased the building in 1942. Because workers built parts for the airplanes, the company needed a loading ramp and door, left, to take the parts from Chehalis to the Seattle area for assembly.*

*Jerry Jobe was a journeyman aircraft mechanic. In 1944, he earned $2,947.98 and had $201 withheld for income tax. Crystal Jobe earned $626.70 in 1944 working for the Chehalis Packing Co. and $386.55 at the Central Bus Station.*

"My dad made me a bracelet out of scrap B-17 wing with my initials on it—which I still have.

"My mom and dad received their training as riveters at the Boeing plant in Chehalis. (Whatever training they got was when someone doing the job showed them how to do it.)

*Jerry Jobe made a bracelet for his daughter Winne from scrap B-17 metal.*

"My parents bought the house on Duffy Street in Chehalis while working for Boeing's. They paid $4,300 for the four-bedroom home, and I am still living there now, having moved back to take care of my dad in his last years.

"I believe women workers were required to wear head coverings and I think they were required to wear slacks.

Everyone was anxious to defeat the Japanese and there was a lot of propaganda to encourage the national spirit and to encourage the will to defeat the Japanese. There were jokes about the Japanese leader Tojo and photos all showed the Japanese with large teeth and slit eyes.

"My dad and mom paid union dues. I think it was $1.50 a month initially and then $2 per month after February 19, 1945."

MARGARET LANGUS

*Margaret Langus served as a nurse at the plant*

plants. The first inspector in Chehalis was Richard Boyle, who came from Plant 2.

During the same year, Boeing's Wichita plant started manufacturing the B-29s, or Superfortresses. In the spring of 1944, Boeing started converting its B-17 production plants to construction of the B-29s, and in the fall of 1944, Boeing opened a branch in an old Safeway store and garage in Hoquaim to boost B-29 production.

## Establishing the Chehalis plant

THE COMPANY FOUND A BUILDING owned by the Lewis County Public Utility District and occupied by a motor company. In August 1943, Boeing leased that building and others to establish a branch plant.

With so many people working in so many plants, everything had to be put in writing. The company's common refrain was VODG—or Verbal Orders Don't Go. For example, in November 1943, John A. Dean, branch plant supervisor, issued company rules for ordering work, stating that the form "will be made out in quadruplicate by person requesting work." It had to be signed by the general foreman and assistant superintendent. The blue sheet, or original, along with two pink sheets were forwarded to the facility supervisor for approval.

Boeing's public relations division published a monthly newsletter for employees, and during 1944 they created separate pages for the branch plants, such as Aberdeen and Chehalis. Le Claire Flint, a public relations division employee, coordinated and attended most of the major events of the Chehalis branch plant.

The newsletters promoted competition among the plants for purchases of war bonds. They also encouraged ride sharing to conserve gasoline. They advocated job attendance as a patriotic duty. And they urged employees to provide suggestions for job improvements and listed the winners each month, stating in January 1944 that "more than $21,000 has been paid out to Boeing employees for their ideas." Some suggestions earned an employee $100.

Because so many of the employees were women, Boeing added women supervisors and counselors to the branch plants "to solve many of the personal and plant problems confronting effeminate employees," stated the

*Reporter Virginia Harlow, right, talks to workers Marjorie Fuhrman and Imogene Pease on Dec. 11, 1943, at the Boeing branch plant in Chehalis.*

while her husband, Allan, fought in hand-to-hand combat as an infantryman in the Philippines.

"With my husband overseas and everything, I wanted to do my part."

## JUNE G. AYRES O'CONNELL

"I worked at Boeings in Chehalis from 1943 to 1945. My job title was mechanic assistant and tool room attendant.

"Glad to go to work every day. There was such a feeling of unity, just like a big family. Also the feeling of doing something constructive for our friends and loved ones in the service. We had a very positive attitude that made each day better. Of course there were the jokes people played on each other and it could be your day. (Ha!)

"One experience I really recall is the fact that the government rejected my fingerprints twice and I was so upset. My hands were frostbitten in my teenage and I had no fingerprints there. Finally they must have decided mine were so different that it would work with the thumbprint. What a relief."

## RICHARD ZORN

"I worked at the Chehalis plant during summer vacation from high school in 1944 so I only worked there a few weeks. My job title was bucking rivets.

Every day, he "passed by guards at gates. They checked badges and lunch boxes. Shift changes took place. I bucked rivets on wing panels and at times helped move completed ones for shipment. Since me and my school-

*Richard Zorn's old Boeing ID badge disappeared in his car years before his brother found it while cleaning the vehicle in 1951.*

Jan. 21, 1944, issue of the Boeing News, a publication of the company's public relations division.

The same issue credited the branch plants with helping to boost the B-17 production record, quoting Boeing operations manager Robert A. Neale as saying the situation improved when the manpower issue was resolved in the fall by tapping into reservoirs in Aberdeen, Bellingham and other communities.

"In November, output of these branch plants was felt to an appreciable extent for the first time—an extent that has been continually growing," he said.

The newsletter article stated that branch plants accounted for 15 percent of Flying Fortress production in Seattle, although only Aberdeen was operating at full capacity. Bellingham had attained 80 percent capacity, Everett 75 percent and Chehalis 65 percent. The two Tacoma plants were operating at 60 percent capacity.

The company added construction of "inboard rib assembly" at the branch plants, noting that Chehalis would work on "inter-spar ribs" while nose section and pilot seats now built at Chehalis would be moved to Aberdeen and Bellingham, respectively.

In January 1944, Boeing delivered two Fortresses for every one plane delivered the same month a year earlier. Production in January 1943 rose 8 percent from December, which was 92 percent above January 1943, according to the February edition of the Boeing News.

## Wage disparity

But operation of the Chehalis plant didn't happen without a few hitches, including a two-hour work stoppage to discuss why workers there received less pay than at any of the other branch plants.

Boeing initially hired workers at the Chehalis plant for 67½ cents an hour, but a January 1944 Boeing News article stated those workers would receive a five-cent-an-hour pay raise retroactively under a ruling by the Regional War Labor Board.

The rate, plus the eight-cent-per-hour shift differential, appeared on checks received Saturday, Jan. 15. Retroactive payments only applied to those who

# Halt Work at Boeing Plant

## Production Held Up at Chehalis While Workers Meet To Protest Wage Scale

The Chehalis' plant's share in the production of the famed Boeing Flying Fortress and parts for the new Boeing Superfortress stopped completely for two hours Wednesday afternoon, when approximately 500 employes gathered for a union meeting in protest to the present wage scale.

Wanted by the Chehalis employes is elimination of a 10-cent lower wage rate in all classifications of work performed in the local plant, as compared to wages paid in all other Boeing operations throughout Western Washington.

The meeting came in protest to a recent decision by the War Labor Board appeals panel in Washington, D. C., which turned down the appeals by both the Aeronautical Mechanics' Union No. 751 and the Boeing Aircraft company itself for a

(Continued on Page 6, Column 2)

---

# Halt Work At Boeing Plant

### (Continued from Page One)

wage scale the same as that paid in the other plants.

**Chehalis Scale Lower**

The minimum starting wage in the Chehalis plant has been set by the WLB at 72½ cents per hour, with eight cents additional per hour for those working on the swing shift. In all other Boeing plants the scale begins at 82½ cents, with 10 cents additional for swing shift workers.

Only eight factory employes clocked in for the second shift at four o'clock. Included in these was one woman whose son has been reported as missing in action following aerial combat over Europe.

Frank Owens, manager of the local plant, declared production was back to normal Thursday and that 85 percent of the workers returned to work Wednesday evening after the two-hour layoff to protest the wage scale.

John D. Glann, president of the Chehalis Chamber of Commerce, went to the meeting following a hastily called session of the chamber's board of directors and told them the board had passed a resolution to be presented to the WLB and to members of congress asking immediate reconsideration of the wage dispute, and also asking that the scale be made the same as that prevailing in other plants.

Union representatives had called two meetings for Wednesday, one for 1:30 o'clock for workers on the swing shift, and another at 4 o'clock for those on the day shift, it was reported. Those attending the earlier meeting, however, voted to attend the 4 o'clock meeting, thus halting production, the report declared.

**"Union Means Business"**

Production was halted, workers declared, in order to show the WLB "we mean business." The board, Floyd Vert, union business agent, said, had declared the workers in the Chehalis plant were not too interested in a wage increase, because there had been no stoppage or slowdown of production. The walkout was to counteract this statement, workers said.

Main fruit of the mass meeting, which was held in the John Wert hall, was to elect a committee of workers representing the Chehalis employes, which will meet in Seattle Monday and will go to the wage stabilization director of the WLB with an appeal direct from the employes.

Named to the committee were Bert Pones, Maxine Betts, Mary Mathews, Tom Davenport and Roy Deshler.

Presiding at the session was Harold Farris, shop committeeman of the second shift. Principal speaker was Jack Bentley, international representative, who reviewed the history of the wage fight and how it had been handled up to the present appeal.

**Board's Action Follows Survey**

The 10-cent lower wage scale was adopted by the WLB following investigations in the Twin City area by which it was determined lower living costs would make a lower wage scale equitable.

Bentley declared that when the new payroll was established the situation changed materially. "Prices went up when the payroll began.

---

...crimination eliminated," Mrs. Maude Meyers, secretary of the Twin City central labor council, who also expressed on behalf of the affiliated unions their "wholehearted support," and John Adams, financial secretary and business agent of the retail clerks' union, who declared "I think you have been treated very unfairly."

After the session Bentley declared the union officials in Seattle "had no idea the workers in the Chehalis plant felt so strongly about this" until they came to Chehalis and attended the meeting.

Owens said he had been informed those who returned to work Wednesday evening "were very industrious," and production did not appear to have suffered greatly.

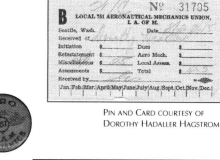

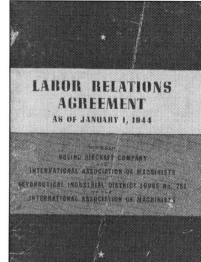

*The Local 751 Aeronautical Mechanics Union represented most of the employees at Boeing, although some belonged to the International Association of Machinists. The union and the company asked the War Labor Board to allow Chehalis workers to receive the same pay as other Boeing employees in Western Washington. Although they received an increase in pay, they still earned less than their counterparts elsewhere in the state.*

*mates were to be there for such a short time, we weren't trained in other duties.*

*He said he received "about one day's training on how to hold a bucking bar to rivet with [the] right amount of pressure.*

*"Friends always inquired how my Army brother was doing and when he was coming home.*

*He drove to work with three of his classmates and their history teacher, Mr. Frame, in his 1934 Ford that he bought with earnings from a job at Yeager's bakery.*

*"I recall that the plant did have a lot of ladies working there and there were a lot of older men also.*

*"The workday was very noisy. I don't remember any kind of ear protection for noise provided. I also remember that the aroma of perfume was quite present. The ladies I worked with as riveters were very nice and mostly hard workers.*

*"I graduated from high school the following year. I tried to join the Navy but didn't make it. I got a job with the local telephone company.*

*"In 1951 I went on duty with the Air Force reserves stationed in Japan during the Korean War. My younger brother wrote me a letter saying he had found my old Boeing Co. badge in his car they were getting cleaned up to trade.*

*"I also recall that nearly everybody smoked at break time. So the break areas were usually very smoky."*

### R. J. BOB MORGAN

*"I worked at Boeings in Chehalis, Aberdeen, and Hoquaim during 1943 through 1945. My job title*

started at 67½ cents an hour, so the new scale put their wages at 72½ cents an hour.

However, it turned out they still didn't make as much money as their counterparts in all the other branch plants.

On May 24, 1944, Boeing workers in Chehalis stopped work for two hours to meet and protest the wage scale established by the War Labor Board, which determined it cost less to live in Chehalis than in the other communities so the workers there didn't need to be paid as much.

Work stopped while about 500 employees met with union officials to protest receiving ten cents an hour less than the other branch plant workers in Western Washington. Minimum starting wage in Chehalis was 72½ cents per hour, while Boeing workers elsewhere in the state started at 82½ cents an hour. Swing shift workers earned an additional eight cents an hour in Chehalis and ten cents an hour elsewhere.

Boeing and the Aeronautical Mechanics Union No. 751 had appealed the wage disparity, but the War Labor Board denied the appeal.

"Only eight factory employees clocked in for the second shift at 4 o'clock," The Chronicle reported May 25. "Included in these was one woman whose son has been reported as missing in action following aerial combat over Europe."

Production resumed after the brief work stoppage and plant manager Frank Owens said employees who worked Wednesday evening "were very industrious, and production did not appear to have suffered greatly."

Union and company officials continued discussing the wage disparity and the Chehalis Chamber of Commerce joined the fight by enlisting support from Congressman Fred Norman. On May 29, The Chronicle noted Norman's written response: "Personally consider it extremely poor judgment to thus discriminate against employees of any plant, and will do my utmost to have such injustice rectified."

Finally, in July 1944, Chehalis Boeing workers saw their wages increased an average of seven cents an hour. They didn't receive the full amount requested, noted the July 13, 1944, issue of The Chronicle, but workers could have their starting wage increased by ten cents an hour after a thirty-day training period, and the top Chehalis scale went to $1.52½ an hour, compared with $1.60 an hour in Seattle.

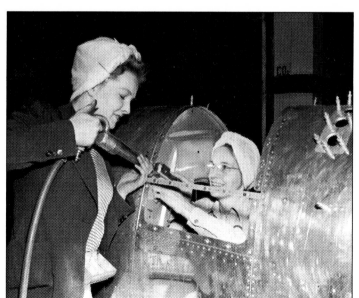

In the photo at left, reporter Virginia Harlow talks with Barbara Jennings in final assembly with two girls in the nose section behind them Dec. 11, 1943. Below, Betty Stockwell, left, rivets with help from her bucker, Martha Smith.

was head electrician (A).

"Checked all electrical to see if it was operating properly. First on the list was the air compressor in the basement. After that, I worked on installation of new equipment, lights and outlets where needed.

"When all the maintenance was done, at lunchtime I often played my guitar and sang while everybody ate.

*R.J. Bob Morgan still has his Boeing ID badge.*

All work had to be approved in writing, referred to as VODG (Verbal Orders Don't Go). His training consisted of "working with another electrician and a correspondence course." He also received additional technical information at Seattle to maintain equipment.

"I wanted to help … It was hectic. We didn't waste any time. We had a job to do and we did it.

"Morale was high at work and home. We had a lack of a lot of things, but very few people complained.

"My wife took care of the family while I worked."

He belonged to the Boilermakers Ship Builders No. 751 D and International Association of Machinists electrician (maintenance and construction) 751 B.

SHIRLEY PADHAN ERICKSON

"I worked at Boeing in Chehalis from 1944 to 1945. My job title was bucker-riveter. My starting salary I think was 65 cents an hour. I believe my pay was $1.10 when the plant closed. We got time and a half Saturday and double time Sunday.

*(Continued on page 120)*

# Flying Fortress stops

Thousands of Chehalis Boeing workers, family members and residents turned out in the rain to see a B-17 when it landed at the Chehalis Airport on Sunday, April 16, 1944.

About 7,000 people defied the rain to inspect the Flying Fortress, which stopped as part of a tour designed to give Boeing workers and local citizens a close-up look at the company's finished product. The plane arrived at 10:30 a.m. and took off again for Seattle at 4:30 p.m.

Flying the bomber was Major Felix Waitkus, chief engineering liaison officer at Plant 2 in Seattle. Later in the year, he visited several branch plants to address the employees.

The bomber also stopped at other branch plants, drawing 64,000 people altogether in Bellingham, Everett, Aberdeen and Chehalis. Aberdeen drew the largest crowd of 28,000, while Bellingham drew 18,000.

Additional stops were planned June 11 at McChord Field so Tacoma plant workers could see the finished product.

In May 1944, the Boeing News carried an article about the 5,000th Flying Fortress built since the Japanese attack on Pearl Harbor, as well as a photo showing the plane at Plant 2 after employees covered it with autographs and christened it "Boeing Five Grand."

"I wish this B-17 at least could fly low over our branch plants so our workers there could see the plane to which they have contributed so much," said Nick Carter, superintendent of final assembly for the Seattle Division, during the celebration marking completion of the 5,000th Flying Fortress. The branch plants contributed many parts to the 1,800 planes built since the fall of 1943.

The public relations department sold eight-by-ten photos of the 5,000th B-17, called the "Five Grand," at branch plants for twenty cents each.

Chehalis remained near the top among branch plants for attendance, with 10 percent absenteeism. But that was still less than Seattle, which averaged only 7 percent absenteeism while some plants were as high as 14 percent.

Thirty-four Chehalis employees were listed in May on the honor roll for

## MARGARET EVELYN COWLEY WHITFORD

*"Some of my family are in the picture. We got to go inside and looked for our riveter's stamp number on parts we might have worked on.*

*"It was exciting when they brought a B-17 to the Chehalis airport and we got to look inside."*

## R. J. BOB MORGAN

*"When landing, one of the lights on the wing tip struck the speakers stand and knocked the light off."*

## DORIS M. YEARIAN

*"It was one special day for everyone—young and old."*

## DOVIE R. WELLCOME (LONG, HALVERSON)

*"I went to the airport and looked at it. Lots of people were there. I don't remember any other details."*

## JANE DUELL MINEAR

*"Lots of excitement. A feeling of patriotism."*

## VIVIAN CURRY WOOD

*"I saw it. Very impressive."*

## EDWARD JOHNSON

*"I remember the day but I don't remember much about it other than people making speeches."*

## MABEL COOK

*"I remember feeling very proud."*

*About 7,000 people flocked to the Chehalis airport in April 1944 when a B-17 Flying Fortress made a stop to show Chehalis Boeing workers the end product of their labors.*

"Get up early—catch a ride with Ed Johnson. Get to work, go upstairs and check out a bucking bar (after I became a riveter, I checked out a gun, drill and any small tools I needed). Work until noon—rushed lunch so I could go shopping or go to the bank. This was the only time to do such things. Worked all afternoon. Go back home, eat dinner, write a letter to my husband and go to bed.

"I didn't receive any training. I started work in the fall of 1944 after graduating from Centralia High School. I bucked rivets on the B-17; when I became a riveter, I worked on the B-29.

"I don't remember the B-17 coming to the airport, but I remember the B-29 coming. I remember getting a B-29 pin. I think my boys got away with it.

"I started work to save money for a house. My husband was a carpenter and we wanted to build a home.

"Working seven days a week was tiresome. We did have good times with the people we worked with.

"We had to wear pants, sturdy shoes, and cover all our hair. No hair showing. Ed Johnson (the man who had the gasoline allotment) picked us up early. I think we were at work at 7 a.m. or 7:30 a.m. After we put in our day, we went home, unless Barney and Ed stopped for beer."

Morale "was very good. We all thought we were helping."

"I was married and didn't flirt with the men. In those days men were always more important (at least they thought so).

"There was some talk about the war, but life was pretty much the same as usual."

Major Felix Waitkus

Altogether during its visits to cities in Western Washington, more than 65,000 people turned out to view the Flying Fortress. Flying the bomber to Chehalis was Major Felix Waitkus, right, chief engineering liaison officer at Plant 2 in Seattle. His photo and the one below appeared in The Boeing News during the summer of 1944.

Chehalis people, defying heavy rains, came by car, foot, and horse-back to the Twin City airport recently to inspect the new Flying Fortress that is making a tour of all branch plant cities. In stopping at four cities, the bomber has drawn 55,000 spectators, with the largest crowd turning out at Aberdeen, where 28,000 persons flocked to the new Moon Island airport.

*Eloise Nugent Evans, right, Rose Ormbrek Menish, center, and Ruby Savage were riding horses after school when they saw the B-17 Flying Fortress at the airport, so they rode over to see it. Because of rationing, they had little gas and few car tires, so Eloise said they often rode horses to get around.*

*Workers at the Boeing plant in Seattle signed the 5,000th B-17 or Flying Fortress produced by the company since the Japanese attack on Pearl Harbor. Above, two Seattle workers paint their names on the bomber, affectionately dubbed the Five Grand. Photo is courtesy of Harry Hokanson of Chehalis.*

### EDWARD JOHNSON

*"I think about all the riders that I transported to work every day for two to three years. Shirley Padhan and her cousin were a couple of my riders.*

*"I always got started late and then I drove wide open. One morning a cop stopped me in Centralia and he asked me, 'Do you drive this way all the*

perfect attendance—many of whom hadn't missed a single day of work since the plant opened November 15.

In early July 1944, a thousand friends and relatives of local Boeing workers toured the Chehalis plant on Family Day. Each received color photographs of the B-17 and literature describing the plane.

Earlier, nearly 4,000 people had toured the three other Boeing branches, including 900 in Aberdeen, 1,303 in Everett and 1,726 in Bellingham. More than 30,000 people attended a similar family day affair held at the main Boeing plant in Seattle in 1943, according to The Chronicle.

## Army-Navy 'E' awarded

On July 18, 1944, the Chehalis branch plant shared in Boeing's success when its workers received sterling silver pins showing the Army-Navy "E" for a sustained excellence of production and the local plant raised the Army-Navy flag.

"These awards are not lightly given, and the Chehalis plant has reason to be proud of the flag that will be flown from it," Frank Owens, plant superintendent, said in making the announcement.

The afternoon ceremony took place outside at the corner of Pacific Avenue and Prindle Street, where several hundred employees gathered outside the building to see guards raise the white, blue and gold flag on the company's flagpole, beneath the Stars and Stripes.

"In 12 months we have gotten these branch plants to the point where we are entitled, along with our 'big Brother' in Seattle, to fly this 'E' award," said A.W. Jacobson, general superintendent of branch plants.

After receiving the flag from Jacobson, Owens handed it to Page Bennett, a shop committeeman who represented all the employees who qualified for the award—those who had been on the payroll as of April 15.

"We will continue to work together and we will win together," Bennett is quoted as saying in the July 19, 1944, edition of The Chronicle.

Boeing received its first "E" award in August 1942, and three stars were subsequently added.

Employees at the Western Washington branch plants helped the Boeing Co. achieve an Army-Navy 'E' award in 1944. Chehalis workers gathered for the presentation, top right, and listened to speeches made by company officials and representatives of the workers, top left. The item at lower left appeared in The Boeing News' Chehalis edition. Below are pages from the Army-Navy 'E' Award booklet.

**Chehalis Plant Receives "E" Flag**

Tom Davenport spoke impressively of the high regard in which the employees held the E flag at the presentation ceremony in Chehalis last week. On the speakers' stand, are: A. W. Jacobson, general superintendent of branch plants (left); Frank Owens, plant superintendent; Tom Davenport, Mayor Louis Virmont and Le Claire Flint.

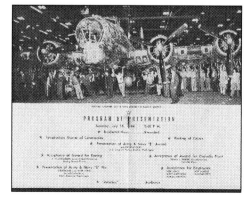

time?' and I said 'yes.' I thought he meant the same route. He smiled and said, 'Go on.'"

### DORIS M. YEARIAN

*She worked as a mechanic at Boeing in Chehalis, where she said everyone was working each day to do their part "for our country and world."*

*"I had never worked, only in our home."*

*She found the job "through radio and [the] local newspaper. And they needed to get workers for the Boeings substation. Few men left so was up to ladies to do our part." She said the pay was $1.50 an hour and "no one complained."*

*She said everyone arrived on time and ended work on time, doing what they had to do, complying with the dress code, leaving home "dressed to go right to work."*

*"Lunch at noon and back to work, until time to quit for the day.*

*"No problems [with morale] at work but hard on families where both dad and mom worked. I worked days and husband with the RR [railroad] at night so family was never left alone as many homes were. We had two boys, six and ten years old.*

*"We were all like one family. The war was our interest yet no TV. Radio and newspapers and mouth-to-mouth with neighbors and friends."*

### DOVIE R. (LONG, HALVERSON) WELLCOME

*"I worked at Boeing in Chehalis and began near the opening and worked until its closing. My job title was Rosie the Riveter with the frozen rivets. My starting salary was one dollar an hour.*

# Boeing president dies

An article in August 1944 mentioned the fact that when the German surrender, only part of the battle would be won.

"Our war is not over until Japan has surrendered," Boeing President Philip G. Johnson declared. "Our job is to do everything in our power to hasten that day."

Rumors about a holiday being declared on V-E day were untrue, he said, since the war wouldn't be over until the Allies won in the Pacific.

He never lived to see that victory.

On Sept. 4, 1944, Johnson died at 49 in Wichita and workers across the country stood for a moment of silence to honor his memory.

*Boeing president Philip G. Johnson died before Allied forces achieved victory in WWII.*

According to a Sept. 29, 1944, Boeing News article, many expressions of sympathy throughout the nation referred to Johnson's great contributions to the military power of the country, specifically referring to the vital role played by the B-17s and B-29s.

The telegrams came from people who admired his "quiet friendliness" and "inspiration." He had been active in the airplane industry for twenty-seven years. The son of Swedish immigrants, he was born Nov. 5, 1894, in Seattle. He studied engineering at the University of Washington, where William E. Boeing recruited him for the company he had started on the shore of Lake Union. Johnson became company president in 1926.

# War bond drives and employee features

In the first week of the Sixth War Loan, employees making the Superfortresses invested $231,160 in war bonds, the Boeing News reported in November 1944. That figure includes $2,193 in cash sales at the Chehalis plant, No. 685, and $1,578 to be deducted from the payroll accounts—a total

*Security guards at Boeing's Chehalis branch plant are, front row, left to right: Clarence Arnold, W.A. Buchanan, J.W. Hawkins and D.H. Canino. Back row, left to right, are: Sgt. Lou G. Clinton, Ralph Lindquist, Clifford Lohtt, Floyd Tharp and Harry Miner. The photo above also appeared in the Chehalis edition of The Boeing News in 1944. Photo provided by Peter Lahmann.*

# Chehalis #685

Contributing Editor: AVARD MANDERY

## They Make It Soft tor B-17 Pilots

Assembly of pilots' seats by the Chehalis plants has been an important contribution of the branch plants to the B-17 production picture. When work started at Chehalis, the Seattle plant was down almost to its last seat, but these Chehalis men — Henry Wilson [left] and Alvin McClure — quickly built up a supply that assures a seat for every Fortress pilot.

The first wing rib to leave the Chehalis branch plant is inspected here by General Foreman Ed Rasmussen [left], while Keith Bidleman and Charles Anderson provide the finishing touches.

## Chehalis Nymph

To prove that more than fish swim in the Chehalis river, 685 presents this snappy shot of Vivian Curry, swing shift bathing beauty. We hope the boys notice, as Vivian stirs up a ripple, that there's water in the river!

*Boeing's public relations division produced a newsletter for employees with feature stories and news. During 1944, they also provided separate pages for the branch plants. All of these items appeared in the newsletters during 1944.*

Don Toney    H1945

## Destroyer Veteran Busy on Home Front

A NEW EMPLOYEE is Donald M. Toney, who served as electrician's mate first class at the head of a maintenance crew on a destroyer recently sunk in the Pacific.

He was in the Navy from January 16, 1942, to November 2, 1943, when he was given a medical discharge. He was in nine major and five minor engagements, including Wake, Midway, Marshalls, Gilberts, Coral Sea, Guadalcanal, Western Solomons, Bismark Sea, Tulagi, Savo Sea and Attu.

## School Girls by Day, Riveters by Night

Working a full shift at Boeing as riveters on the second shift and taking a full course of studies at Adna high school has made the last year a busy one for Grace Anderson [left], Della Tyler and Evelyn Cowley. They all have taken an active part in school activities, such as the school band and senior class play, and have made the honor roll for scholastic standing. Grace also is editor of the school Annual and Della contributed art work to its pages.

that amounted to 95 percent participation among employees.

"Plant 685 is expected to purchase $36,750 in bonds, and indications are that the quota will be reached. The first three days of the drive netted $7,000," the newsletter reported.

Shop people helping in the drive were Kathleen Baxter, Joyce Markstrom, Mildred Fetters, Robert Titus, Aileen Jacobs, Ted Arnold, Mary Matthews and Harold Faires. 685's slogan was, "Buy Bonds Build Boeing Bombers."

An article in the Boeing News noted that a B-29 tail gunner's enclosure was on display at the Chehalis plant as an added attraction to boost participation in the Sixth War Loan drive.

Other articles in the Boeing News featured former veterans who had taken defense jobs to continue fighting the war on the home front, such as Lyle Harold Andrews, who served two years and ten months with the field artillery of the 41st Division before his discharge from a Walla Walla hospital with a purple heart. He lost a brother, Private Cecil M. Andrews, in Belgium. He said he liked working at the Boeing branch plant because "I feel like I'm still in there pitching."

David Mason, who was released from the Navy after a year and nine months in the South Pacific, said his interest in working was "not the job and pay, but to help get the war over as soon as possible. B-17s and B-29s will help do that, he says," a Boeing News article stated.

One feature in the Boeing News focused on three young girls who worked swing shift at the Boeing plant and attended school at Adna during the day.

One article mentioned Japanese weapons on display in the office of Ethel Zirkle, women's supervisor, who received the souvenirs from Lorraine Arrington, whose husband Sgt. Ray Arrington, had collected them and sent them home from the South Pacific.

A March 1944 story described the training of branch plant guards, most of whom were businessmen working at the plants during the war. They received five-day intensive instruction in Seattle before starting work. They were considered members of the "auxiliary military police under the Army Air Forces, subject to 24-hour call, and their passes are honored any place within the United States." Most were hired locally or transferred to jobs in their hometowns to cut down on commuting.

In September 1944, a story featured Capt. Robert Crawford, a former

*"I had to go to work for survival. It paid the best. Started at one dollar an hour and finished at $1.10. It just paid the bills.*

*"I went to work swing shift—from 2 to 11:30 p.m. I worked on the wing panels using frozen rivets. We couldn't visit outside of our work area so I didn't meet many people. The rivets were in a freezer and you had to use them before they thawed.*

*"At lunchtime we used to go to a restaurant a couple times a week. The restaurant was where Sterling Bank is located—owner Mary Meadows Carson.*

*"Trained at the Boeing plants. Holes were drilled in the panel. The panel was on a rack. I placed the rivets in the panels.*

*"At home, we just worked, worked, worked on our farm clearing land and planting.*

### ETHEL NELSON

*She worked at Boeing's Chehalis branch, earning about a dollar an hour, she said, in her job as "Rosie the Riveter."*

*"My sister, Nina Hallman, who is deceased, and I lived with my mother in Chehalis on Fourth Street. We had a day shift so made our lunch and walked to work. Both worked as riveters so with heads covered with a scarf we were ready for work. We were both riveters for airplane wings. I was a riveter but sometimes would relieve the bucker.*

*"Coming home from New York [after] traveling with my husband, the Boeing plant was just starting up. Thought it was one way to help all servicemen.*

*"Came to work with our heads covered—slacks and good sturdy shoes.*

*"As I remember, everyone was there to do their best work and as I remember everyone seemed to get along. Worked hard and relaxed on our breaks."*

## EUGENE DONALD "DON" CASTLE

*"I worked at [the] Boeing branch plant in Chehalis during the summers of 1945 and 1944. My job title was machinist helper, rivet bucker. I can't remember [my starting salary]—80 cents an hour I think.*

*"Summer of 1944—I drilled rivet holes in the B-17 wing ribs.*

*"Summer of 1945—I bucked rivets on the B-29 wing ribs. A Rosie the Riveter and I replaced defective rivets after the rib was assembled and inspected. We didn't have much to do. The repair team I was on became so boring that I quit Boeing and went to work for Palmer Lumber Co. I really worked hard there.*

*"In the fall of 1945 I went to work for a grocery store in Centralia delivering groceries after school. Before I worked for Boeing I was the official bread wrapper for Daviscourt Bakery in Centralia after school in the evening.*

*"I was a high school student on summer break from school. There was no formal training [at Boeing]. I was supplied an electric drill and needed bits and shown what to do. The women (two) put a wing rib together in a jig and I drilled the holes where needed."*

## EUNICE L. HOWARD

*"Worked at Boeing in Chehalis from 1944-45. Job title was office worker in the personnel office. No special training. Worked for an accountant and also bookkeeping at Chevrolet Garage prior to working at Boeing.*

Chehalis resident and author-composer of the Army Air Force Song. The article states that he was born in a gold mining camp in Alaska and moved at an early age to Chehalis, where he took his first music lessons and later graduated from Chehalis High School. He lived in Chehalis for a while after graduating and performed with a local quartet.

"Maybe there is something in the rhythm of a rivet gun that inspired Willard Hudson, assistant production supervisor, [Chehalis Plant] 685, to write five popular songs and have them all accepted at one time," begins a story in the Nov. 30, 1944, edition of the Boeing News.

Hudson, who was better known as Bill Hudson, had already published "Keep 'Em Flying," but recently had five other songs accepted: "Caution Me," "Tonight I Walk With Angels," "Every Little Bird Will Sing a Song of Love," "Who Is It?" and "Riding on a Cloud."

"It's a wonderful feeling to know that I've finally made the grade," said Hudson, who made his first stage appearance when he was six at the Alaska Yukon-Pacific Exposition in Seattle in 1909.

He had worked with Eddie Cantor, Jimmy Durante, Sophie Tucker and Horace Heidt and, as a professional banjo player, played with Al Pierce and his gang. He also performed a role in *The Winning of Barbara Worth* along with Gary Cooper, Ronald Colman and Vilma Banky. But he recalled that living in Hollywood for nine months proved embarrassing as he had to have his hair bleached and marcelled—made wavy with a curling iron—for a role in *The Volga Boatman*.

"It took Hollywood nine months to film the picture," he says, "and all that time I had to go around looking like a dandified play boy. Anyway, I became well acquainted with Max Factor because he always had to make up my coiffure."

After creating California Rhythm Rogues, he traveled throughout the country for fourteen years playing in the dance halls. He met his wife, La Verda, who went by "Torchy," while playing in his hometown of Seattle. She worked as chief clerk at the Chehalis plant.

An article in the Dec. 30, 1944, edition of the Boeing News chastised employees for losing 32,000 pounds of rivets each month—rivets needed to build B-17s and B-29s.

*Shirley Padhan Erickson, left, who provided this photo, is seen riveting with help from bucker Peggy Friese at the Chehalis plant.*

*"We all worried about the war."*

## JULIA R. FORD MEADOWS

*"I worked at Boeings in Chehalis from June 1944 to 1945. My job title was riveter-bucker. My starting salary was 50 cents an hour.*

*"Swing shift—check in at 4 p.m., check tools out, got rivets from freezer and go to work. Got off at 12 p.m. I riveted wing ribs that were sent to Seattle to be assembled at their plant into the wings.*

*"On-the-job training. Training was all the time due to different jobs. At first I was a bucker for a riveter then was promoted to riveter.*

*"Wore slacks or jeans. Hard-toed shoes.*

*"I had one sister who worked at the Chehalis plant for two weeks and ended because [of an] appendicitis operation. (Luella Ford Vandal, deceased)*

*"I had two sisters and one brother-in-law who worked at Boeing in Seattle. Also several cousins. (Helen Ford Erdman, deceased; Rhoda Jean Ford Ray, who later became a WAVE, deceased; Gilbert Lloyd Erdman, deceased; Kathleen Ford and Dick Ford)*

## MARGARET EVELYN COWLEY WHITFORD

*"I worked at [the] Boeing branch plant in Chehalis from December 1943 to March 1945. My starting salary was 90 cents an hour. My job title was Riveter 'B.'*

*"A friend, Della Tyler, had worked at Boeings in Seattle during the summer, so when Boeing opened the plant in Chehalis we applied and were accepted for jobs. We went to school days and rode to town with Della's dad to work.*

"Rivets aren't peanuts, and if they were, employees wouldn't lose 27 percent of them getting them into their mouths," the article began.

To build a Flying Fortress, employees need 450,000 rivets, and the Superfortress requires 600,000 rivets.

"If rivets were bullets, employees would be horrified at a 27 percent loss of vital materiel so urgently needed by the men behind the guns at the front," the article contended. "But rivets used by employees behind the rivet guns on the home front serve an equally vital place in the war effort."

## Pachy arrives at Chehalis on anniversary

In November 1944, the Chehalis plant celebrated its first anniversary with a turkey dinner and music at the St. Helens Hotel. The celebration featured music by Byron Seeley, foreman, who played the violin, and accompanist Evelyn Duncan, another Chehalis employee.

The only damper on the evening came with the arrival of Pachy.

To encourage safety, the company established a white elephant—Pachy—who traveled each month to the plant with the highest accident rate. It arrived in Chehalis once in 1944, an arrival reported in the November edition of the Boeing News.

"The pachyderm inopportunely appeared on the scene as Frank Owens, superintendent of the Chehalis plant, had finished eating a sumptuous dinner at St. Helens hotel during 685's anniversary celebration. Owens, however, wouldn't shake hands with the little beast when it cutely sat up, waggled its ears and offered a chubby pad.

"'You're certainly not welcome here, Dumbo, and I'm sure you weren't invited,' said the superintendent, as he picked up the elephant as though it had rattlers on its tail. 'As soon as our accident frequency goes down, I'll see that the inspection department hangs you with a rejection tag.'"

Boeing public relations workers also arranged for branch plant employees and their families to view two films, the *War Department Report* (taking workers behind enemy lines to view footage from captured German and Japanese films) and *Fortress of the Sky* (filmed in color at Boeing Seattle plants following the B-17 from its birth on engineering boards through fac-

## 'Pachy' Packs His Trunk to 685

Frank Owens, 685, is the new member of the Royal Order of Mahouts, an "honor" that goes with the bestowal of the white elephant upon the superintendent of the branch plant with the month's highest accident frequency. Superintendent Owens held the elephant as if he were afraid it would bite him and up the accident frequency. Attendants at Owens' initiation into the "pachyderm club" were Mrs. Al Jacobson [left], Mahout Owens, Mrs. Frank Owens, Al Jacobson, general superintendent of branch plants, and Dave Williams, Jr., assistant general superintendent of branch plants.

*Chehalis branch plant manager Frank Owens isn't exactly thrilled with the arrival of Pachy, a white elephant given to plants with the highest accident frequency, as noted in this Boeing News item. Below, clockwise from lower left around the group of rivets, are a stainless steel rivet, a B-29 rivet used upstairs at the Chehalis plant, a frozen rivet that exploded because it became too warm and a defective rivet.*

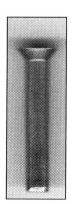
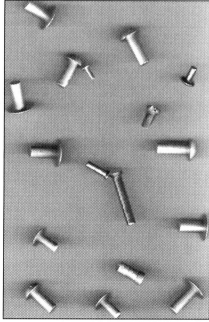

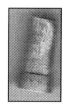

RIVETS COURTESY OF SHIRLEY PADHAN ERICKSON

"At 2:30 my friend Della Tyler's dad would pick us up and take us to Chehalis. We would stop at a restaurant and get something to eat. Then walked to the plant and checked in. Our lunch boxes were opened so the guards could check them. We would then get our tools, rivet guns and motors, and go to our stations to work.

"We were teenagers and met a lot of other teens working there. My bucker, Evelyn Saunders Connadi, and I became best friends and still keep in contact though she lives in Nevada. Some of the people called us the 'Gold Dust Twins' as we were both Evies. We worked on rib parts for the Flying Fortress B-17s and later on B-29 parts.

"We worked till 12 midnight then checked out and had our lunch boxes checked again. My mom also worked there then and we both rode home with a neighbor, Ray Davis, who also worked there.

"I started out as a bucker for a riveter and was soon made a 'C' riveter at 90 cents per hour, then a 'B' riveter at $1.065 and hour. I later was earning $1.165, good money at that time. I worked swing shift.

"We wore bib overalls, no loose sleeves or blouses that could get caught on machinery. We also wore our hair covered with a scarf.

"Morale was good at work and home. Everyone felt they were doing what they could to help end the war."

### MARTHA LAHMANN LOHRER

*She worked as a bucker at Boeing in Chehalis during 1944.*

"Early morning, walk one mile to Rochester highway for carpool to Chehalis. Worked with a riveter

*This photo, provided by Peter Lahmann, shows B-29 Superfortresses, probably in Seattle. The Chehalis plant converted to making parts for the B-29s in the spring of 1944.*

tory assembly and into Army flight formations). Chehalis workers saw the films at the St. Helens Theatre in February 1944.

## Converting to B-29s

In early April 1944, an article in The Chronicle reported that the Chehalis branch plant would start producing B-29s. Five other plants also would be converted to production of the Superfortresses.

"News of this changeover from Flying Fortresses to Super Fortresses lends even greater importance to the Boeing factory here," Owens said.

"It means we are now charged with responsibility of directly helping to turn out the biggest military airplane ever produced anywhere on a large scale. I am confident that, with the same fine cooperation from employees and the community, we can meet B-29 production schedules as we have done on the B-17."

Owens said local employees helped Boeing establish a world record for single-month heavy bomber production.

The Boeing Co. announced its big Seattle plant No. 2 and five Western Washington branches would be converted to the building of B-29s.

President Philip G. Johnson said conversion would be started immediately and extend over several months, with all manpower utilized during the changeover.

The Boeing plants at Renton, Washington, and Wichita, Kansas, already produced B-29s.

An article in late April stated that Bellingham, Tacoma and Chehalis would be the first branch plants to start producing parts for B-29s and start shipping them by June 1.

The article said that while Boeing plants would focus on producing the B-29s, the B-17s would continue to be built at California plants of Douglas Airplane Company and Lockheed Vega Aircraft Corporation.

About the same time, the Boeing News quoted Army officials as warning employees against speaking too freely about the B-29 or Superfortress. The article had the headline: "Employees Talk Too Much About B-29 Work, says Army."

*as a bucker on airplane wings. Half hour [to eat] lunch from home—long enough to go to the bathroom and eat a sandwich and return to work. Then carpool ride ... to drop off at highway and walk one mile to my home. This was a summer job before my senior year at Rochester High School.*

*"My mother, Astrid Lahmann, also worked on a drill press at the plant.*

*"Before my junior year in high school, I was able to get a job at Fort Lewis in the PX in [the] cafeteria (summer). Carpool with other workers. Don't remember wages. I needed money for school clothes. We had on-job training, learning how to mix raw hamburger into patties and cook; had to clean the grill; run cash register; worked in soda fountain.*

*"When I was in nursing school, work and school studies were first priorities. That was the time the men were returning, all branches of service. They sure didn't want to talk about the bombings and ships sinking in English Channel."*

### MARY JACOBSEN KLAUS

*"I worked at Boeings in Chehalis.*

*"Widowed in 1940 and two brothers in service. Was very worried about the war. Had a new car and had four riders. Was pleased to be able to help. When daughter became very ill had to quit. Now it all seems like a bad dream!"*

*She had two children at the time. "Every morning had to take them to Mother."*

### VIVIAN CURRY WOOD

*She worked at Boeing in Chehalis from 1943 to 1945. "My job title was riveter—countersink riveter, pickup riveter, yoke riveter—icebox rivets.*

*"Can't remember my starting wage or quitting wage. I got several raises along the way."*

*She described morale as "very good."*

*"I worked on the swing shift by choice. During the day I helped my folks on the farm, putting up hay for the cattle, helping milk the cattle [in the] mornings."*

## ELANOR WILBER

*She worked as a mechanic at Boeing in Chehalis in 1945, where, she said, "we had a lot of good times."*

*"My starting salary was approximately 75 cents per hour. I worked the swing shift. On Saturday nights it was not uncommon to meet my husband and the 'gang' to go out to Plaquato and dance. I believe there were some spirits available too. We also went to Chehalis Eagles #1550 to dance. They were located over Garbey's Tavern on Chehalis Avenue.*

*"A typical day was to take care of my family. Rodney owned and operated his own logging trucks so his day started very early. We had a son and daughter that had not started school yet. I would go to work as I remember about 2 p.m.*

*"We were very much in need of extra money. The country was still in a depression. The logging industry was changing. I did not have any training except the initial introduction to the job. I applied at the Boeing hiring center.*

*"Dress code? I do not know that anyone knew about that. The one exception was that it was OK to wear pants (long, that is) and tie your hair up*

The Army said people tended to talk about the plane in letters or to friends on buses, in taverns or in other public places.

"This increase in security carelessness has led government intelligence agencies to investigate the sources of the chatter," the article states. "At Boeing field, some cameras have been nabbed from photographers trying to sneak photos of the big bomber.

"Facts that employees definitely must NOT talk about are the most interesting features of the Superfortress: speed, altitude, bomb load, construction details, and information about the plants where it is being manufactured."

The article said Boeing workers should refrain from discussing anything they weren't sure had been released by the government.

"That's just one more part given to workers to play in the war," the article concludes.

In late May 1944, The Chronicle reported that the first deliveries of B-29 parts from branch plants to Seattle would be made "early next week," with Chehalis "expected to lead the parade, with its first delivery booked for June 3." Bellingham was expected to follow a week later, then Tacoma and Aberdeen.

In mid-June, the newspaper ran a story describing details about the B-29s after reporters toured three Boeing plants in Seattle over two days but withheld publishing any information until the bombing of Japan began—and after sending a copy to Washington, D.C., for censorship. The headline stated: "Latest Boeing Mystery Plane Is Giant Craft."

Written by John B. Edinger, the June 15 story described the Superfortress, also known as the B-29, noting that each of the newspapermen who toured the plants had been "sworn to secrecy" and told to keep publication of their stories under lock and key until military officials decided it was time to inform the public.

He noted the plane outstripped other bombers, flying higher, faster and farther at higher altitudes with better targeting than any other bomber. "It does everything the B-17 can do, only better," he wrote.

Twice as large as the B-17, the B-29 featured rivets that were countersunk, a 141-foot wingspread and an aluminum alloy skin giving a perfectly smooth surface. Noting the visit of the B-17 to the Twin Cities in the spring, Edinger said that the Flying Fortress "could be run under the wing of the

*Richard Larson provided this copy of a photo Boeing sold showing the Five Grand, the 5000th Flying Fortress built since the attack on Pearl Harbor. Seattle employees painted their autographs on the plane.*

in a bandanna. I worked as a mechanic. I will never forget the smell when we drilled the asbestos out of tubes that went into the wing structure. It ... had an odor that was unforgettable.

"I had a baby sitter. My son was five but not in school and my daughter was four."

### ELLEN IRENE KAIN

"I worked at Boeing in Chehalis during the summer of 1945.

"They announced at a school assembly that they needed workers at the plant in Chehalis. My two friends and I applied and got jobs.

"I was a driller and we had to wear navy coveralls and tie our hair in a bandanna.

"I worked with a good group. They were great. Morale at home was fine. Great fellow workers. Lunch together in lunchroom.

"We were trained on the job. We drilled holes for the riveters to finish."

### JEAN DeSPAIN

"I worked at Boeing in Chehalis from June to August 1944 as a drill press operator.

"Aunt and uncle (Gordon and Alice Hoover) worked at Chehalis Boeing and encouraged me to work there.

"Draw drill bits, set up drill press, drill holes in wing assembly and pass on to riveter. All day, all week, all summer.

"It was on-the-job training. One day. Morale was good to high everywhere."

*Reporter Virginia Harlow is seen near a body section of a plane in final assembly during her tour of the Chehalis Boeing plant in December 1943.*

Superfortress." He described the bomber as 98 feet long—23 feet longer than the B-17—shaped like a huge cigar with a small plastic nose, tapering wings and completely retractable "tricycle landing gear." He said it carried a crew of ten: pilot, co-pilot, bombardier, flight engineer, radioman, navigator and gunners and was armed with 20mm cannons and .50-caliber machine guns.

When Boeing announced plans to convert plants to building the B-29s, the company said Lockheed and Douglas Company in California would continue to build the B-17s.

## Branch plants continue to grow

As the company converted to construction of the B-29—and still strived to meet its B-17 schedule—each of the branch plants increased in workers.

To meet the heavy B-29 production schedule, Boeing planned to enlarge the Everett plant and open a new plant in Hoquiam.

On June 12, 1944, the Chehalis branch launched its graveyard shift.

War needs also ruled out vacations for employees, who had to work on the Fourth of July to help meet the demand for B-17s and B-29s.

The June 1944 Boeing News described the need for suspending vacations, quoting H.O. West, executive vice president: "The new critical nature of the production problem is due to the acute manpower shortage, and the extreme difficulty of obtaining additional qualified personnel. He pointed out that if vacations were taken it would result in the loss of enough manpower to build more than 80 Fortresses. Employees will be awarded extra pay in lieu of vacations this year."

"It is the company's policy and its desire to give employees vacations whenever this policy can be carried out without interference with production," West said. "However, due to the important task of rushing our B-29 conversion program ... and the important heavy production schedule of both the Superfortress and the Flying Fortress, it is necessary for everyone to keep on the job."

According to the Oct. 31, 1944, edition of the Boeing News, about 5,500 workers would be building parts for the Boeing B-29 at eight Western Washington branch plants by the end of the year.

Tacoma, which would employ 1,500 by the end of the year, would see the greatest increase in late 1944. Aberdeen and Hoquiam were expected to add 800 employees.

According to A.W. Jacobson, branch plant supervisor, the company expected employment totals of Jan. 1, 1945, to be:

| | |
|---|---|
| Aberdeen | 650 |
| Hoquiam | 500 |
| Chehalis | 500 |
| South Tacoma | 700 |
| Tacoma | 1,500 |
| Everett No. 1 | 750 |
| Everett No. 2 | 400 |
| Bellingham | 500 |

RUTHIE A. KRAUSE, COURTESY OF
HER DAUGHTERS ARLENA ZADINA AND
LOIS KRAUSE WELLBROCK

*"My mother was 32 or 33 years old when she worked at Boeing [in Chehalis]. My mother was a riveter in 1945. Her name was Ruth A. Krause. They made B-29 bomber wings.*

*"We lived in Napavine at the time. We did not own a car but she rode to work with a neighbor lady, Reba Milam. She worked the shift from 4 p.m. to midnight. My aunt, her sister Esther Miller, also worked there. She was a bucker.*

*"They wore a snood-type thing around their heads to keep hair covered. It had a bill, something like a baseball cap, to keep anything from flying down into their eyes. They used rivets of various sizes and colors and sometimes they would be in her pockets. She said they were refrigerated at the plant. We had to remove them if we were helping her with laundry, so they did not go through the washing machine.*

*"We lived about eight miles from her job, and that put her going to work before we got home from school most days. Our father was a carpenter who was on a construction crew working on various projects throughout the [West]. He was one of the crew who helped to build a big supply depot at Clearfield, Utah. There were four of us girls. One of the oldest sisters had to baby-sit each day. Our brother stayed in Minnesota (with relatives) to finish his school year. If things were late for Mom to get home at night, she would sometimes need to sleep in [the] mornings.*

*"We needed to get to school, so we learned to get ourselves up and breakfasted and walked to school without her some days. We lived just a few blocks from school."*

# The end of an era—Boeing's last B-17

In April 1945, Boeing held elaborate ceremonies in Seattle to mark completion of the company's contract for manufacturing B-17 Flying Fortresses.

Riveter Lorraine Hamilton attended the ceremonies to represent typical workers at the Chehalis branch plant.

The company delivered more than 5,000 Flying Fortresses to the Army before shifting its focus to building "the now famous B-29 Superfortress," The Chronicle reported April 5, 1945. Wartime production had boosted the total of B-17s from only a handful when the Japanese bombed Pearl Harbor to more than 12,000 by May 1945.

Meanwhile, on April 12, 1945, President Franklin Delano Roosevelt died at the age of 63.

The Chehalis Eagles held "Boeing Night" in late April 1945, featuring combat films and other shows pertaining to the aircraft industry, as well as members of a C-97 crew that established a speed record from Seattle to Washington, D.C.

Workers at the Chehalis Boeing branch plant heard news flashes of the B-29 raid on Japan broadcast over the public address system June 15, 1945, beginning at 11:55 a.m.

Later, employees throughout Boeing received high praise from the military.

"I wish to express to the personnel of your company my sincere appreciation for the splendid effort displayed by them in making it possible for me to have had the honor of initiating the first of the Strategic Air Forces attacks against industrial Japan," Brig. Gen. K.B. Wolfe, commanding general of the 20th Bomber Command, wrote to company president Philip G. Johnson.

Thousands of employees showed up at the Chehalis airport on a Sunday in May 1945 to view a completed Boeing B-29 Superfortress as well as a United States Airlines mainline plane. Altogether, about 12,000 people gathered to view the Superfortress and participate in ceremonies dedicating the airfield, which had been converted over the past twenty years from a small cow pasture to a distinguished airport. State Sen. Virgil R. Lee served as master of ceremonies.

## Boeing Makes Its Last B-17

Elaborate ceremonies in Seattle Thursday marked the completion of the Boeing Aircraft company's contract for manufacture of Boeing B-17 Flying Fortresses, and representatives of branch plants throughout Western Washington were participating in the event.

Going from the Chehalis plant to represent the employes here was Lorraine Hamilton, a riveter, who attended the ceremonies as a typical worker from the local plant which aided in the completion of the large contract.

The Seattle plant of the Boeing company, with the co-operation of the branch plants, has delivered to the Army well over 5,000 Flying Fortresses. In addition, other plane manufacturers throughout the nation have built the huge ships, and some of continue to manufacture them on Boeing specifications.

THE CHRONICLE AT CENTRALIA

That same month, a veteran Superfortress pilot visited workers at the Chehalis branch plant.

Capt. Norman F. Watkins, who participated in the first B-29 raid over Tokyo, told workers about his experiences during an informal talk. He said thick flak bored holes in the plane's wing.

"I was plenty scared. In fact, everyone was scared. And anyone who tells you he wasn't, is a liar," he said, as quoted in the May 16, 1945, issue of The Chronicle. "But those holes in the wing didn't bother that B-29 at all."

He said the Japanese referred to the bombers as "diabolical destroyers of Japanese culture" after they demolished a dictionary that had been twenty-three years in the making.

He also said people who were absent from work should compare their lot with those in the air forces, where they worked twenty-four hours a day, seven days a week without time and a half or double time for Sundays.

"I am not here to criticize you or ask you to do any better than you have been doing," he said. "All I ask is to keep the status quo; that you continue to turn out good ships. Because the B-29 is a good ship and is about the best bomber the allies have."

"We lived close to Fort Lewis, an Army base, and McChord Air Force Base at Tacoma. If there were a blackout, we would have to make sure our windows were covered and no lights peeping out, if she was not at home to be in charge.

"It was an interesting time in our lives. Radio, reading and school functions [were] our main entertainment.

"She passed away in May 2001 so she cannot tell you her story herself."

### GEORGIE BRIGHT KUNKEL

"I worked at Boeing in Seattle one summer in the office and again one summer at [the] Boeing plant in Chehalis in the summer of 1945, the year the war was over. I was a mechanic. I don't remember what my salary was.

"I remember that I drilled holes in wing panels for the B-17 bomber. I worked with a retired man on this job. One day the supervisor came by and said that our wing panels had some crooked holes. He wanted us to show him how we were drilling. Of course, they asked me to show my drilling skills first. I was perfect. So it was my partner who was drilling crooked holes.

"I received on-the-job training. Someone taught me to drill holes and then I was left to go ahead with a partner drilling holes in wing panels."

## The Air Force Song—Full Lyrics

*By Robert Crawford*
*Courtesy USAF Heritage of America Band*
*http://usmilitary.about.com/od/airforce*
*/l/blafsong.htm*

*Off we go into the wild blue yonder,*
*Climbing high into the sun;*
*Here they come zooming to meet our thunder,*
*At 'em boys, Give 'er the gun! (Give 'er the gun now!)*
*Down we dive, spouting our flame from under,*
*Off with one helluva roar!*
*We live in fame or go down in flame. Hey!*
*Nothing'll stop the U.S. Air Force!*

*Additional verses:*
*Minds of men fashioned a crate of thunder,*
*Sent it high into the blue;*
*Hands of men blasted the world asunder;*
*How they lived God only knew! (God only knew then!)*
*Souls of men dreaming of skies to conquer*
*Gave us wings, ever to soar!*
*With scouts before And bombers galore. Hey!*
*Nothing'll stop the U.S. Air Force!*

*Bridge: "A Toast to the Host"*

*Here's a toast to the host*
*Of those who love the vastness of the sky,*
*To a friend we send a message of his brother men who fly.*
*We drink to those who gave their all of old,*
*Then down we roar to score the rainbow's pot of gold.*
*A toast to the host of men we boast, the U.S. Air Force!*
*Zoom!*

*The late Joyce Markstrom Venemon told a reporter in 1989 that she felt like a millionaire while working at Boeing's branch plant in Chehalis.*

# Defense jobs pose dangers

Working at Boeing brought with it high wages—but a few dangers as well with people working around the clock.

Joyce Markstrom Venemon told a Daily Chronicle reporter in 1989 that she earned good pay as a welder at Boeing's Chehalis plant—less than a dollar an hour.

"God, I thought I was a millionaire!" she said. "It was fun work and I knew the people there.

But Malcolm "Bud" Berg remembers seeing a woman working across from him on the swing shift suffer a nasty shock.

He said he warned her against using a particular drill, telling her: "I wouldn't do that if I were you. I'd take that drill and trade it in for another one. It's got a bad cord on it. It's liable to curl your hair."

But she said it was all right—and it was—"right up until she touched that drill to the wing.

"I was watching for it. It grounded her—boy, it was twisting her up like a clock-spring. I jerked the cord out. It turned loose and everything was out," he remembered. "If she'd had a bad heart, that could have been a bad one. Took about an hour for her to get stabilized again. That was a terrible shock."

Berg remembers they took the drill to the tool room. "I called the foreman and I said, 'Howard, get rid of this drill. Get rid of it before someone gets hurt seriously.'"

Although defense industry jobs could pose dangers, Berg said: "I never saw anything any worse than that—at least not on my shift."

He remembered the women had to wear bandannas over their hair.

"I never saw any of them get hooked with the drill," Berg said. "In Seattle I did. I saw one girl—that drill went in and grabbed her hair; she was inside one of the wings."

"I did see girls get a chunk of hair pulled out of the scalp," he recalled, saying they'd let out a shrill scream. "I couldn't say as I blamed them."

Mary Jacobsen Klaus recalls one injury while working at the Chehalis plant.

"A spike hit me on the forehead," she said, adding: "I survived."

Vivian Curry Wood, now of Alaska, said she ran a drill through her hand.

"We had a good nurse on the job and she took care of it."

Jean DeSpain of Hayden Lake, Idaho, a drill press operator, said most injuries were smashed fingers or a drill bit going through a hand.

An on-duty nurse at the plant could handle most on-the-job injuries, which primarily consisted of cuts from aluminum and the closeness of machinery, said Frances Nugent, who worked at Boeing as a mechanic from June to August 1945.

Margaret Langus, who was the day-shift nurse, said she didn't see too many injuries at the plant, primarily cuts and scrapes, although she remembers one man who drove a rivet into his thumb.

Dr. Duncan W. Turner, who practiced medicine in an office across the street, helped during emergencies.

"Some machinery could be dangerous," Margaret Shaver Shields said. She had seen her predecessor nearly sever his thumb on the electric saw. He

PHOTO COURTESY OF MARGARET LANGUS

*Margaret Langus worked as nurse on the day shift at the Boeing plant while her husband, Allan, fought in hand-to-hand combat as an infantryman in the Philippines. She didn't see a lot of injuries, primarily just cuts and scrapes.*

*Off we go into the wild sky yonder,*
*Keep the wings level and true;*
*If you'd live to be a grey-haired wonder*
*Keep the nose out of the blue! (Out of the blue,*
*boy!)*
*Flying men, guarding the nation's border,*
*We'll be there, followed by more!*
*In echelon we carry on. Hey!*
*Nothing'll stop the U.S. Air Force!*

*Notes: Crawford didn't write "Hey!"; he actually*
*wrote "SHOUT!" without specifying the word to be*
*shouted. Wherever they appear, the words "U.S.*
*Air Force" have been changed from the original*
*"Army Air Corps." Words in parentheses are spo-*
*ken, not sung.*

rushed to the nurse's office and no longer worked at the plant afterward.

"They could send workers out to a doctor or hospital if necessary and the worker was covered," Shields recalled.

"No one was hurt where I worked, although I did sprain my back while turning a 'jig,'" recalled Eva (Perona) Hauck.

"I remember there were a lot of safety rules," said Jane Duell Minear. "My job was in an office so I wasn't close to work areas. I don't remember any accidents on our shift but there must have been some."

Langus also remembered there was a great deal of noise, although she was fortunate to have an insulated office of her own.

"There were some riveters outside my door," she said. "But whoever insu-lated the place did a real good job."

The noise in the plant posed problems for many of the workers.

Venemon's daughter, Lori Venemon Phillips, said her mother told her about working at Boeing.

"She said it was very noisy in the plant. She must have mentioned this to my grandmother, Blanche Markstrom, at some point. Being a nurse and a concerned mother, my grandmother insisted that Mom wear ear protection while working. Mom said she was one of the only ones wearing earplugs at work but it really helped with the 'ringing in the ears' problem she had been having.

"Of course now it would be mandatory to wear ear protection. I feel sure this helped preserve her hearing ability too!"

*Employees earned good wages at the Boeing plant, especially considering that in 1945, shoppers could buy a quart of milk for 14 cents, a steak for 41 cents per pound and a gallon of gas for 21 cents.*

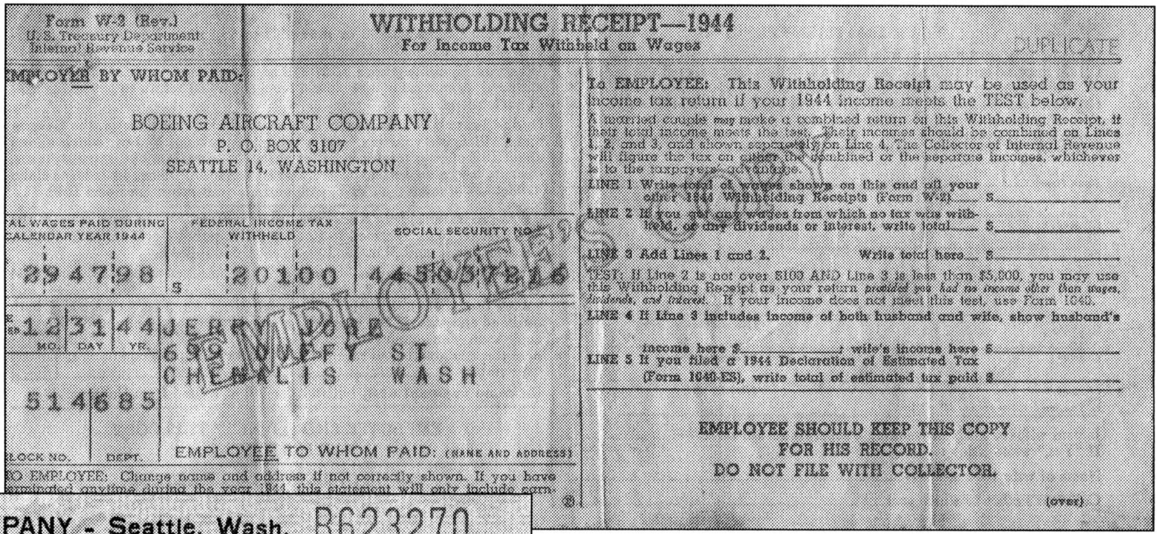

Form W-2 (Rev.)
U. S. Treasury Department
Internal Revenue Service

WITHHOLDING RECEIPT—1944
For Income Tax Withheld on Wages

DUPLICATE

EMPLOYER BY WHOM PAID:
BOEING AIRCRAFT COMPANY
P. O. BOX 3107
SEATTLE 14, WASHINGTON

| TOTAL WAGES PAID DURING CALENDAR YEAR 1944 | FEDERAL INCOME TAX WITHHELD | SOCIAL SECURITY NO. |
|---|---|---|
| 2947 98 | $ 201 00 | 445 [illegible] |

12 31 44 (MO. DAY YR.)

JERRY JOBE
699 DUFFY ST
CHEHALIS WASH

514 685 (CLOCK NO. / DEPT.)

EMPLOYEE TO WHOM PAID: (NAME AND ADDRESS)

TO EMPLOYEE: Change name and address if not correctly shown. If you have terminated anytime during the year 1944 this statement will only include earn-

To EMPLOYEE: This Withholding Receipt may be used as your income tax return if your 1944 income meets the TEST below.
A married couple may make a combined return on this Withholding Receipt, if their total income meets the test. Their incomes should be combined on Lines 1, 2, and 3, and shown separately on Line 4. The Collector of Internal Revenue will figure the tax on either the combined or the separate incomes, whichever is to the taxpayer's advantage.

LINE 1 Write total of wages shown on this and all your other 1944 Withholding Receipts (Form W-2) $
LINE 2 If you got any wages from which no tax was withheld, or any dividends or interest, write total $
LINE 3 Add Lines 1 and 2. Write total here $
TEST: If Line 2 is not over $100 AND Line 3 is less than $5,000, you may use this Withholding Receipt as your return *provided you had no income other than wages, dividends, and interest.* If your income does not meet this test, use Form 1040.
LINE 4 If Line 3 includes income of both husband and wife, show husband's income here $ ; wife's income here $
LINE 5 If you filed a 1944 Declaration of Estimated Tax (Form 1040-ES), write total of estimated tax paid $

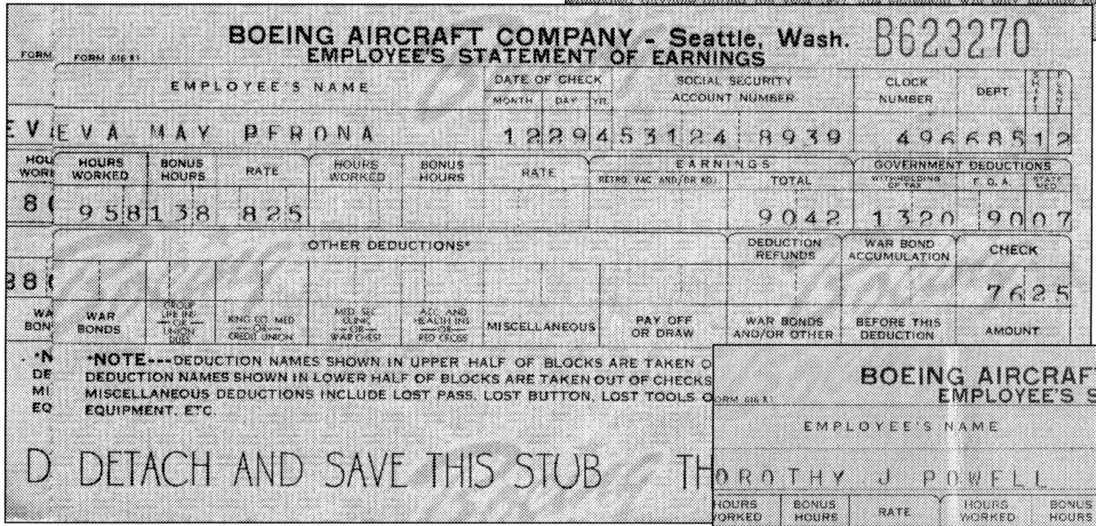

EMPLOYEE SHOULD KEEP THIS COPY
FOR HIS RECORD.
DO NOT FILE WITH COLLECTOR.

(over)

MEMORABILIA COURTESY OF WINNIE NICHOLS

FORM 516 B1

BOEING AIRCRAFT COMPANY - Seattle, Wash. B623270
EMPLOYEE'S STATEMENT OF EARNINGS

| EMPLOYEE'S NAME | DATE OF CHECK (MONTH DAY YR.) | SOCIAL SECURITY ACCOUNT NUMBER | CLOCK NUMBER | DEPT |
|---|---|---|---|---|
| EVA MAY PERONA | 1 22 9 | 453 12 4 8939 | 4966 | 85 1 2 |

| HOURS WORKED | BONUS HOURS | RATE | HOURS WORKED | BONUS HOURS | RATE | EARNINGS: RETRO. VAC. AND/OR ADJ. | EARNINGS: TOTAL | GOVERNMENT DEDUCTIONS: WITHHOLDING OF TAX | F. O. A. | STATE MED. |
|---|---|---|---|---|---|---|---|---|---|---|
| 95 8 | 13 8 | 8 25 | | | | | 90 42 | 13 20 | 9 | 0 07 |

OTHER DEDUCTIONS* — WAR BONDS | GROUP LIFE INS. OR UNION DUES | KING CO. MED OR CREDIT UNION | MED. SEC. CLINIC OR WAR CHEST | ACC. AND HEALTH INS. OR RED CROSS | MISCELLANEOUS | PAY OFF OR DRAW | DEDUCTION REFUNDS: WAR BONDS AND/OR OTHER | WAR BOND ACCUMULATION: BEFORE THIS DEDUCTION | CHECK: AMOUNT 76 25

*NOTE---DEDUCTION NAMES SHOWN IN UPPER HALF OF BLOCKS ARE TAKEN O
DEDUCTION NAMES SHOWN IN LOWER HALF OF BLOCKS ARE TAKEN OUT OF CHECKS
MISCELLANEOUS DEDUCTIONS INCLUDE LOST PASS, LOST BUTTON, LOST TOOLS O
EQUIPMENT, ETC.

DETACH AND SAVE THIS STUB TH

MEMORABILIA COURTESY OF EVA (PERONA) HAUCK

FORM 516 B1

BOEING AIRCRAFT COMPANY - Seattle, Wash. B460202
EMPLOYEE'S STATEMENT OF EARNINGS

| EMPLOYEE'S NAME | DATE OF CHECK (MONTH DAY YR.) | SOCIAL SECURITY ACCOUNT NUMBER | CLOCK NUMBER | DEPT |
|---|---|---|---|---|
| DOROTHY J POWELL | 6 30 4 | 535 20 9870 | 2346 | 85 1 2 |

| HOURS WORKED | BONUS HOURS | RATE | HOURS WORKED | BONUS HOURS | RATE | EARNINGS: RETRO. VAC. AND/OR ADJ. | EARNINGS: TOTAL | GOVERNMENT DEDUCTIONS: WITHHOLDING OF TAX | F. O. A. | STATE MED. |
|---|---|---|---|---|---|---|---|---|---|---|
| 96 0 | 8 0 | 7 25 | | | | | 75 40 | 4 40 | 7 5 | 0 9 |

OTHER DEDUCTIONS* — WAR BONDS | GROUP LIFE INS. OR UNION DUES | KING CO. MED OR CREDIT UNION | MED. SEC. CLINIC OR WAR CHEST | ACC. AND HEALTH INS. OR RED CROSS | MISCELLANEOUS | PAY OFF OR DRAW | DEDUCTION REFUNDS: WAR BONDS AND/OR OTHER | WAR BOND ACCUMULATION: BEFORE THIS DEDUCTION | CHECK: AMOUNT 70 16

*NOTE---DEDUCTION NAMES SHOWN IN UPPER HALF OF BLOCKS ARE TAKEN OUT OF CHECKS DATED THE 1ST THRU THE 14TH
DEDUCTION NAMES SHOWN IN LOWER HALF OF BLOCKS ARE TAKEN OUT OF CHECKS DATED THE 15TH THRU THE END OF THE MONTH.
MISCELLANEOUS DEDUCTIONS INCLUDE LOST PASS, LOST BUTTON, LOST TOOLS OR TOOL CHECKS, SAFETY GLASSES, DRAFTING EQUIPMENT, ETC.

DETACH AND SAVE THIS STUB THIS IS NOT A CHECK

MEMORABILIA COURTESY OF DOROTHY POWELL

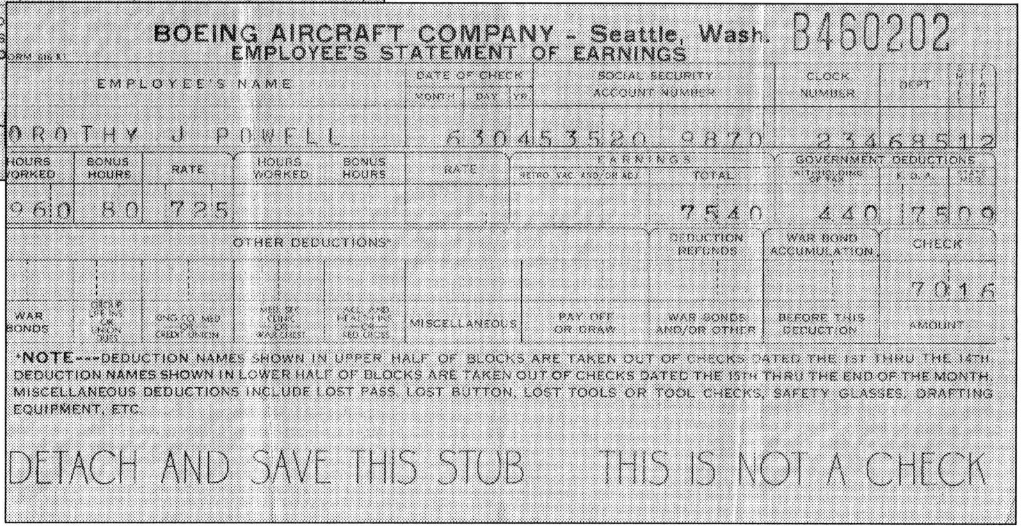

*Avard Mandery starts us off by doing all the hiring,*
*Assigning workers to the jobs, to them will be least tiring.*
*Walt Minear is on his toes, Harry Johnson, too;*
*That Bill Storm is a busy man, he sure had lots to do!*
*Leo Johnson gets around, in a business way—*
*Doing more than his full share, with never much to say.*
*Eddie Ratcliffe shies at girls, apparently immune,*
*But when he leaves the Boeing Plant—*
*Well, that's a different tune!*
*Bill Robison just makes things hum from morning until night,*
*But when he gets a job all done, you know it's all done right.*
*Georgie Jordan has a grin that really is contagious,*
*To think of him without a smile would be almost outrageous.*
*What does Donald Waldo do? He really gets about,*
*The busiest man in all the plant, of that there is no doubt.*
*Then there's Roy Herrin, he's the guy who watches over all*
*Responsible for every job, whether great or small.*
*Byron Seeley is the kind who'll never bawl you out—*
*But just try shirking on the job when you think he's not about.*
*Robin Hartnagel? Who is he? Why, everyone knows Robbie!*
*A friend to all the Boeing folks, and baseball is his hobby!*
*Mr. Thornton—he deserves more than a little praise,*
*For passing all our pay-checks out to us on Saturdays.*
*Clair Stafford—a mighty man, who does amazing things*
*He rose from transportation's gang, to sit among the Kings.*
*They say that Scottie Boyle is Scotch, but is that really so?*
*I've often wondered about that—I'd really like to know.*
*Donald Ward—oh, dearie me, he's very near perfection,*
*A toast of all the pretty girls, and master of inspection!*
*The Sergeant really is O.K. and pretty good at hunches,*
*He greets us at the door each morn, and peeks into our lunches.*
*Another new one on the job, the workers call Bugs Bunny*
*I really don't know him at all, but his name is sure a honey.*
*Ethel Zirkle is my choice for Matron, you can bet*
*Another gal to fill her boots would sure be hard to get!*
*Mr. Owens wouldn't care to be sorted from the rest*
*For he's a very regular sort, who always does his best.*
*And last but never least of all, (I almost forgot Duke Olson)*
*He's been with us so very long, without him we'd be lonesome.*
*Take them all in all, they are above the average run*
*And we won't soon forget them when our 685 is done!*

# Remembering the bosses

THE TALL RED-HAIRED SUPERINTENDENT at the Boeing Aircraft Co.'s Chehalis branch plant proved to be the youngest man holding such a position in all of the company.

Frank Owens started working for Boeing almost fifteen years before taking over as the Chehalis branch plant superintendent. The March 1944 issue of the Boeing News identified him as the youngest branch plant superintendent, but didn't report his age. He had previously worked at Seattle Plants No. 1 and 2 as well as at the Renton plant. He had held a supervisory position since 1940.

"I was just 18 years old and I think I thought of Mr. Owens like my school principal," recalls Dorothy J. Powell. "I didn't want to get in any trouble with him (and lose my job). So I never even spoke to him. I'd exchange office papers with his secretary, Vivian Johnson, but he was busy at his desk."

"I recall that he seemed humorless to me, but I could be very wrong," said Jane Duell Minear. "It was 'crazy' times and he was more serious than most.

"Frank Owens, to me, seemed a very reserved person."

Eva M. (Perona) Hauck said she doesn't remember the plant superintendent well—"only that he came around to see how we were progressing."

"He was a very good guy," recalled Vivian Curry Wood of Ninilchik, Alaska, describing him as "cooperative."

"He was a tall red-haired fellow," Edward Johnson recalls. "Didn't say very much, at least to me."

Doris M. Yearian remembers Owens as "a very understanding manager."

In 1989, The Chronicle interviewed Owens for a feature story headlined: "Remembering Rosie the Riveter."

At the time, he explained about the branch plants and recalled trouble the first few months working as fast as required.

"The first month or two we were hard up keeping up with the demand from Seattle," he said. "But we didn't slow down!"

Quoting from a 1944 pamphlet published by Boeing, the article states: "If it

# Branch plants and what they built

*(Information below comes from a paper at the Boeing Historical Archives in Bellevue, Washington.)*

WWII B-17 Subassembly Effort

6-24-1943—Boeing News, Renton Weekly announced plans.

Branch plant manager: Albert W. Jacobson

Assistant plant facilities manager: Roger Holman

The U.S. Employment Services recommended building locations.

On-site two-week training provided while the plants were under construction, enabling skilled workers to begin making parts with low or no time loss. Management and very few workers were transferred to the branch plants, mostly labor was local.

Purpose: To locate subassembly manufacturing in localities of available labor force. These parts were then trucked to Seattle for final assembly.

## PLANT 685 CHEHALIS (three buildings)

Pacific Avenue and Park Street: 33,050 square feet

Manager: Frank Owens

Began production: 11-15-1943

First Shipment: 11-20-1943

Subassemblies:

Pilot and co-pilot seats

Wing leading edge

Lower turret mounting assemblies

## PLANT 681 ABERDEEN

G Street and Railroad Avenue: 38,700 square feet

Manager: Wesley Hohlbein

First occupied: 8-15-1943

Began production: 9-1-1943

First shipment: 9-18-1943

Subassemblies:

Stinger turret

Top gun emplacement

Side gun panels and other subassemblies

EVERETT, Second branch plant to open; date unclear as to products/manager of both sites listed.

## PLANT 682 NORTH EVERETT

Grand Avenue and California Street: 47,100 square feet

## PLANT 687 SOUTH EVERETT

Rucker & Pacific Avenue: 33,300 square feet

Manager: Robert Duxbury

Began production: 10-13-1943

Subassemblies:

Bulkheads

Radio operator's section complete with all installations and camera well

## PLANT 683 BELLINGHAM

W. Magnolia and Commercial: 49,630 square feet

Began production: 10-4-1943

Subassemblies:

Engine control stands

Control columns plus 253 other subassemblies

## PLANT 689 HOQUIAM (two buildings)

7th and J streets: 29,035 square feet

## PLANT 684 SOUTH TACOMA

62nd and So. Tacoma Way: 37,086 square feet

Manager: William Pratt

Began Production: 10-15-1943

Subassemblies:

Trailing edges—wing

## PLANT 686 NORTH TACOMA (EXPOSITION HALL) last to open

26th and Bay Streets: 51,000 square feet.

Manager: Thomas Nelson

Began production: 12/1943

Subassemblies:

Control cabin enclosures

Dorsal fin

Training edge wing ribs

Top turret windows

Elevator hinge and fairing

Drag struts

Supercharger ring

*Dorothy Powell provided this poem about the first-shift supervisors at Chehalis Plant 685. She doesn't know who composed the poem.*

had not been for Chehalis, and the other branches, Boeing Aircraft Co. never could have set its record in March (1944) for production of completed four-engine bombers. And the 5,000th Flying Fortress since Pearl Harbor wouldn't have rolled off the production line for many weeks after it did."

"He never bothered any of us," Malcolm "Bud" Berg, who had transferred to Chehalis from Seattle in April 1944, said of Owens. "He had his hands full trying to get things done, because it was a new crew down here."

Elanor Wilber remembers her son attended the University of Washington with Frank's son and the two young men became friends.

The supervisor in the Chehalis personnel department, Avard Mandery, who wrote stories for the Chehalis page of the Boeing News, had quite a career in college football before working for Boeing.

He played halfback for the Nebraska Cornhuskers in 1924, according to a story in the Feb. 18, 1944, Boeing News. The following year, he was high scorer for Nebraska—and scored a touchdown in a University of Washington match-up that ended in a tie game.

Mandery, who also participated in track, taught and coached high school students before starting work in the Boeing personnel department in 1942.

"Mr. Mandery, the personnel manager, was my boss," Powell said. "He was very nice to me. But I worked in the general foreman's (Ed Rasmussen's and later Byron Seeley's) office, so they were more my boss. All were very nice to me—never an unkind or crabby word."

Hauck recalls her immediate supervisor was Rex Hess, assistant foreman, who lived at Salzer Valley where he cared for a stable of riding horses. In May 1944, he agreed to organize a riding club for women on the swing shift, according to the May 1944 Boeing News. The idea came from Evelyn Duncan, women's supervisor. The girls rode the horses over forty miles of trails.

"He lived up Salzer Valley and had a string of horses," Hauck recalled. "My 'boyfriend' Clarence Hauck would come and get me on Sundays to trail ride."

Larry Sellers, assistant superintendent, had worked for Boeing five years. He moved to Chehalis from Seattle with his wife and children, said Jane Duell Minear, recalling her immediate supervisor. She described him as "a handsome man—a bit of a flirt!"

# Chehalis #685

**Contributing Editor: AVARD MANDERY; Reporter: ALICE McNEIL**

## Sing Some More, Say Girls to Supervisors

*Chehalis girls like the singing of their supervisors, judging from the expressions on their faces when this photograph was taken during a recent rest period.*

*Avard Mandery, bottom right, edited the Chehalis edition of the Boeing News, which featured stories about supervisors and employees at Plant 685. These photos all come from the newsletter. At top right is Frank Owens, plant superintendent. At right center are Torchy and Bill Hudson, both supervisors at the plant and singers. At center is Rex Hess, assistant foreman who organized a riding club. At left are female employees asking their supervisors to sing.*

## Other Superintendents Call Him Junior

Superintendent Frank Owens [right], shown here with General Foreman Jim Rasmussen, is youngest branch plant superintendent with Boeing, a check last week revealed. He started out in the shops almost fifteen years ago and since has worked at Plants 1 and 2 and at Renton, as a supervisor since 1940. Under his direction, the plant has met all production schedules, despite some unusually difficult problems.

Torchy and Bill Hudson

R.J. "Bob" Morgan, the branch plant's electrician, worked for Don Waldo. "He was always busy," Morgan said.

"My supervisor at Chehalis was Jack Duryear," said Edward Johnson, who came to Chehalis from the Seattle and Renton plants. "He and I were the first ones in the plant besides Frank Owens and other managers."

Julia R. Ford Meadows worked directly under Walt Minear, whom she described as a "very pleasant person to work under."

Ellen Irene Kain doesn't recall her supervisor's name, but she hasn't forgotten him completely. "He was very nice and very good-looking!"

Vivian Curry Wood of Ninilchik, Alaska, worked for Max Olds, a "very good guy" who was "helpful to explain any problems."

Bud Berg remembers his supervisor, Howard Stafford, whose family came from Adna.

"He was a nice guy," Berg said. "Nice to work for. I gave him a black-and-white dog and he took it home. The first day his dad delivered oil, the dog bit him!"

# She worked while working

**D**OROTHY J. POWELL REMEMBERS gathering around a radio with co-workers at Boeing Aircraft Co.'s Chehalis plant and listening to the news as an armada of Allied troops crossed the sea to land on the beaches of Normandy, France, on D-Day.

June 6, 1944—D-Day—the day she turned 19.

She felt certain her husband, Harold, was in England, so she figured he'd be aboard a tugboat as part of the armada of 156,000 Allied troops.

"I had heard on the radio before going to work that the invasion of Europe had begun," she remembers.

"At morning break at work, all gathered in the big wide hallway (for trucks also) and listened on someone's radio to the report of thousands of boats in the English Channel going to France."

"How worried I was and how anxious everyone was. Everyone had someone over there."

June 6 later proved to be the same day Harold won a promotion to staff sergeant. He didn't participate in the D-Day armada.

She and Harold had married February 8, 1943, and she followed him from one base to another until he shipped overseas. Then she returned home to her parents in Riffe and looked for work.

"I heard from Harold's sister who worked at Boeings in Chehalis that I should see there as the pay was twice what I could get as a secretary," she recalled. "I had no training for Boeings. I started out on swing shift for two weeks or so bucking rivets for 'Rosie.' Then I got on day shift in the personnel office."

She had received office practice in high school.

"I got about 70 cents an hour for the first month, then to 80 cents and after a girl left, I got 90 cents. The last few months I was in charge of the general foreman's office and got 96 cents an hour. We were paid time and a half for Saturdays, and double time for Sundays."

She worked at Boeing from May 1944 until after the war ended in August 1945. She and her aunt lived together on Fifth Street about three-quarters

*Above, Dorothy Powell is still wearing her name tag after work. At left are two good friends from her office, Eloise Scott and Ailene Wilson, who are seen at Deep Lake Aug. 12, 1945.*

PHOTOS COURTESY OF DOROTHY POWELL

*Chehalis employees who never missed a day of work or arrived late in six months received a trip to Seattle to tour the Boeing plant there. Dorothy Powell, who is standing on the first step below the platform wearing a tied jacket and white blouse, worked sixteen months and never missed a day.*

april 8, 1943

Miss Dorothy McMahon, who was recently married to Harold Powell, now in the armed forces and stationed in Texas, was honored with a bridal shower Thursday at the home of her mother, Mrs. Steve McMahon. Mrs. Powell expects to join her husband as soon as school is out.

Present at the shower were Mesdames Jerry Belcher, Wallace Osborne, John Christian, Norman Riordan, Roy Hanger and sons, J. W. Powell, G. W. Peters, Frank Core and Daughter, Tom Quinn and daughter Ruth, Les Wright and daughters, S. H. Senter, J. W. Peters, Evelyn Stinson, Glen Overstreet, Harold Belcher and daughter Jean, L. F. Bartley, Ted Landes, E. D. Overstreet and the Misses Betty Donaldson, Fay Brooks, Jeanne Brown, June Ayers, Norma Birley and Marie Walters. Those sending gifts were Miss Dolores Brown, Mesdames Evman Cusick, Abe Cole, Jacobsen, Arthur Blankenship, Ernest, Hamilton, Jesse Osborne, O. R. Schoonover and Beula Riffe, Walter Rose, Bill Graham, Herbert Workman, Nora Watkins, W. S. Kiser, Dick Russell and Dixie Rose, Calvin Brown, Norma Davis, Helen Halderman, Marie Taylor, Mr. and Mrs. Elmer Jacobsen, Mr. and Mrs. Harold Mabeffy, Mr. and Mrs. Jim McMahan, Mr. and Mrs. Niel McMahan and Mr. and Mrs. Clarence McMahan.

February 4, 1943

**MARRIAGE LICENSE APPLICATIONS**

Beacher A. Jefferson and Opal F. Gunsolley, both of Chehalis.
Holmes B. Moore, Fort Lewis, and Edna M. Gosselin, Detroit.
Harold Lee Roy Powell, Salkum, and Dorothy Josephine McMahon, Ajlune.
Stanley O. Smiley, Portland, Ore., and Ila Crooker, Auburn.
Joseph Lewis Keepers and Mary Irene Oster, both of Centralia.

of a mile from the plant, so they usually walked. One of her aunts had four sons—and all four were in the military.

"We checked in past the two guards and with the timekeeper. My office was next to the shop, which was so noisy with so many tools. Our office was heavily insulated—you could hardly talk outside.

"First thing I'd go to Personnel and get papers concerning hirings and terminations, plus any changes made in employees' job ratings. I had a chart I kept current for each shift—how many men and women in each job classification—with the total employees. And I kept all the changes to the seniority list. Each week I typed up seven new copies of it all.

"The rest of the day was spent often looking up employees in the work area to give papers to or have them sign. The last three months the girl over us left and I did her job, which has a huge chart of where we kept track of all parts made there.

"We had a name tag to get admitted. We were fingerprinted when we were hired.

"We wore slacks unless you were in an office that didn't require you to go out into the working area. We had to wear a scarf to completely cover all our hair when in the working area. Most women used large white flour sacks. Men's work hankies were a little small as a rule."

She said workers had to be careful using tools and make sure they didn't catch hair or clothing in a drill.

"One day my good friend was a mechanic helper (near my office) and the drill caught her slacks—ripped the seam from her crotch to the feet. She came to our office and we pinned her pants together and she walked home—several blocks—and got another pair of pants."

Although Powell didn't have children at the time, she said most working women with children left them with friends or relatives. "I don't think there were any public (or private) day cares."

One day, workers with perfect attendance were treated to a trip to Seattle. Powell recalled working six days a week and sometimes Sundays—and once she worked twenty-eight straight days without a day off.

"I got to go to Seattle with twenty others who were taken for free to Boeing's Seattle plant to see the B-17 and B-29s," Powell recalled. "We went inside the B-29. This was a reward for not missing any work for six months. Absenteeism was frowned upon—unpatriotic also."

She said she's always looked askance at unions after working at Boeing.

"I saw the union leaders at our union meetings as troublemakers," she said. "I saw how hard my boss (general foreman) worked with employees, and the union would just make it look like the bosses were so uncaring, etc. I heard outright lies and it made me angry."

On warm sunny days during lunchtime, often the workers from Boeing would sit at the curb along the street near the plant eating their lunches.

"Often I and a couple girls from my office would go the block up to the lawn in front of the Chehalis City Hall and sit on the grass and eat our lunch," she remembered.

They also had to work on the Fourth of July 1945, when the four girls from her office brought picnic lunches—probably sandwiches, pork and beans and cookies—and put a tablecloth on the lawn at City Hall and had a quick picnic. "It was a little extra fun for us."

"One day two of the girls said I just had to go with them to get this new kind of ice cream cone they'd had a couple of times. It was at the St. Helens Cafe (I think) and it was a soft freeze ice cream. The first we'd had in Chehalis. It was a nickel a cone so I didn't eat many as I was saving all the money I could. Also I was trying to lose weight."

Ethel Zirkle, the women's supervisor, helped organize married girls whose husbands were overseas. In August 1944, the Boeing newsletter reported that she and a dozen women held their first meeting of the Servicemen's Wives' Club, enjoying steak dinner at the St. Helens Hotel. They shared news and stories about their husband's military service and told how good-looking each man was.

"We'd have a potluck at one's home and played games (board games) etc. I only [went] to two or three for some reason."

She said her bosses discovered one of the girls, Ailene Zerowick Wilson, possessed a talent for art, so they asked her to draw pictures of equipment needing repairs.

"From then on for about a year, she was Boeing's 'draftsman.' They didn't

February 11, 1943

**19 Leave Thursday For Army Service**

Nineteen selective service men will leave at 11:15 a.m. Thursday for Fort Lewis for induction in the army, according to the Chehalis draft board.

The men are John W. Clark Jr., Don Coleman, Edwin Reir, Herbert H. Spatz, Harley Cook Jr., Norman Jones, Robert Weber, Ernest E. Rose, Glen A. Ellingson, Sherwood C. Sjoblom, Marlin M. Hackney, Frederick D. Hendricks, Albert D. Bott, Willard E. Moses, Eugene R. Burris, Harold L. Powell, George E. Williams, Louis W. Smith and John A. Bett.

Weber was named acting corporal to take charge of the group until their induction.

*An article in The Chronicle Feb. 11, 1943, mentions the departure of Dorothy Powell's husband, Harold, who served on a tugboat in the European theater during World War II.*

March 25, 1943

**COMMENCEMENT SPEAKERS**

Three commencement speakers have been chosen. Dorothy McMahan leads the class as valedictorian with an average of 3.75. June Ayers places second highest with the average of 3.38. As class speaker, the seniors chose Bob Stinson. The faculty has yet to choose the other spea-

*The photo above, provided by Edward Johnson, shows the men in the jig shop. He said the first person from the left, in the back row, wearing a suit and tie ,is Jim Rasmussen, assistant superintendent. The sixth person from the left is Johnson, who is standing next to his supervisor, Jack Duryear. At left, Frances Nugent recalls eating lunch on the lawn at Chehalis City Hall while working at Boeing.*

PHOTO COURTESY OF FRANCES NUGENT

have anyone available as manpower was pretty short. That is just an example of making do with what was available."

When she went home to see her folks at Riffe, Powell had two girls from her class ride with her to Salkum and Mossyrock—June Ayres O'Connell and Helen Locke Alderman.

"A few times another girl from Mossyrock and her little girl also rode with me (five of us in a coupe). The speed limit was 35 mph but I doubt it if I drove more than 25 miles an hour. (No freeway as such)."

In the small general foreman's office where she and four others worked, the assistant foremen came in during breaks to smoke. So did her boss, "Torchy" Hudson.

"Sometimes the air was a blue haze," she recalled. "We had one little window that hardly opened. Finally our boss got the janitor (or maintenance man) to fix the window so we could get more fresh air."

She described morale at the plant as pretty high.

"Everyone had an object in mind—no division of minds like today. Most young women (at work) were married or engaged to be married and so we had a lot in common. The older ones also had sons or brothers in the service so we were always interested in each other.

"There didn't seem much on anyone's mind but winning the war so loved ones could get home."

---

# Berg recalls working as a riveter in Chehalis

MALCOLM "BUD" BERG WORKED as a fix-it man at Boeing in Seattle in the summer of 1941.

"I didn't do too much riveting in Seattle," he recalled. "If the girls would poke a gun die through the wing, I'd have to put a patch on it."

When Boeing opened a branch plant in Chehalis, Berg applied for a transfer so he could be closer to his hometown. But it didn't come through and finally he went to the office, found his request and moved it to the top of the pile.

"The guy said, 'You don't want that,'" Berg recalled. "And I said, 'That's exactly what I want. I want that transfer. I'm going to Chehalis. That's where my home is.'"

He arrived at the Chehalis branch plant in late April 1944. He said he worked on the seventh B-17, since "things hadn't got lined out to where the bugs were out." He later worked on the B-29s.

His sister, Autumn Beam, also worked at the plant in Chehalis,

having transferred from the Seattle plant with her husband, Leon.

He described morale on the job as "pretty good."

"They treated people pretty well."

At the Chehalis plant, where Berg worked as a riveter, he said he'd come in for his swing shift and see where others on the day shift had left off. He'd look at the wing panels, doors and aluminum skin that needed to be riveted together.

"There was a row of gang nuts, every two inches, all the way around these doors, and they were on the underside and they had holes where the bolts would go through and it would suck them right in when the tank was put in," Berg recalled. "Gang nuts— they had them in strips. They were riveted underneath there … just enough to make a bump.

"Then these aircraft bolts went through there, shiny devils, and bolted them up."

They also made wing covers for the doors that covered gas tanks.

*The December 1944 issue of The Boeing News featured the tallest employee and the two shortest employees at the Chehalis plant. The caption below the photo in the newsletter states: 'What it really proves, however, is that no one is too tall or too short to help build Boeing Superfortresses. The shortest and tallest employees from left are Adelaide Lumsden, Lowell Cairns and Wanda Leach. Photo provided by Peter Lahmann.*

"I was working on these wing doors and sometimes all I did was repair them if they screwed up somewhere," he recalled.

He remembers having an inspector who would check for errors and record them on the blue papers, because "Verbal Orders Don't Go."

"Everything had to be on a paper or you'd best not do it," he said. "That was their saying. Get a VODG on it."

He said sometimes he'd find three or four repair jobs waiting for him.

He belonged to the Aeronautical Engineers union, No. 751, and said he paid $15 a month in union dues.

While working as a riveter, he said he worked most closely with his bucker, Art Fagerstrom of Winlock. He said frozen rivets had to be handled while they were frozen.

"If you tried to drive it when it was warm, they'd split like shrapnel."

## VERBAL ORDERS DON'T GO

Inter-Departmental Memo                                          Date 1-7-44

This is Not a Scratch Pad

To ALL EMPLOYEES

The Boeing Employees Manual under "General Plant Rules"
lists the following offense as proper cause for discharge, quote:

"Leaving work stations before the end of the shift and/or
washing up or changing clothes before the end of the shift."

You are allotted five minutes to turn in tools at the end
of the shift. After tools are turned in you are to return to your
work station and remain there until the whistle sounds. You are
not to close your tool box and generally get ready to leave the
plant until the shift end.

General Foreman
Chehalis #685

## VERBAL ORDERS DON'T GO

Inter-Departmental Memo                         Date 1-10-44

This is Not a Scratch Pad

To SHOP PERSONNEL

It should be understood by all shop employees hired in under the 57¢
per hour rate, that rate is no longer in effect.

Also, 67¢ rates are being changed to 72½¢ per hour by order of the
War Labor Board.

It should also be understood, under this new order, that there are
no automatic increases. All up-grading is entirely up to the individual, and all such raises are at the recommendations of the Supervisors and must conform to the job classifications as set down by
the War Labor Board.

*Chehalis employees had their photograph taken outside the plant on the day the company received its 'E' award for excellence.*

# Chapter Eight

# Movies, Dances and Athletic Activities

## USO gives servicemen a home away from home

## WINNIE NICHOLS, DAUGHTER OF JERRY AND CRISTLE JOBE

"Mom and Dad went to a lot of dances—at Woody's Nook, Plaquato, Swede Hall, etc. My folks loved the dances, which they attended with my mom's sister and brother-in-law and my mom's brothers who lived with us.

"About once every week or two weeks, my dad, my mom and my sister Bennie, my brother O.J. and I walked downtown to the Pix Theatre to watch a movie. The movie house showed a continued episode of 'Tarzan' and cowboy movies every week. My favorite was Roy Rogers.

"My dad also loved cowboy movies, as did my mom and us kids. Our other entertainment was family gatherings, picnics, hunting deer, fishing the many rivers—Cowlitz, Toutle, Willapa—and digging clams."

## R. J. BOB MORGAN

"Before the war I played and sang on KELA [radio station]. First live talent. After the war I played for dances. I still play and sing for dances."

## DOROTHY HADALLER HAGSTROM

"Listened to the radio. Visited local neighbors, grandparents and relatives at Harmony, Salkum, Ethel."

## HELEN C. (JONES) KLINDT

"Moose Lodge. Davenport, Iowa. My favorite film was 'Gone With the Wind.'"

## FRANCES NUGENT

"Movies—Centralia's Fox. [USO] dances. Crowded. Well-behaved. Very young."

# Fun on the home front

DURING THE WAR, most people on the home front pitched in to help out. They worked in defense jobs, watched for enemy planes, gave blood, organized book drives, bought war bonds and collected grease, paper, aluminum and metal.

But a special group of girls entertained servicemen as part of the United Service Organization.

A year before the United States entered WWII, President Franklin D. Roosevelt challenged six organizations to provide on-leave recreation for the armed forces. Rising to the challenge, the private groups—the YWCA, YMCA, National Catholic Community Service, National Jewish Welfare Board, Traveler's Aid Association and the Salvation Army—created the USO, which incorporated Feb. 4, 1941, in New York, and grew to more than 3,000 chapters throughout the nation by 1944.

The USO, with its slogan "Until Every One Comes Home," brought entertainment to the troops overseas, a tradition that started with Bob Hope's visit in 1942 and continues today—more than sixty years later. Hope continued entertaining military men and women for fifty years.

The USO also provided a "home away from home" by opening clubs throughout the United States where military men would gather for dances, card games, ping-pong and other recreation. During World War II, the ranks of the military grew from 50,000 to 12 million, according to the U.S. history Web site: http://www.u-s-history.com/pages/h1673.html

By entertaining the servicemen, whose ranks had grown by 1944, young women performed their patriotic duty and enjoyed themselves as well.

Enid Rogerson, whose son Ron was born in 1943, lived with her mother and worked at the welfare office in Chehalis. She often brought her son to the USO on Sundays "and guys really enjoyed him," she said.

"I attended the dances both in Chehalis and at Fort Lewis. When a big band came to Fort Lewis, they would call me to get the girls together and they would send a bus down to pick us up.

"The day the bomber landed at the Chehalis airport, I was called to get the girls to come to the Elks Club to dance with the guys. This was a Wednesday."

*Young girls entertained servicemen at USO dances in Chehalis. The USO held dances to celebrate Christmas, top right, and St. Patrick's Day, above, as well as other holidays. At right, singer Harold Quick performs at the USO. He also served as Lewis County's treasurer.*

PHOTOS COURTESY OF PEARL MILLER

*Soliders from Fort Lewis often arrived by bus at Chehalis to attend USO dances. The Chehalis USO opened in November 1942.*

Helen Holloway recalls the USO in Chicago as "a place where service people could take a shower."

"Volunteers were available to put a quick crease in pants," she said. "There were desks with paper and envelopes (service people needed no stamps). There was always coffee, cookies and possibly sandwiches. Also there were a few comfortable chairs where one could sack out. Last but not least, music—maybe only canned—and girls decked out in their finest to dance with and talk to. I danced some and also volunteered in the kitchen."

Holloway often worked nights but Chicago "was a 24-hour place" so they would bowl, swim at large hotel pools or attend movies and watch the newsreels, which always started "somewhere in the Pacific" or "somewhere in Europe" until after the battles had been won.

"Dances were always fun. The service people were lonely for family and their girls and wives. For us, we were missing our boyfriends and husbands and for a little while the person you danced with became your missing dance partner. In my case if I saw a familiar shoulder patch (insignia), I zeroed in on the individual just in case he had heard news of where my loved ones might be.

"We always had chaperones. We were not to make dates or meet on the outside but as in all things, some broke the rules. I have always been a straight arrow—always following the rules—but I promised to wait for my soldier and that I did for three years."

"My only association with the USO was in the Army camps and nearby towns," said Dorothy Powell, who followed her husband Harold to his stateside bases until he was shipped overseas. "I always went to them for a room to rent in a home in the town. They were very helpful."

For recreation beyond the USO, men and women often went to movie theaters for the latest double feature. Sometimes the theaters offered light shows, comedies and cowboy movies. But Hollywood also cast John Wayne and many other actors in starring roles as military men.

"The movies of this era concentrated on the war effort," John Alexander Jr. said. He remembers seeing amphibious landings, PT boat squadrons, carrier operations and jungle warfare.

"I remember one grim jungle scene where our soldier, surrounded by the enemy, finds time for a last cigarette before he is shot. So the media of that

## JUNE G. AYRES O'CONNELL

*"Shirley Temple shows."*

## MARGARET SHAVER SHIELDS

*"Some movies. Chehalis. Don't remember any [favorites]."*

## RICHARD ZORN

*"Fox Theatre, Centralia. Favorite film 'King Kong.'"*

## SHIRLEY PADHAN ERICKSON

*Grange.*

## ETHEL NELSON

*Movies at St. Helens and Pix in Chehalis.*

## EUGENE DONALD "DON" CASTLE

*"High school activities. Church services at the Centralia Church of the Nazarene.*

*"I visited a USO club in Fukuoka, Japan, a number of times. No dances. I do remember some free donuts."*

## MARTHA LAHMANN LOHRER

*"Rarely [went to the movies]. Olympic Theatre in Olympia, Washington. Was a nursing student. No [USO dances], but many big bands were very popular and dancing was our best recreation."*

## VIVIAN CURRY WOOD

*"USO dances. Didn't have any certain ones—dance partners. We just all had a good time together. The special dance partners I enjoyed the most were ones who were good jitterbug dancers.*

*"Working swing shift was the wrong time of day for any movies."*

DALE ALEXANDER

*"Dances, movies. Shirley Temple."*

RICHARD LARSON

*"I belonged to the Eagles Lodge. Played baseball."*

EDWARD F. PEMERL

*"Movies in Seattle. Also vaudeville."*

RUTH HERREN

*"Went to movies, roller rink.*

*"I went to some USO dances. Went to dances, met and dated a soldier one week before he was shipped out. Corresponded until his letters stopped coming; never knew what happened."*

SARAH CIRANNY ZOPOLOS

*"Dances. We gals danced but didn't really belong. Danced a lot. Jitterbugging was in—no real boyfriend—we gals danced with all the guys.*

*"[We] went to a lot of movies. Fifth Avenue in Seattle. Liked them all."*

THERESA "TERRY" (WALZ) VANNOY

*"Went to the movies at the Paramount Theatre and the naval base at Lake Union with my future husband.*

*"USO dances, occasionally we went to a dance. It was sixty years ago. I can't remember anyone I danced with. We couldn't leave with any of the boys."*

day kept the struggle on our plate constantly."

"We went to the movies," recalled Jane Duell Minear. "I don't think I missed one. We went mainly to the St. Helens Theatre in 'downtown Chehalis.' Many war-themed movies were made. I had loved movies since a child. Love them all!"

"We went to the movies and we went to the fountain at the St. Helens Hotel and just hung out and I usually had my favorite—root beer float," recalled Helen Riedesel-Knoechel. "I believe my favorite film of all-time was *The Good Earth*, with Louise Rainer and Paul Muni."

"I went to a lot of movies during the war years," said Georgie Bright Kunkel. "We could go on Saturday for not more than a dime and I would sit through them twice. The one I really loved was *Seventh Heaven* with James Stewart.

"I remember going to Plaquato just outside Chehalis to the Saturday night dances. Everyone thought I should be married because I was in my early twenties so a friend introduced me to a farm fellow at the dance. I knew that I wouldn't make a good farm wife so I, in turn, introduced him to another of my friends and she married him. They lived in Adna for many years and are now both dead."

Powell recalls attending movies at the St. Helens Theater in Chehalis and the Fox Theater in Centralia. Once in a while, she and her friends would make an outing.

"In the summer of 1945, Ailene Wilson and Eloise Scott (later Eloise Ellis) and I planned an outing one Sunday to Deep Lake at Millersylvania Park near Tenino," she said. "I picked up Ailene and her mom a few miles south of Chehalis. Then my mom, who lived with me at that time in Chehalis, and Eloise, who lived in Centralia.

"I had Harold's 1935 Plymouth coupe so the two moms rode with me and we put a blanket in the trunk, left the trunk door up, and Ailene and Eloise climbed in and sat back there for the 25-mile one-way trip. It was okay except the car exhaust made them a little sick. But I guess getting around in those gas shortage days warranted abandoning your pride sometimes."

Swing shift workers couldn't see the movies much, but they did enjoy late-night bowling for recreation. And dances. Sometimes they went to Plaquato for dancing.

Enid Syers Rogerson, bottom left, holds her two-year-old son Ron, who accompanied her to the USO on Sundays. In the top left photo, Enid Syers Rogerson and Helen Tausher Emerson, a co-worker in the welfare office, were vacationing in Vancouver, B.C., on Aug. 15, 1945, when the war ended. They came home early to celebrate with family members and friends. Above, Pearl Miller is seen second to the right of the man holding the binoculars. She is also pictured at right. Below are members of the USO in Chehalis with servicemen.

TWO PHOTOS ON LEFT COURTESY OF ENID ROGERSON

THREE PHOTOS ON RIGHT COURTESY OF PEARL MILLER

## EDWARD JOHNSON

*"There was a movie that I thought was pretty good. "It Happened One Night." Clark Gable and ? [Claudette Colbert]. I can't remember the actress's name."*

## CLAUDENE MOLLER

*"Movies with friends. Played baseball with other shipyard workers."*

## BUD BERG

*"No USOs. I wasn't a dancer. The only place I danced was in a ring. I loved fighting. Boxing. When I was a kid in school, I was on the boxing team. Loved fighting. My hands don't like it today."*

## JUNE (WEESE) JOACHIM DESKINS

*"Dances, bond drives. I think blood drives. Navy [dances]—mostly Coast Guard from Astoria.*

*"Telephone gals were always invited every place. Dances, etc. We were all fingerprinted, background-checked and could not discuss anything from office or work!"*

## MABEL COOK

*"Just enjoyed being there [at the USO] and enjoyed dancing with the servicemen."*

## ELLEN IRENE KAIN

*"Didn't belong but attended. They [dances] were fun and some very good dancers. Corresponded with a couple for a while."*

## ELANOR WILBER

*"St. Helens Theater, Chehalis. Pix Theater,*

"We used to go to dances at the hall in Claquato, where a lot of men in the service went," recalled Margaret Evelyn Cowley Whitford.

Other times impromptu dances took place, such as the time in 1944 when forty-four men flying fifteen Navy torpedo planes set down at the Chehalis Airport in bad weather, and their commanding officer thanked the city and the mayor for the hospitality shown by citizens Aug. 31. An informal dance was arranged at the Chehalis Elks for the men.

An article in The Chronicle Sept. 20, 1944, quotes Lt. Cmdr. B. E. Cooke: "On behalf of the squadron I want to take this opportunity to thank you and your fellow townsmen for the many kindnesses and the hospitality extended to my officers and men. Your local field proved a godsend at a time of real need. I hope you will convey our appreciation to all who made our visit so enjoyable in every respect."

The Chehalis USO center opened downtown on weekends starting in November 1942 to entertain visiting servicemen. When the center closed for the summer in 1944, Nina E. Terrill, hostess, told The Chronicle that more than 5,000 servicemen had been entertained there since its opening.

"Nina Terrill, a prominent Chehalis businesswoman, promoted the USO locally," Duell Minear said. "She got a lot of us young gals signed up to come to the dances, etc. We would go to Fort Lewis, too, by bus, to dances there.

"I can remember all those young men—many of them from states far away from Washington. I can remember dancing one time with a young fellow from New York—a 'zoot-suiter,' and, I suppose, a terrific dancer—New York-style —definitely not mine! The chaperones were great. I honestly don't remember the food."

After the 1943 Christmas party, Col. P.E. LeSturgeon of the 4th infantry wrote to USO Committee Chairman J.A. Wright, saying: "The reports that have reached me concerning this trip [to Chehalis] indicate each man had a most wonderful time, and the hospitality of the citizens of your city is unexcelled in warmth and friendliness."

In just the first six months of 1944, visitors signing the guest book hailed from thirty-eight states as well as two each from England and Scotland.

After listing the USO committee members, the June 14, 1944, article in The Chronicle states: "Assisting Mrs. Terrill at the center on weekends were a

The top right photo shows Nina Terrill, a chaperone and major organizer of USO events, at a Christmas party. Among those volunteering to help at the party were Mayor Louis A. Vimont, on the left in the photo at right, and Virgil R. Lee, behind the counter. The bottom right photo shows Ben Dusnowsky, one of the young men entertained at the USO. In the group photo below, the girls in the front row, from left, are Alice May, Helen Riedesel-Knoechel, Peggy Riedesel-Dalzappo and Nina Terrill, chaperone. Carmen Justice is in the back row. On the left are more group photos of the girls with servicemen.

PHOTOS COURTESY OF HELEN RIEDESEL-KNOECHEL

*Chehalis. Fox Theater, Centralia."*

## JULIA R. FORD MEADOWS

*"Movies at St. Helens Theatre and Fox Theatre."*

## PAGE G. BENNETT

*"We went to some movies. Went to Chehalis and Centralia."*

*Helen Riedesel-Knoechel refers to these men as the New Jersey cowboys. They had never been on a horse until they visited Chehalis.*

loyal group of senior and junior hostesses and local girls, who were aided from time to time by various organizations of the city."

Among those young women were Pearl Miller, Helen Riedesel-Knoechel and Enid Rogerson.

Riedesel-Knoechel worked at Coffman-Dobson Bank in Chehalis from 1942 until 1953 as a bookkeeper, teller, secretary and receptionist. But on weekends, she volunteered at the USO.

"We met some wonderful servicemen and sometimes we would take them to my mom's house for her wonderful chicken dinners," she said.

"I attended the dances. We all learned to jitterbug. That was before drugs, etc. It was all good clean fun. We were certainly naive and innocent compared to today.

"There was certainly a 'man shortage' during the war years, but we girls kept busy. We played tennis. We would catch a bus to the beach and stay the weekend. There were always ships in with lots of sailors, or we would rent horses and ride along the beach or rent bicycles to ride. We never did anything risqué, but completely behaved ourselves.

"Many of the boys were from 'back east' like New Jersey or New York, so we would take some of them out to Melton's farm and let them ride the horses. They had never been on a horse, and maybe some of them had never seen a horse. They thought that was really fun."

Georgie Bright Kunkel sang in church choirs and took music lessons from a voice teacher in Centralia, so she'd ride her bike from Chehalis for her lessons.

"We would often go to Deep Lake for Sunday picnics and also to the park on the Chehalis River in Chehalis," she said. "I belonged to the Wesleyan Society of the Methodist Church."

She also belonged to the United Service Organization.

"We were told that we were never to date the fellows we met in the hall above the fire station in Chehalis," she said.

"One time we were taken by bus in our formal dresses to Fort Lewis for a Valentine Day dance. They had a big heart constructed out of wood and decorated on the stage and we were told to walk up behind the stage and

*Girls found a lack of young men to date during the WWII years, when so many men served overseas. Often the girls would ride horses, pedal bikes or take trips to a lake or beach for fun. The photo at lower left shows a group of servicemen and girls, probably on a Sunday. In the top left photo, back row, from left, the girls are Mildred, Helen and Margaret Green, and in the front row, from left, are Enid Rogerson, Carmen Justice, Anne Melton, Katie (last name unknown), Helen Riedesel-Knoechel and Peggy Riedesel.*

PHOTOS COURTESY OF HELEN RIEDESEL-KNOECHEL

come out of this heart and stand there to be chosen by some soldier to dance with.

"This was one of the most embarrassing moments in my life. I never will forget it. It was like being served up like a dessert for the male's pleasure."

## Eva M. (Perona) Hauck

*"About three weeks after I had been working at Boeings, they gave a picnic for all Boeing employees at Offut Lake. I went out to the picnic with some people and came back with Clarence Hauck (my future husband).*

*"I do remember someone wanted me to enter the bathing beauty contest. I didn't bring a swimsuit. I wouldn't have entered anyway. I was too shy for that kind of exposure."*

*(Winner of the bathing beauty contest at the July 7 picnic at Offut Lake, attended by three hundred, was Lorraine Hamilton, who wore an 1890 coal-black bathing suit.)*

*"My boyfriend and I did attend movies on Sundays. I attended some of their [softball] practice sessions as my boyfriend at the time (Clarence Hauck) was on the team. We later became engaged and married."*

## Dorothy J. Powell

*"I went to a couple games with a girl from my office whose boyfriend, Barney, played on the team. I just had a lot of other things to do—as we worked six days a week."*

## Jane Duell Minear

*"Attended the picnic—but not baseball games. I don't remember any social activities."*

## Julia R. Ford Meadows

*"Swing shift bowling. I set pins for bowlers."*

## Margaret Evelyn Cowley Whitford

*"I remember going to a roller skating party after*

# Bowling for Boeing

Boeing Aircraft Co. must have adhered to the adage that "all work and no play" makes Jack—or in this case Rosie and the guys—dull people.

The Chehalis branch plant offered plenty of recreational opportunities for the men and women who toiled drilling and riveting wing parts for B-17s and B-29s.

The Boeing News often shared the latest victories of the champion Boeing Greens softball team or the highest scorers in the bowling leagues.

"Vivian Johnson, secretary to Frank Owens, topped the women's bowling league recently with a 192 game," the March 1944 newsletter reported.

In January 1944, the newsletter noted that Lowell Cairnes wanted to form a basketball team. "The company will furnish jerseys and a basketball and will rent a practice area if enough employees are interested."

Ethel Zirkle organized a girls' bowling team. The plant also had a girls' softball team. Sometimes the company organized roller skating parties. And, under the direction of Bill Hudson and a committee, the company organized semi-monthly swing shift dances at the West hall where 150 people moved to the jukebox and ate sandwiches, pie and coffee.

The newsletter shared items about employee's hobbies, births, engagements and marriages. It also listed promotions and deaths.

In the Sept. 29, 1944, issue, the Boeing News stated: "Evelyn Clumpner [Chehalis employee] has received word through the International Red Cross of the death of her husband, Lt. Alfred Clumpner, co-pilot on a B-17, during a raid over Germany. Executives and employees of 685 express their deepest sympathy to Evelyn."

The newsletter also listed the names of people who left Boeing to join the service and featured stories on veterans who continued fighting the war at home in the defense industry.

In Feb. 18, 1944, the Boeing News ran an article with the headline: "Destroyer Veteran Busy on Home Front."

"A new employee is Donald M. Toney, who served as electrician's mate first class at the head of a maintenance crew on a destroyer recently sunk in the

## They Are 685's Pin-Up, Pin-Down Boys

Like the kegler vets they are, this Chehalis quintet was careful not to step over the foul line but went as close as it could without being declared out of bounds. Tossing a mean cannonball on the Centralia City League alleys are Denny Ward [left], Karl Hermanson, Roy Herren, Ed Rasmussen and Ralph Lindquist.

BATHING CONTEST PHOTOS COURTESY OF EVA (PERONA) HAUCK

Boeing employees formed teams to pursue their recreational activities, including the bowling team, above, and the softball team, right. These two items appeared in The Boeing News during 1944. In the top right corner are three photos from the bathing beauty contest at Offut Lake in the summer of 1943. Winner of the contest was Lorraine Hamilton, standing on top of the car in an 1890 coal-black bathing suit.

## Boeing Greens Are Champs

The Boeing Greens, 685, were conceded the championship of the Chehalis Softball league several weeks before the end of the season's play because of the team's outstanding record of wins. Back row, left to right: Ed Rasmussen, Avard Mandery, Grant Lewis, Newt Stedhan, Lyle Nordlund, Ed Johnson, Jack Duryea and Page Bennet. Front row, left to right: Sam Shultz, Kemp Hall, Bill Thornton, Robin Hartnagel [holding the championship trophy], George Jordan, Joe Christian and Albert Ring. Ted Carlson, also a member of the team, does not appear in the picture.

*our swing shift was over, in Centralia, I think. A lot of the workers went.*

*"Another time we had a Halloween party in a bar on old Highway 99 south of Chehalis. We even had a ride on a hay wagon."*

### PAGE G. BENNETT

*"I played on the team. I was the catcher and played left field."*

### VIVIAN CURRY WOOD

*"The girls also had one (baseball team). I was the pitcher on it."*

### EVA STAFFORD

*"Howard had his picture taken with his team."*

### EDWARD JOHNSON

*"I remember the Sunday we played a team from Fort Lewis that had some professional players on their team. They didn't beat our team very much—9 to 6?"*

### SHIRLEY PADHAN ERICKSON

*"We lived in the country and our ride left after work so [I] didn't socialize."*

### JOHN ALEXANDER, JR.

*"The current PUD Office was a busy site with the local Boeing plant. I remember that workers on their lunch breaks used Pacific Avenue for impromptu baseball practice."*

### EUGENE DONALD "DON" CASTLE

*"Some of the swing shift crew said they went 'skinny-dipping' in the Chehalis River at Claquato after*

Pacific. He was in the Navy from January 16, 1942, to November 2, 1943, when he was given a medical discharge. He was in nine major and five minor engagements, including Wake, Midway, Marshalls, Gilberts, Coral Sea, Guadalcanal, Western Solomons, Bismark Sea, Tulagi, Savo Sea and Attu.

"Since his discharge, Toney has been home in Packwood, resting and hunting cougars. He says he has bagged seven cougars and two bobcats in recent months."

In April 1944, a group of Chehalis businessmen planned to tour the Boeing Aircraft Co. plant in Seattle, courtesy of Frank Owens, manager of the Chehalis branch plant.

When Mr. and Mrs. Wilbert Brewer celebrated their twentieth wedding anniversary, the Chehalis plant's song group serenaded them with "I Love You Truly" while Mr. Waldo presented them with a flower-filled vase.

"Francis Porter, production department, presented a steelhead to each member of the personnel department this week," the April 1944 Boeing News reported. "Porter states that fishing is good in the Cowlitz. To prove it he has landed 34 this spring."

In May 1944, the Boeing News' Chehalis page reported: "Bonnie Poindexter, clerk in maintenance on the first shift, has good reason to be proud of her husband, T/Sgt. Victor Poindexter of the U.S. 15th Air Force. He is credited with shooting down a Messerschmitt in a recent raid over Italy and also with aiding in bringing his damaged Flying Fortress to a safe landing following a raid on Cassino."

"Engagement rings are sparkling on the hands of Rose Fleming and Clara Stanslowski," the July 28, 1944, Boeing News' Chehalis page reported. "To them, congratulations, and a note to remember the safety regulations about when and where to wear jewelry."

In December 1944, the Boeing News noted that "Richard Browning of Chehalis won a suggestion check for proposing the installation of bases on the bottoms of electrical outlet boxes. This will keep boxes upright."

The same month, Chehalis worker Frank Thomas also won for a money-making suggestion and Joe Zavolosich won for two of his ideas to prevent damage and save time.

★ MAJOR LEAGUE STARS ★
TO SHOW IN
CHEHALIS BASEBALL
"Grand Finale"

MILLETT FIELD,
Chehalis, Wash.

Sunday, Aug. 5, 1945
2 p. m.

Bremerton Eagles
vs.
Boeing All Stars

Farewell Appearance. "Bobo" Palica, pitcher, Cleveland Indians; Ed Kuhl, infielder, Chicago White Sox; "Ollie" Byers, outfielder, Indianapolis.

Welcome
To
Celebrities

Boeings' of Chehalis deeply appreciate the opportunity of climaxing a very successful season with the Bremerton Eagles. We extend a cordial welcome to Judge Joseph Mallory, president of the State of Washington Eagles. We salute Bremerton's outstanding drill team.

Howard Stafford, holding the bat, is pictured with the
Boeing softball club in this photo provided by Eva Stafford.
Team players are from left, top row, Tod Carlson, Gordon
Therault, Ralph Ralston, Ray Herrin, Louis Miur and
Keith Booth, and in the bottom row, from left, are Bill
Hudson, Henry Louis, Stafford, George Jordan, Ben Rome
and Joe Zavolosich. The same photo appeared in The
Boeing News. At right are pamphlets touting baseball
events featuring the Boeings of Chehalis.

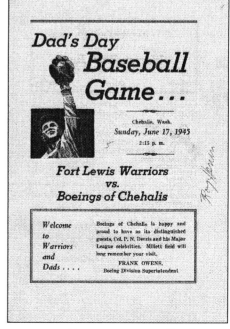

Dad's Day
Baseball
Game...

Chehalis, Wash.
Sunday, June 17, 1945
2:15 p. m.

Fort Lewis Warriors
vs.
Boeings of Chehalis

Welcome
to
Warriors
and
Dads ....

Boeings of Chehalis is happy and proud to have as its distinguished guests, Col. P. N. Derzis and his Major League celebrities. Millett field will long remember your visit.

FRANK OWENS,
Boeing Division Superintendent

SEATTLE SHIP YARD WWII
PLANT "A" AND "B" BASEBALL TEAM
Middle row 4th from left
CLAUDENE MOLLER

*Todd Shipyards also provided recreational teams for employees, including the Curves softball team. Claudene Moller is in the middle row, second from the right.*

## Boeing Greens Are Champs

The Boeing Greens, 685, were conceded the championship of the Chehalis Softball league several weeks before the end of the season's play because of the team's outstanding record of wins. Back row, left to right: Ed Rasmussen, Avard Mandery, Grant Lewis, Newt Stedhan, Lyle Nordlund, Ed Johnson, Jack Duryea and Page Bennet. Front row, left to right: Sam Shultz, Kemp Hall, Bill Thornton, Robin Hartnagel [holding the championship trophy], George Jordan, Joe Christian and Albert Ring. Ted Carlson, also a member of the team, does not appear in the picture.

*The Boeing Greens won the championship in the Chehalis Softball League in 1944, according to the photo above printed in The Boeing News. At right is a telegram from Avard Mandery regarding the baseball team.*

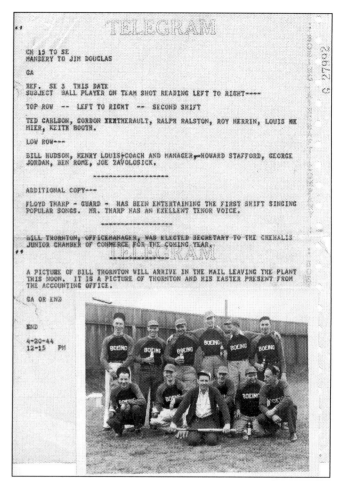

The same issue told about mail catching up with Phyllis Buzzard, who worked in the personnel department, when she received several letters from her husband, who was stationed in the Alaska area with the Navy.

"When she read the letters, she learned that her husband had received 50 of her letters at one time."

As for marriages and weddings, Eva Perona and Clarence Hauck married April 8, 1945, in Chehalis with their Boeing co-workers looking on from a window.

"When I got married, a light skiff of snow had fallen," Eva Hauck recalled.

*the shift was over. I didn't go! I was sixteen and seventeen years of age.*

*"I didn't know they had either (baseball games or picnics)."*

### JEAN DESPAIN

*"Went to movies in Chehalis and Centralia. 'Trail of the Lonesome Pines.'"*

## Miss Eva Perona, Clarence Hauck Have Church Wedding

An impressive afternoon wedding united in marriage Miss Eva Perona, daughter of Mr. and Mrs. John Perona, of Centralia, and Clarence R. Hauck, Centralia, son of Mr. and Mrs. William H. Hauck, Gladstone, Oregon.

The service was read April 8 at 2 o'clock by the Rev. E. J. K. Burzlaff in St. John's Evangelical church, Chehalis. The young couple repeated their vows before an altar flanked on either side with tall baskets of daffodils, iris and huckleberry greens and a background of candlelight. About 50 guests witnessed the ceremony.

Presiding at the organ was Mrs. E. J. K. Burzlaff and Miss Jeanette Burzlaff sang "Oh Perfect Life" and "The Lord's Prayer."

The bride, who was given away by her father, was charming in a white wedding gown with a high round neckline and three-quarter sleeves. Her veil was held in place with a sweetheart cap and her only jewelry was a string of pearls, a gift of the groom. She carried a lovely bouquet of stock, carnations and gardenias.

Miss Stella Perona, sister of the bride, was maid of honor, and she and Miss Barbara Moe, bridesmaid, were in pastel shades. Miss Perona carried a bouquet of daffodils, and Miss Moe carried carnations.

Best man for the groom was Harold C. Calhoun, a close friend.

The bride's mother was dressed in a black dress trimmed in blue. Her corsage was of carnations and gardenias.

Immediately following the wedding ceremony, a reception was held at the home of the bride's parents for 25 guests. The all-white cake was attractive with the miniature bride and groom and silver wedding bell. The bride and groom cut the first piece of cake and Miss Freda Yocum, of Olympia, completed the serving. In charge of the guest book was the bride's sister, Mildred Ruth Perona.

The new Mrs. Hauck was in a poudre blue suit and top coat and wearing a corsage of gardenias when she and Mr. Hauck left for a short wedding trip to the coast.

Out-of-town guests were Mr. and Mrs. John Orloske, grandparents of the bride, from Yakima; Mr. and Mrs. H. E. Rowett, Seattle; Mr. and Mrs. M. L. Orloske, Adna; Mr. Arnold Orloske, Woodland; Miss Harriet Sprague, Tacoma; Mrs. H. C. Calhoun, Chehalis.

Unable to attend were the groom's parents, Mr. and Mrs. R. Hauck of Gladstone, Oregon, his brother, Benjamin Hauck; his sisters and brothers-in-law, Mr. and Mrs. Paul Holsworth, Oregon City, and Mr. and Mrs. Melvin Troudt, Houlton, Oregon.

Mrs. Hauck is a graduate of the Centralia high school and has been employed at the Boeing plant in Chehalis. Mr. Hauck is the assistant foreman of the same plant.

The new Mr. and Mrs. Hauck are now at home in Salzer valley.

## Marriage Licenses

Applications for marriage licenses have been filed with the Lewis county auditor by Chester Vander-ool and Mary Wright, both of ....ndle; Daniel Walters and Violet ....almatier, both of Chehalis; Walter ... Jinnings and Genevieve Lusk, ...oth of Ryderwood, and by Clarence ... Hauck and Eva May Perona, ...oth of Centralia.

*Co-workers of Eva Perona and Clarence Hauck watched from the plant's windows as the couple entered St. John's Lutheran Church to marry April 8, 1945. At left is The Chronicle article about the wedding and the marriage license application. Above are the newlyweds with Eva's parents, John and Margaret Perona, and grandparents, John and Alice Orolske.*

"St. John's Lutheran Church was kitty-corner from the Boeing plant. My father picked me up and carried me into the church door. People [from Boeing] were looking out the window and waving.

"There weren't many people at my wedding. My grandparents, John and Alice Orloske, my aunt and uncle Max and Dora Orloske and their four children. His side of the family could not attend as they lived in Oregon and gas rationing was in effect. The photographer took our wedding picture in his studio. I had two baskets of the flowers with daffodils and greenery. These were brought in and used in our wedding pictures."

Chapter Nine

# War Ends in
# Allied Victory

## Dropping atomic bombs

## forces Japanese surrender

RUTHIE A. KRAUSE, COURTESY OF
HER DAUGHTERS ARLENA ZADINA AND
LOIS KRAUSE WELLBROCK

*"The war ended in August with the Japanese surrender and Ruth walked the floor and cried for joy. The plant closed almost at once and Ruth was out of a job. Ruth worked as a waitress and we kids worked in the fields, picking beans, cucumbers, strawberries, raspberries or whatever was in season. Baby sitting, yard jobs, whatever came along for us to help with clothes and school needs. The war was hard on our family but we coped and grew up and married and have had happy, productive lives. None of us went to college but learned early to work hard and all have had good employment in our great country."*

### BUD BERG

*"After Boeing I went back to loggin', and then I ran my own outfit for a while."*

*He also worked as a logger for other people, falling timber and topping trees. After running his own mill near Mossyrock for a while, Berg did logging and other work for Grasser's Auto Wrecking before moving into highway construction, working for S.D. Spencer and Sons of Vancouver. As a road construction worker, he helped build part of Interstate 5 near Lynnwood as well as roads in the Long Beach Peninsula area and in Oregon. Later, he worked at the Centralia coal mine for more than fifteen years.*

### HATSUE HIRATA YOSHIDA

*She finished business college, married in 1948, raised four children—three boys and a girl—and then worked as a secretary for the 1,100-patient state hospital at Kaneohe for twenty years. She now has eight grandchildren, many attending college.*

# War ends in victory

MARGARET LANGUS REMEMBERS AUG. 14, 1945, when office worker Dorothy Greeley read over the Teletype machine that the Japanese had surrendered.

The war was over!

"When it came through on the Teletype that day, they closed down the plant and let us leave," said Langus, who retrieved her car from its parking spot across the street and, with a friend, joined an impromptu victory parade driving around and around between Centralia and Chehalis.

"We told the rest of the town about it," she said.

Joyce Markstrom Venemon told a reporter in 1989 about the euphoric celebrations throughout the town when the Japanese surrendered. People rushed outside, laughing and cheering.

"I know I went downtown and everyone was hollering and singing," she said.

But she also turned around to see a young co-worker whose husband wouldn't be coming home.

"I saw her leaning against the wall, crying," Venemon said. "It kind of took the zip out of it.

"You thought you were real excited and relieved, but then you'd see someone who lost her husband. It kind of brought back the really serious and terrible thing the war was. It was a bittersweet kind of thing—it came back to you how many wouldn't be coming back."

President Harry Truman announced the Japanese surrender to the American people at 4 p.m. Pacific War Time, and within minutes, people poured from houses and businesses, clinging to one another in joy and relief. In New York City, people rushed into Times Square to hug one another and celebrate. In Seattle, air raid sirens wailed starting at 4:36 p.m. while motorists in cars honked their horns in glee.

"One day on the job the horn blew and an announcement was made, 'The war is over. Everyone go home,'" recalled Georgie Bright Kunkel. "That was the last I ever set foot in the plant."

*An impromptu victory parade through Centralia took place as soon as people heard the news of the Japanese surrender. At right is the Teletype received at Boeing sharing the news.*

```
TO-----ALL BRANCH PLANT SUPERINTENDENTS
FROM    PUBLIC RELATIONS

     THE FOLLOWING CONFIDENTIAL ANNOUNCEMENT IS FOR USE ON YOUR LOUD SPEA
SPEAKER SYSTEM, IF AND WHEN, OFFICIAL CONFIRMATION OF JAPANESE SURRENDER
IS RECEIVED.
     THE SPECIAL WHITEHOUSE ANNOUNCEMENT WILL BE TRANSMITTED TO YOU BY
TELETYPE AND IS TO BE INSERTED IN THIS MESSAGE AT THE POINT INDICATED.
     YOU ARE NOT /REPEAT NOT/ TO PUT THIS ANNOUNCEMENT ON YOUR PA
SYSTEM UNTIL DIRECTED TO DO SO BY SEATTLE PUBLIC RELATIONS, CONFIRMED
BY DAVE WILLIAMS.

     YOUR ATTENTION PLEASE
     YOUR ATTENTION PLEASE     /REPEAT UNTIL SHOP NOISE QUIETS DOWN/

     WE ARE ABOUT TO GIVE YOU THE NEWS YOU.VE ALL BEEN WAITING FOR.  IN
ADDITION WE HAVE AN IMPORTANT ANNOUNCEMENT CONCERNING THE COMPANY,S
POSTWAR OPERATIONS.  PLEASE LISTEN CAREFULLY TO THIS COMPLETE REPORT.
/PLEASE EMPHASIZE THIS SENTENCE FROM IMPORTANT TO END OF SENTENCE./

     WORD OF JAPANESE ACCEPTANCE OF THE FOUR POWER SURRENDER TERMS HAS
BEEN RECEIVED AND OFFICIALLY CONFIRMED BY THE WHITE HOUSE.

     HERE IS THE OFFICIAL WHITE HOUSE ANNOUNCEMENT.
       /READ BULLETIN/


     XXXXX
     YOUR ATTENTION PLEASE----  PLEASE LISTEN CAREFULLY.  THIS IS IMPORT
ANT TO EACH OF YOU.  THE BOEING COMPANY NOW HAS ORDERS FOR CONTINUED WORK
ON ADVANCED MODEL B-29 SUPERFORTRESSES AT A REDUCED  ONTHLY OUTPUT.

THERE WILL BE NO IMMEDIATE CUTBACK IN EMPLOYMENT, BUT A REDUCTION WILL
WILL TAKE PLACE DURING THE NEXT TWO MONTHS.

     ALL REGULAR WORK SCHEDULES WILL CONTINUE TOMORROW AND THEREAFTER
UNLESS A NATIONAL HOLIDAY IS DECLARED IN THE MEANTIME.

     OFFICIAL V-J DAY HAS NOT YET BEEN DECLARED, BUT THOSE OF YOU WHO
WISH TO TAKE THE REMAINDER OF THE DAY OFF MAY DO SO.  PLEASE BE SURE TO
PUNCH OUT ON YOUR TIME CARD AS YOU LEAVE.  FOR THOSE WHO WISH TO REMAIN,
WORK WILL CONTINUE AS USUAL.

     PLEASE DO NOT RUN IF YOU LEAVE.

     WE REPEAT-----  THOSE OF YOU WHO WISH TO TAKE THE REMAINDER OF THE

AND NO RUNNING PLEASE.  /REPEAT IF NECESSARY/

FOR THOSE WHO WISH TO FINISH OUT THE DAY, WORK WILL CONTINUE WITH THE
SOUNDING OF THE WHISTLE.

AND TO REPEAT AGAIN----  ALL REGULAR WORK SCHEDULES WILL CONTINUE
TOMORROW AND THEREAFTER UNLESS A NATIONAL HOLIDAY IS DECLARED IN
IN THE MEANTIME.
```

*Frances Nugent, left, expresses elation at the news of the Japanese surrender and the end of the war. Downtown streets became the scene of parades in cars, bicycles and on foot as Twin Cities residents celebrated the end of a long ordeal.*

PHOTOS COURTESY OF FRANCES NUGENT

"The day the siren blew and the war was over, I was working upstairs in the tool room," said June G. Ayres O'Connell. "I never saw people vacate so fast and I froze. Finally I could move and join in.

"Then I received a telegram from my husband in the submarine service that he was fine—[it] all happened so fast."

Altogether, the war cost the lives of more than 400,000 Americans—plus millions of other servicemen and civilian men, women and children throughout the world. Allied military and civilian losses came to 44 million—20 million of those in the Union of Soviet Socialist Republics—while the Axis nations of Germany, Japan and Italy lost 11 million, according to the 1997 Microsoft Encarta Encyclopedia.

All told, three-fourths of the world's population in sixty-one countries took part in World War II, according to the encyclopedia. The United States spent $341 billion, including $50 billion for the lend-lease program. During the war, U.S. companies had manufactured 300,000 aircraft, 100,000 tanks, 88,000 warships, 2.5 million machine guns and 44 billion bullets.

The war had ended, but at what a cost.

On Aug. 6, 1945, the B-29 Superfortress Enola Gay dropped the first atomic bomb on Hiroshima at 8:15 a.m. Within seconds, the fireball killed 66,000 people and destroyed four city blocks. A mushroom cloud rose 40,000 feet into the air.

The United States dropped a second atomic bomb on Nagasaki three days later, killing 80,000 people.

"I remember when we first heard about the atomic bomb. It was a terrible realization that there was a bomb that powerful," Kunkel said. "I was very naive about the war. However, I used to have nightmares about the Nazis coming after me."

Hatsue Hirata Yoshida, who lived in Honolulu, said none of her Japanese relatives died when the United States dropped the atomic bombs on Hiroshima and Nagasaki.

When she heard about the bombs, she said, "Why, I thought that was the ... saddest thing. ... I don't know. I mean—that's the only way you can stop the war, I guess there was ... but that killed lots of people. Plus, I mean, the Americans on December 7th got killed but ... I don't know."

*"I had four children so I didn't go to work, you know. My husband worked for the state so we moved to Kaneohe, and this is a very removed kind of area but now I just love this area."*

### MARGARET SHAVER SHIELDS

*After the war, she "went back to sales clerk in Sears in Chehalis."*

### DOROTHY HADALLER HAGSTROM

*"I returned home and worked on the farm until I married in April 1946."*

### ENID ROGERSON

*"I continued working at the welfare office until 1947 as clerk typist."*

### FRANCES NUGENT

*"Went to college."*

### RICHARD ZORN

*"Worked as a telephone tech."*

### R. J. BOB MORGAN

*"Drove bus for North Coast."*

### EDWARD JOHNSON

*"I went back to work in the logging industry again, falling and bucking timber."*

### ETHEL NELSON

*"Went to work at Kraft cheese in Chehalis on Cascade Avenue."*

## Helen Riedesel-Knoechel

*"I always worked. Our generation I think was the first to have both husband and wife working to a large extent. After I had my family, I went to work for county schools superintendent Florence Kennicott and then was supervisor in the audiovisual department for a five-county school area."*

## Eugene Donald "Don" Castle

*"I enlisted in the army of occupation in July of 1946 after I finished high school. I went to Japan for a year."*

## Eunice L. Howard

*"When the war was over in August 1945, our personnel office moved to the employment office and we worked in the unemployment division and began paying out compensation to the Riveters and also to the G.I.s coming home from the war. After that I worked at the Lewis County PUD for over thirty years."*

## Julia R. Ford Meadows

*"Yes, cannery."*

## Martha Lahmann Lohrer

*"After graduating from high school, I was accepted in [the] United States Nurses Cadet Corps and graduated. If [the] war were still going, I would have been a commissioned officer. Needed to give [the] military two years' service for educating me!"*

## Vivian Curry Wood

*"As soon as the plant shut down I went to work over at the Darigold plant in Chehalis. I worked on weights and balances—made tests in the lab."*

But after the Japanese surrender, Americans remained in the country to help it recover from the war.

"When the Japanese surrendered and after that America went into Japan … to help the Japanese, and now the Japanese in Japan are more Americanized than people here in Hawaii," she said.

"Many of them, they don't want to eat rice and they would rather eat potatoes and bread. Why—it's insane."

A week after V-J Day, the Chehalis Boeing plant was emptied. Only a few office workers and supervisors remained on the payroll to close the plant and take items back to Seattle.

The leased Boeing plant building reverted to its owner, the Lewis County Public Utility District, which is located there now.

During the twenty-two months it operated, Boeing paid $2.2 million to employees at the Chehalis plant.

According to a September 8, 1945, Daily Chronicle article, A.W. Jacobson, Seattle, general superintendent of Boeing branch plants, described the Chehalis plant as "the most outstanding of all those operated in Western Washington by Boeing and said the type of labor employed here was of exceptionally high standard."

"When the plant left, the whole town suffered," Langus said, adding that people depending on the job for salaries had to find other work.

A survey of women employees by the United Auto Workers in 1944 showed that 85 percent of the women who worked during the war wanted to keep their jobs in peacetime.

In another survey at the Springfield Arsenal in Springfield, Massachusetts, 81 percent of women employees wanted to continue working—but every one of them had been fired within a week of V-J Day, according to *The Lives and Times of Rosie the Riveter.*

A propaganda machine that had encouraged women to enter the work force now begged them to return to their homes and families, making room for the millions of returning U.S. servicemen. Newsreels, magazine articles and newspaper items all talked about the need for mothers to remain home with their children. Blame for rising divorce rates and juvenile delinquency was placed on working women.

*The end of World War II meant that Ethel Nelson, a Chehalis Boeing plant employee and a Rosie the Riveter, lost her job. But it also meant that her husband, E.R. Bud Nelson, would be returning from the South Pacific where he served on a destroyer.*

PHOTO COURTESY OF ETHEL NELSON

After the war, many women workers voluntarily left the work force to marry and raise families. Others were laid off. By 1946, more than 3 million women had left the work force.

Birth rates soared after the war, creating today's Baby Boomer generation.

Locally, many of the Boeing workers opted to marry and stay home, such as June G. Ayres O'Connell and Margaret Evelyn Cowley Whitford.

"I got married March 31, 1945, and didn't work until my two children were older," Whitford said. "Then I worked at times in several different jobs."

"I did not continue to work," said Eva M. (Perona) Hauck. Instead, she "started to raise a family."

### WINNIE NICHOLS, DAUGHTER OF JERRY JOBE AND CRISTLE JOBE

*"Jerry Jobe worked for many a construction company, the cannery, Borden's creamery, and helped put in many of the sewer lines in westside Chehalis, worked on the Mossyrock and Mayfield dams and helped put in the Interstate 5 freeway from Vancouver to Olympia.*

*"My mom, Cristle Jobe, went on to work at the Greyhound bus depot as a waitress, then Gishes' Lunch as a cook, at the cannery, and for many restaurants. Eventually, Jerry and Cristle Jobe bought their own restaurant, the "Koffee Kup Kafe."*

### ELANOR WILBER

*"I worked in retail stores. Sears Roebuck and Peoples Store. In 1953 I went to work for LPA Fred Convery in the accounting office."*

### THERESA "TERRY" (WALZ) VANNOY

*She married October 6, 1945, and then worked for AT&T as an operator for two years before moving to Olympia and working at Penney's till her first child was born. After her children started school, she returned to Penney's for four years.*

### PAGE G. BENNETT

*"After Boeing left Chehalis, I didn't want to go back to Seattle so went and drove truck for West Coast Grocery in Chehalis."*

### DORIS M. YEARIAN

*"We lived in Chehalis seventeen years (when war broke out) left there when [the] logging railroad closed. Returned to Salmon and seventeen years traveled until illness of my husband. We remained*

*in our home in Salmon, Idaho. He passed away twelve years ago."*

## SARAH CIRANNY ZOPOLOS

*She married November 22, 1947, and left Seattle and continued to work several small jobs until her son was born in 1950.*

## GEORGIE BRIGHT KUNKEL

*"I was not married during the war. My future husband was overseas for two years between 1943 and '45. We were married in 1946. Our children came after that. Our first in 1947, then 1949, then 1955 and 1959.*

*"I continued working after the war because I never left my teaching job. I worked very hard to try to help establish a teacher's union after the war."*

## JEAN DeSPAIN

*"Attended Centralia College and University of Washington. Degree in civil engineering. Was city engineer of Olympia for ten years; director of public works for King County for eleven years; and Bechtel Engineering for fifteen years.*

*"In August 1944 I had appendicitis and was operated on at St. Helens Hospital. A very pretty and caring girl from the B plant came to visit me when I was recovering and did much to raise my spirits. (At that time patients were confined to hospital for about ten days.)*

*"I do not recall her name but she was certainly an Angel as well as a Rosie. If any of the attendees at your great event recalls this, please give her my address or phone number or send me her address so I may express a long, long overdue appreciation."*

"I raised four children and kept books for my husband's business," said Shirley Padhan Erickson.

"As soon as the plant was closed, I went home and my husband went back to work," recalled Dovie R. (Long, Halverson) Wellcome.

Jane Duell Minear worked at Puget Sound Power & Light Co. until she became pregnant with her first child in 1945.

"I married December 1, 1945, to Walter Minear, who was the night foreman I mentioned I was dating!" Jane Duell Minear said. "We were married for 54½ years till he died in August 1999."

Looking back at the war years, Eva Stafford offered this observation:

"Let us just hope and pray that we will never need Rosie the Riveter and the Guys again."

# Atomic bombs killed many

DOROTHY POWELL ARRIVED AT WORK in the personnel department at the Chehalis Boeing plant Aug. 6, 1945, to find her boss and several foremen talking excitedly about a nuclear bomb the United States had dropped on Hiroshima, Japan.

"The one thing I especially remember was their concern of what else might happen," she said.

"There hadn't been an atomic bomb dropped before and there was concern that it might start a chain reaction that could start a world catastrophe. That made for some scary thoughts for us for a while, but we all had hopes this would hurry up the end of the war."

Three days later, she arrived at work Aug. 9 to news that a U.S. plane had dropped a second atom bomb—this time on Nagasaki, Japan.

"The devastation of those bombs was hard to fathom and you couldn't help but feel sorry for the Japanese civilians," Powell said. "But the Japanese had started the war and they had been so brutal in their actions against civilians and prisoners of war that the thought was—it's better that it's them than more of our men being killed by them."

She knew that five months earlier in the thirty-six-day battle for Iwo Jima, nearly 7,000 U.S. personnel had been killed and more than 19,000 wounded. Altogether, the war cost the lives of more than 400,000 Americans.

"One can only imagine how many thousands more Americans would have died if it had not been for the atomic bomb," Powell said.

"Many of us had loved ones who had survived the war in Europe who were going to be sent to the Pacific area for the invasion of Japan proper."

Harold Powell, Dorothy's husband, remained in France waiting for deployment to the Pacific. A sign over the camp entrance stated: "On to Tokyo." Dorothy hadn't seen him in seventeen months, and since they were heading to the Pacific, he wouldn't be home for any furloughs either.

Then came the atomic bomb.

"The very thought that now the war might soon be over and that we would be seeing our loved ones soon was very exciting indeed," she recalled.

*When he left for the war, Harold Powell took with him these photos of his wife, Dorothy, who returned to the Riffe area of Lewis County and later worked at Boeing's Chehalis plant.*

PHOTOS COURTESY OF DOROTHY POWELL

Five days after a pilot dropped the second atomic bomb, the Japanese surrendered. The news arrived at the Boeing plant and spread like fire.

"I really can't remember what happened next except that I and everyone else was just overjoyed," she said. "There were lots of tears of happiness.

"The bosses said for everyone to just stop working and go celebrate. I don't think we realized it right then but that day really ended work for good at Boeing's Chehalis plant."

She and two co-workers—one whose husband was in Europe and the other waiting for her fiancé overseas—walked a mile to her apartment and climbed into Harold's '35 coupe.

"We drove around town and over to Centralia," she said. "The church bells were ringing and car horns were honking and everywhere people were just so happy. A block or two was roped off in downtown Centralia that night and people danced in the street.

"We were there before it began but since we didn't like to dance and it didn't seem right to dance without our husbands we went to a movie."

At the request of her boss, Powell continued working at the plant packing items for Seattle.

"For the next week there were just a few of us at work, which seemed so quiet after all the bustle of so many workers working plus all the noise from the machinery that made it hard to even talk out in the shop.

"It had been a good job, especially after the hard years of the Great Depression with not much money or jobs, and people wondered where they would find work now.

"But we were happy to think we soon would be living normal lives again with our loved ones safely home."

Dorothy continued working for three months, employed by the Lewis County Extension Service office compiling 4-H records into a book. Then she worked in the credit department at Sears Roebuck and Co. in Chehalis.

Finally, on January 7, 1946, Harold arrived home.

"I planned to work while he went to the university but I got pregnant and very sick so that was the last of my working—except as a farm wife raising six kids on one income."

EVERNDEN STUDIO · CENTRALIA, WN.

PHOTOS COURTESY OF DOROTHY POWELL

*Harold Powell kept the photos of his wife on a shelf above his bunk on a barge where he and others working on a tugboat slept. The end of the war meant the return of loved ones from the battlefield. He said she was the only thing on his mind.*

# The long wait is over

Hitchhiking home from work, Helen Holloway and a friend sat perched above surrounding cars on the seat of a pickup heading into downtown Santa Barbara, California.

Suddenly the truck stopped amid a mass of emptied cars.

"The people are going crazy," said the man who gave the two girls a ride. "What's going on?"

"Everybody was crying and screaming and hugging each other," she recalled. "I mean, it was just chaos.

"The streets, everything was so crowded. People came out of their homes. I don't know where everybody came from. But it was just bedlam!"

They finally heard the news: The war is over!

"When we finally realized what they were saying, everybody was crying and hugging each other," she said. "But it was kind of like we couldn't believe it."

She cried, too.

"That was a long war. We were all so happy because then we knew that the people we loved would be coming home.

"The war was over and Americans would no longer die on foreign battle-fields."

She and her friend squeezed through the crowd to return to the rooming house where they lived.

Helen Holloway worked at an Army hospital just outside Santa Barbara. She had moved from Chicago to California in May 1945 when her fiancé's letters started sounding as though he'd be home soon. It turned out he suffered from jungle pneumonia so he was in the hospital, thinking he would be sent home because of it.

Since he was serving in the Pacific—at Luzon just then—she figured he'd be returning home to the West Coast. She wanted to be there when he arrived.

*All the time she worked in the defense plants in Chicago, Helen Dilbo Holloway waited for the safe return of her sweetheart, Merle Foote, who is pictured here at Fort Lewis.*

Merle Foote is seen above at Fort Gordon in 1942, before he was sent overseas. He served in the motor pool in New Guinea, which is pictured at the top right. The men in the motor pool are seen at right, with Merle Foote standing, sixth from the left, the last man standing without a shirt on.

PHOTOS COURTESY OF HELEN FOOTE HOLLOWAY

"I was bound to wait for my soldier 'Merle.' I almost died of homesickness in the interim."

At Hoff General Hospital, she worked in the office doing the morning report, counting all the patients and identifying which men were assigned permanently to the base. She also took orders for shoes and helped present medals to patients who had earned them.

She remembers the day a B-29 pilot dropped the atomic bomb on Hiroshima, August 6, 1945.

"Poor President Truman had some terrible decisions to make. The atomic bombs were dropped over Nagasaki and Hiroshima—even the horror that ensued seemed worth it," she said.

"From the reports we heard and everything, it was just so horrendous. You couldn't even imagine what had happened."

Three days later, a B-29 dropped another bomb—this time on Nagasaki.

Then people started talking about the coming of peace because the Japanese couldn't endure another attack.

"It was just so horrendous that the human mind couldn't even imagine what that bomb did."

Having helped build B-29s in Chicago, she said she felt good that a plane she might have helped build would be instrumental in ending the war.

Later, in November 1945, she started working as a long distance operator.

A month later, she noticed in the newspaper that the USS Grant would be arriving in San Francisco, bringing home her sweetheart, Merle. But she knew that thousands of boats crowded San Francisco Bay and many soldiers, once they were put ashore, hitchhiked out of town so they could catch a bus or train in a less crowded community. She called the harbormaster, who told her that the USS Grant had docked, let the men come ashore and left again to go overseas. But that didn't seem quite right.

So she waited.

At the rooming house where she resided, the family treated her like one of their own. The couple had four sons, including 3-year-old Billy, who followed Helen everywhere.

*Merle Foote relaxes outside a tent in New Guinea, where he served during World War II. He contracted jungle malaria and thought he would be sent back to the States, but he didn't return home until after the war had ended.*

"He was my shadow," she recalled. He loved to look at her photos and ask about them, so he knew what "Uncle Merle" looked like. She would often tell him, when he began rifling through her dresser drawers, to go to the window and see if Uncle Merle had come home.

On December 23rd, she'd asked Billy to look out the window, which he dutifully did. He looked and said: "Yeah, Uncle Merle came home," and returned to the dresser drawers.

"What did you say? Did Uncle Merle come home?"

He responded: "Yeah, Uncle Merle came home."

"So I ran to the window and there he was paying the cab driver. And I could tell it was him by the patch on his shoulder—he was in the third engineers special brigade that was blue and gold. And that just hit me in the face and so by the time I ran downstairs he was coming in the front door. And, oh— what a reunion! It was wonderful!"

It turned out that the USS Grant, while traveling around the Aleutians, encountered a horrible storm that started breaking apart the ship, so when the vessel finally reached San Francisco, the men moved to the front of the line for debarking. The ship went into dry dock and Merle hitchhiked to Santa Barbara.

The couple married January 1, 1946, and moved to Kosmos, Washington, in Eastern Lewis County the following month. Helen worked as a "flunkie" in the cook house for Kosmos Timber, although in Chicago "calling someone a 'flunkie' was tantamount to asking for a fistfight."

She helped cook meals for the men who lived in the bunkhouses, beginning at 4 a.m. to serve them breakfast, going home, and then returning at 4 p.m. to make supper.

"I never saw men eat so much in my life," she recalled. "At breakfast and supper we ran the 'four-minute mile' keeping heaping platters of food coming to those ravenous eaters."

But what she'll always remember is the end of World War II.

"When it was announced that the Japanese surrendered in August 1945, we went wild with joy. We danced in the streets—cried and hugged and cried and laughed some more—and then retreated to our churches and thanked God it was over at last."

*While serving in New Guinea, Merle Foote, second from the right, carved a jewelry box for his sweetheart and engraved her name on the lid. He also brought her home this shell necklace.*

PROCLAMATION

WHEREAS, during World War II, many citizens of the City of Centralia performed an important and vital role in the home front war effort; and

WHEREAS, these citizens, who worked at the Boeing aircraft plants, with the USO, and in other war efforts, have come together as the "Rosies and the Guys" Reunion; and

WHEREAS, these citizens are the unsung heroes who worked diligently to provide quality products and support to the military to help the United States of America achieve victory in World War II; and

WHEREAS, the City of Centralia's Summerfest celebration is honoring these war support workers as Grand Marshals of the 2005 Fourth of July Parade.

NOW THEREFORE, I, Tim A. Browning, Mayor of the City of Centralia, do hereby proclaim Monday, July 4, 2005, as

UNSUNG HEROES' DAY

in the City of Centralia, and I encourage all citizens to join me in honoring all those who supported the home front war effort.

SIGNED, SEALED AND DATED this 28th day of June 2005.

Tim A. Browning, Mayor
City of Centralia

---

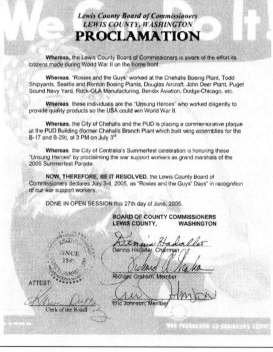

Lewis County Board of Commissioners
LEWIS COUNTY, WASHINGTON
**PROCLAMATION**

Whereas, the Lewis County Board of Commissioners is aware of the effort its citizens made during World War II on the home front.

Whereas, "Rosies and the Guys" worked at the Chehalis Boeing Plant, Todd Shipyards, Seattle and Renton Boeing Plants, Douglas Aircraft, John Deer Plant, Puget Sound Navy Yard, Rock-OLA Manufacturing, Bendix Aviation, Dodge-Chicago, etc.

Whereas, these individuals are the "Unsung Heroes" who worked diligently to provide quality products so the USA could win World War II.

Whereas, the City of Chehalis and the PUD is placing a commemorative plaque at the PUD Building (former Chehalis Branch Plant which built wing assemblies for the B-17 and B-29), at 3 PM on July 3rd

Whereas, the City of Centralia's Summerfest celebration is honoring these "Unsung Heroes" by proclaiming the war support workers as grand marshals of the 2005 Summerfest Parade.

NOW, THEREFORE, BE IT RESOLVED, the Lewis County Board of Commissioners declares July 3-4, 2005, as "Rosies and the Guys' Days" in recognition of our war support workers.

DONE IN OPEN SESSION this 27th day of June, 2005.

BOARD OF COUNTY COMMISSIONERS
LEWIS COUNTY, WASHINGTON

Dennis Hadaller, Chairman

Richard Graham, Member

ATTEST:

Eric Johnson, Member

Clerk of the Board

---

# PROCLAMATION

WHEREAS, the City of Chehalis is aware of the effort its citizens made during World War II; and

WHEREAS, "Rosies and the Guys" worked at the Chehalis Boeing Plant, Todd Shipyards, Seattle and Renton Boeing Plants, Douglas Aircraft, Puget Sound Navy Yard, Rock-OLA Manufacturing, John Deere Plant, Bendix Aviation, and Dodge-Chicago, etc.; and

WHEREAS, these individuals are the "Unsung Heroes" who worked diligently to provide quality products so the USA could win World War II; and

WHEREAS, the City of Chehalis and the PUD is placing a commemorative plaque at the PUD Building (former Chehalis Branch Plant, which built wing assemblies for the B-17 and B-29), at 3:00 p.m. on July 3; and

WHEREAS, the City of Centralia is declaring "Rosies and the Guys" as the parade grand marshals during the annual Summerfest Parade.

NOW THEREFORE, I, Fred W. Rider, Mayor of the City of Chehalis, Washington, do hereby proclaim July 3-4, 2005 as "ROSIES AND THE GUYS" DAYS in the City of Chehalis.

SIGNED, SEALED, AND DATED this 27th day of June, 2005.

Mayor

*The cities of Chehalis, above, and Centralia, far left, as well as Lewis County commissioners, center, all proclaimed July 3-4, 2005, as 'Rosies and the Guys Days' to honor the contributions of local war support workers and volunteers.*

*Bibliography
and Index*

# Bibliography

Bevers, Amanda. *Rosie the Riveter Goes West: The Mobilization and Migration of Women Workers During World War II*, History 400 Final Draft, 16.12.04, on the Internet at: http://www2.ups.edu/faculty/dsackman/400papers/fall2004/bevers.htm

The "Boom-Boom" Girls of WW2 Web site on Triumph Explosives workers on the Internet at: http://475thmpeg.memorieshop.com/Elkton/index.html

Children of the Camps Web site at: http://www.children-of-the-camps.org/history/

Colman, Penny. *Rosie the Riveter: Women Working on the Home Front in World War II*. 1995. Crown Publishers, Inc., New York.

Crawford, Robert. The Air Force Song—Full Lyrics. Courtesy USAF Heritage of America Band on the Internet at: http://usmilitary.about.com/od/airforce/l/blafsong.htm

D-Day Museum information on the Internet at: http://www.ddaymuseum.co.uk/

Densho: The Japanese American Legacy Project. On the Internet at: http://www.densho.org/

Encyclopedia Britannica, Inc.'s Guide to Normandy 1944 on the Internet at: http://search.eb.com/dday

Frank, Miriam; Marilyn Ziebarth and Connie Field. *The Life and Times of Rosie the Riveter: The Story of Three Million Working Women During World War II*. 1982. Clarity Educational Productions, Inc., Emeryville, California.

Michael Furukawa's Web site on the history of the 442nd Regimental Combat Team and the 100th Battalion at: http://www.katonk.com/index.html

Gluck, Sherna B. *Rosie the Riveter Revisited : Women, the War, and Social Change*. 1987. Twayne Publishers, a Division of G.K. Hall & Co. Boston.

Hansen, Linda, et. al. *History and Favorite Recipes of Onalaskans*. 1997. Second printing.

History Channel This Day in History, Dec. 7, 1941. http://www.historychannel.com/tdih/tdih.jsp?month=10272964&day=10272972&cat=10272946%3Cbr%20/%3E

The History Place, World War II in Europe, attack on Pearl Harbor, on the Internet at: http://www.historyplace.com/worldwar2/timeline/pearl.htm

Joyce, Robert. *Astonishing Century: A Rapid Reference Guide to the Events and People We Remember.* September 1999. Hawthorne House, published by Pygmalion Press, Santa Ana, California.

*The Life and Times of Rosie the Riveter* VHS movie. 1987. Direct Cinema Limited, Inc., Los Angeles. Copyright 1987.

Dr. Eric Mayer's Social Science Webzine at: http://www.emayzine.com/lectures/WWII.html

Naval Historical Center Web site, Department of the Navy, at http://www.history.navy.mil/faqs/faq66-1.htm

Nelson, Pam, editor, and Dawn Chipman, Mari Florence and Naomi Wax. *Cool Women: the thinking girl's guide to the hippest women in history.* 2001. Girl Press, a division of 17th Street Productions, an Alloy Online, Inc., company.

The Pearl Harbor Attack, 7 December 1941, Web site at: http://www.janet.org/janet_history/niiya_chron.html, which created a chronology of Japanese American History edited by Brian Niiya (New York: Facts-on-File, 1993).

Remarks on Signing the Bill Providing Restitution for the Wartime Internment of Japanese-American Civilians, August 10, 1988, on the Internet at: http://www.reagan.utexas.edu/archives/speeches/1988/081088d.htm

Shirley, Orville. *Americans: The Story of the 442nd Combat Team.* Sons & Daughters of Los Angeles Chapter. $45.

34th Infantry Division Association home page at: http://34thdivdeathcasualties.homestead.com/HomePage.html

"United States History Video Collection, Origins—WWII: World War II." Vol. 19. 1996. Schlessinger Video Productions, a Division of Library Video Company, Bala Cynwyd, Pennsylvania. Copyright 1996.

University of San Diego history Web site on the Battle of Iwo Jima at: http://history.acusd.edu/gen/WW2Timeline/LUTZ/iwo.html

US Asians.net Web site at: http://us_asians.tripod.com/timeline-2000.html Features Asian Pacific American historical timeline details.

US History.com Web site on the USO at: http://www.u-s-history.com/pages/h1661.html

Wikipedia, the free encyclopedia. Attack on Pearl Harbor on the Internet at: http://en.wikipedia.org/wiki/Attack_on_Pearl_Harbor

Wise, Nancy Baker and Christy Wise. *A Mouthful of Rivets: Women at Work in World War II*. San Francisco: Jossey-Bass, 1994.

Women at War: Redstone's WWII Female "Production Soldiers," on the Internet at: http://www.redstone.army.mil/history/women/welcome.html More than 50 years ago, fire trucks raced through Huntsville delivering an "Extra" edition of the local newspaper.

# Index

# About the Author

Julie McDonald Zander worked for nearly twenty years as a newspaper reporter and editor before leaving journalism to pursue her passion for preserving the past.

In an effort to preserve her own family's stories, she interviewed her parents and father-in-law, transcribed the tapes, scanned photos and wrote and designed several memory books. Her mother-in-law had written her own recollections by hand in a spiral notebook, so Zander also turned those stories into a book.

After completing almost a dozen books for family members, she launched her business, Chapters of Life, in 2001, to help others preserve those stories in oral and book form. She enjoys listening to people talk about the old days, the joys and fears, heartaches and triumphs experienced in their lives. As a newspaper reporter for a decade and an editor for nine years, she's developed the skills to take the raw material from interviews and write interesting, entertaining books that capture clients' hearts and souls, as well as their speech and mannerisms.

Zander served four years as Northwest regional co-coordinator for the Association of Personal Historians. She also served as conference registrar and helped organize the November 2002 APH annual conference in Vancouver, British Columbia, Canada, and she's been asked to serve as manager for the 2006 annual conference, which will be held in Portland, Oregon.

Zander obtained her bachelor's degree in communications and political science from the University of Washington and has continued her education through many life-writing workshops, courses and conferences.

She lives at Toledo, Washington, with her husband, Larry, and their two children.

Her Web site at www.chaptersoflife.com provides more information about her services. To reach her, call 360-864-6938 or toll-free 1-888-864-6937.